This Life Is in Your Hands

This Life

— IS IN —

Your Hands

One Dream, Sixty Acres,
and a Family Undone

MELISSA COLEMAN

HARPER

An Imprint of HarperCollins*Publishers*
www.harpercollins.com

This is a work of nonfiction. The events and experiences detailed
herein are all true and have been faithfully rendered as remembered
by the author, to the best of her ability, or as they were told to the
author by people who were present. Others have read the manuscript
and confirmed its rendering of events. Some names have been
changed in order to protect the privacy of individuals involved.

HarperCollins books may be purchased for educational, business, or sales
promotional use. For information, please write: Special Markets Department,
HarperCollins Publishers, 10 East 53rd Street, New York, NY 10022.

Grateful acknowledgment is made for permission
to reproduce from the following:
"Stupidity Street" by Ralph Hodgson. © 2010 Bryn Mawr College Library.
"Big Yellow Taxi" words and music by Joni Mitchell. © 1970 (Renewed)
Crazy Crow Music. All rights administered by Sony/ATV Music
Publishing, 8 Music Square West, Nashville, TN 37203. All rights
reserved. Used by permission of Alfred Music Publishing Co., Inc.

Map copyright © 1989 Jane Crosen

Designed by Eric Butler

Library of Congress Cataloging-in-Publication Data

Coleman, Melissa.
This life is in your hands: one dream, sixty acres, and a
family undone / Melissa Coleman. — 1st ed.
p. cm.
ISBN 978-0-06-195832-8
1. Coleman, Melissa—Childhood and youth. 2. Coleman, Melissa—Family.
3. Coleman, Eliot, 1938– 4. Coleman, Sue, 1945– 5. Loss (Psychology)—
Case studies. 6. Children—Maine—Penobscot Bay Region—Death. 7.
Drowning—Maine—Penobscot Bay Region. 8. Penobscot Bay Region
(Me.)—Biography. 9. Farm life—Maine—Penobscot Bay Region. 10.
Penobscot Bay Region (Me.)—Social life and customs. I. Title.
CT275.C6857A3 2011
974.1'3043092—dc22
2010024942
[B]

11 12 13 14 15   ID/RRD   10 9 8 7 6 5 4 3

For my sister Heidi

—but beauty is more now than dying's when

—E. E. CUMMINGS

Contents

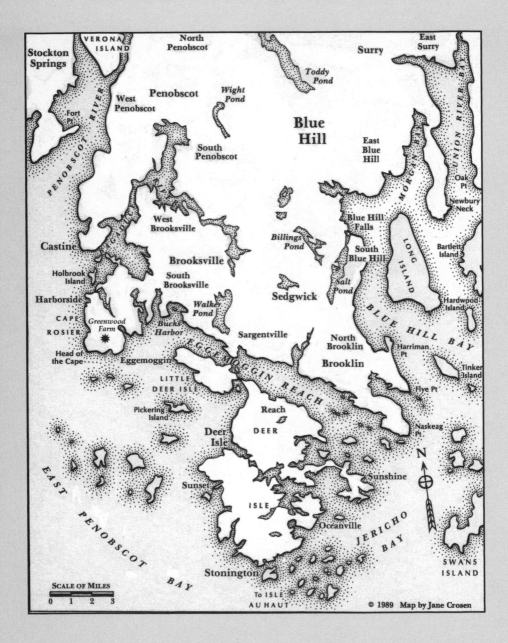

This Life Is in Your Hands

Prologue

WE MUST HAVE asked our neighbor Helen to read our hands that day. Her own hands were the color of onion skins, darkened with liver spots, and ever in motion. Writing, digging, picking, chopping. Opening kitchen cabinets painted with Dutch children in bright embroidered dresses and pointed shoes. Taking out wooden bowls and handing them to my mother, Sue, to put on the patio for lunch. As Mama whooshed out the screen door with hair flowing and child-on-back, the kitchen breathed chopped parsley and vegetable soup simmering on the stove, and the light glowed through the kitchen windows onto the crooked pine floors of the old farmhouse where I stood waiting.

It was a charmed summer, that summer of 1975, even more so

because we didn't know how peaceful it was in comparison to the one that would follow.

"Ring the lunch bell for Scott-o," Helen called out the window to Mama. She liked to add an *o* to everyone's name. Eli-o, Suz-o, kiddos for the kids, Puss-o the cat. We were the closest she had to children.

As the bell chimed, Helen took my small hand and turned it upward in hers. The kitchen was warm, but her skin cool and leathery. Mama returned with Heidi as I stood long-hair-braided and six-years-brave, holding my breath. We knew about Helen that when she didn't have something interesting to say, she'd change the subject. She smoothed my palm with her thumbs and looked down but also in, her cropped granite hair holding the dusty smell of old books.

"Tsch, what's this?" she asked of the marks I'd made with Papa's red magic marker.

"A map," I told her, proud of the artistry on my fingers. "A map of our farm."

"Pshaw." She tossed my hand aside like an old turnip from the root cellar.

So she read Heidi's palm instead. Heidi was a blue-eyed two-year-old, "an uncontainable spirit," everyone said. Even she held still, mouth open, breathing heavy, snug in the sling on Mama's back as Helen smoothed out her little fingers.

"Short life line," Helen muttered, bending toward the light from the window, then paused as if catching herself too late.

"What do you mean by short?" Mama asked, brown eyes alert, mother-bird-like. "Thirty, forty years?"

"Oh, it doesn't mean a thing," Helen said, and began to mutter about the overabundance of tomatoes in the garden.

*   *   *

SEVEN YEARS EARLIER Helen had thought differently, perhaps, as she read my father, Eliot's, hands when he and Mama visited, looking for land. Some say hands hold the map of our lives; that the lines of the palm correspond with the heart, head, and soul to create a story unique to each of us. Understanding the lines is an attempt to understand why things happen as they do. Also a quick way to figure out who might make a good neighbor. Helen and Scott Nearing, authors of the homesteading bible *Living the Good Life*, wanted young people around who would find the same joys in country living as they did. Their philosophy held the promise of a simple life, far removed from the troubles of the modern world. The good life.

"Very strong lines," Helen told Papa that summer of 1968. He had the deepest fate line she'd ever seen, and wide, capable hands. With hands like his, they could do anything. And such a nice-looking couple, too, young and clean-cut—Papa with his sandy tousle of hair, blue eyes, and straight nose, Mama's long, dark hair parted in the middle and kindly chestnut eyes. Shortly after that visit, my parents received a postcard from Helen and Scott offering to sell the sixty acres next door. That's how we came to be back-to-the-landers, living on a farm cut from the woods without electricity, running water, or phone on that remote peninsula along the coast of Maine. Trying something different to see if truth could be found in it.

"THE VEGETABLE GARDEN," the sign at the end of our drive said, "Organically Grown," with the vegetables in season listed beneath: carrots, lettuce, tomatoes, zucchini. Past a gravel parking lot, the driveway thinned to a grassy lane curving around the orchard and down a gentle slope to a wood-timbered stand with wet-pebble shelves full of fresh produce for sale. Customers and farmworkers came and went as the surrounding gardens ripened beneath the pale disk of midday sun and cicadas thrummed regular as your pulse. On the rise by an overarching ash tree sat our small house, its slanted roof and front eyes of windows looking across the greenhouse and gardens below. The only home I'd ever known.

Heidi and I were always outside, naked and barefoot, dancing on the blanket of apple blossoms, skipping along wooded paths, catching frogs at the pond, eating strawberries and peas from the vine, and running from the black twist of garter snakes in the grass. We lay in the shade under the ash tree, gazing up at the crown of leaves and listening to the sounds of the farm—birds calling, goats bleating, chattering of customers at the farm stand, and whispers of tree talk.

When you focused on the leaves fluttering in the dappled light, they vibrated and shimmered into one, becoming a million tiny particles. You felt a shift inside, and you began to vibrate too, on the same frequency as everything else. All secrets were there, all truths, all knowledge. You had to scan with your heart to find what you were seeking. It might not be spoken in words, it might be hidden in rhyme, in song, in images. You knew the tree and the earth were the same as you, made of particles, like you, come together in a different form. You loved it all as you loved yourself.

THERE ARE REASONS why nothing lasts forever.

Papa says it was the little red boat Heidi must have carried down to the pond and set afloat. One of our farm apprentices said she was the kind of child who wasn't afraid of anything. Another thought it was the black crow that hung around the farm that spring, a single crow being an omen of death in the family. Someone else suggested it was her lost caul, the rare birth sac myths say will protect against drowning. Others blamed it on our lifestyle—not a proper way to raise children.

Mama usually says it was the rain. She didn't worry about us girls playing by the pond because it wasn't that deep during the dry months of summer. But when it rained, the pond filled and turned black as the water caught in barrels under the eaves.

None of these things alone tells the whole story. Only in looking back can you see a pattern in the threads of life, interwoven with the events that would tear them asunder, and within that pattern lies the knowledge I'm seeking—the secret of how to live.

CHAPTER ONE

Family

FOR THE FIRST nine years of my life, Greenwood Farm was my little house in the big woods, located as long ago and far away up the coast of Maine as it was from mainstream America. Five hours from Boston, three from Portland, along winding roads that became successively narrower from Belfast to Bucksport to Penobscot, until they finally turned to dirt. If you were a bird, you could shorten the trip at Camden by cutting over the scatterings of fir-pointed islands on Penobscot Bay—North Haven, Butter Island, Great Spruce Head, Deer Isle. Viewed from above, the islands formed bright constellations in the dark sky of water, a mirror of the universe leading you back in time.

Just past Pond Island, you'd see the forested head of Cape Rosier reaching into the sea from the mainland and a sandy line of beach, beyond which a narrow road wound up through a blue-berry field and disappeared into a dappled stretch of forest. A mile in, our land was surrounded by the cape's uniform blanket of fir, spruce, and the purple scrub of blueberry barrens.

On a morning in early April of 1969, as my future parents were clearing brush under the bare crown of the ash tree next to their new home, two sparrows circled once, twice, then alighted on a branch to announce their arrival with a familiar melody of clicks and tweets. Surprised by the song, Mama raised her head to spot the diminutive brown birds with patches of white at the throat. "The white-throat," she exclaimed, an armload of brush resting on the pronounced swell of her belly. She'd always loved sparrows best—so joyous in their simplicity. "They mate for life and come back every year to the same place to build a nest," she added, having checked it in her *Peterson's* before.

"A sure sign of spring," Papa replied, giving a low whistle through his teeth before returning with renewed vigor to his work. Easter would fall that Sunday, though they'd lost track of such dates by then—spring was a resurrection with or without a holiday.

It was not the spring of hyacinth, lily of the valley, and drunken bumblebees, but the New England spring that comes just before. Mud season. The last pockets of snow melted away as rain fell from the sky in steady gray sheets, filling hollows and ruts with dark puddles. Ice crystals released their hold on soil that sank into a primordial muck.

"Son of a gun," Papa said. "The ruts in the driveway are up to my knee." The white VW truck wallowed like a pig when he revved up and tried to drive through. Sometimes he made it, sometimes he didn't.

"Looks like we'd be having the baby at home even if we didn't want to," he said after one unsuccessful attempt.

Mama's belly was the perfect half round of the wooden bread-mixing bowl, a defined mound under her favorite anorak with the fur-trimmed hood. It appeared before her when she exited the outhouse and entered the door of the farmhouse. Her face was round too, glowing like the moon. Standing at the kitchen counter preparing lunch, she looked normal from behind, but when Papa came and put his arms around her, they could rest on the curve of her belly as his hands searched for the shape of a foot or leg.

"There, Eliot, there again," Mama said. "Movement."

His larger hand pressed next to hers, waiting for another kick.

"Yes, I felt it," he said. "I really did that time."

"It could be any day now," Mama said. She felt something changing inside, a slowing down and getting ready.

Scientists say my waiting self could already hear the chirp of Mama's voice, the ha-has of Papa's laughter, the thump of feet and the click of Normie-dog's paws on the wooden floor of the farmhouse. There would have been the shush of sweeping, the crack-shatter of Papa chopping kindling, an explosion of firewood dropped into the bin, the crunch of gravel outside, goats bleating as they waited to be milked, water splashing at the spring. Most of all, I would have felt the constant sound of Mama's heart beating, a steady drumbeat on a rawhide surface, blood rushing through valves into arteries and capillaries, keeping me alive. A new home awaited, one Mama and Papa had worked hard to make safe from what they saw as the dangers of the outside world.

* * *

SIX MONTHS EARLIER, on October 21, 1968, my parents had moved from Franconia College in New Hampshire to a make-shift camper on the sixty wooded acres Helen and Scott Nearing sold them for $2,000. There was no mail service, no telephone or electrical wires, no plumbing. All of that ended a mile down the road at the Nearings'. Mail was picked up at the post office, the one public building in Harborside, a tiny town located four miles from the homestead along the western side of Cape Rosier's coast. Calls were made fifteen minutes away on a pay phone at a store off the cape in Bucks Harbor, also home to the famous Condon's Garage, where Sal gets a spark plug as condolence for her lost tooth in the children's book *One Morning in Maine*.

"Cape Rosier looks like the profile of a moose's head." Mama pointed out to Papa on the map. Holbrook Island and its neighbors to the north made the distinctive shape of horns above the dot for the town of Harborside, a round unnamed pond in the middle was the eye, the head of the cape was the nose, and the Breeze-mere Peninsula hung below like a chin under an open mouth. This moose head appeared to be almost an island, with only a thin neck holding it to the mainland. They laughed when they learned that the Indian name for the cape was Mose-ka-chick, which actu-ally meant "moose's rump."

Their sixty-some acres made a nostril in the moose's snout, about a mile from the ocean and two hundred feet in elevation above it. A dirt road wound up from Nearings' Cove to curve along the southern edge of the property before heading back out to the sea on the other side. Across the way were the undulating rock and scrub of a blueberry barren, and beyond that stretched the uninhabited head of the cape at the tip of the moose's nose.

The site of my future home was only a rise in the forest surrounded by spruce and fir, a cluster of birch, and the large ash with its healthy crown of branches. "This seems like a good place to begin," Papa had said, standing beside the tree. "We'll have to start building right away before winter."

"A home of our own, at last." Mama sighed, and that image alone soothed her. She felt a twinge in her stomach, like a feather stroking the inside, and hugged her expanding belly with her arms. She hadn't realized how homeless she'd been up until that point.

While Mama's father was Harvard-educated and her mother descended from a passenger on the *Mayflower*, they never aspired to be part of wealthy Boston society or had the money to become so. Papa's parents, Skates and Skipper, though not rich, were in the *Social Register* and part of the beach, tennis, and country club circles of Rumson, New Jersey. "Fonsy people," Mama liked to joke with a blue-blood affectation. Young and in love, my parents hoped to make their way without concern for the *Social Register* and Harvard degrees and to leave behind their respective family affairs—shuffling off the shell of the past to grow a future of their own making.

During the last two weeks of October, Papa shoveled out a hole eight feet deep, six feet wide, and ten feet long—where the root cellar would sit beneath the house—and laid the foundation with rot-resistant cedar posts. A self-taught carpenter and woodworker, Papa learned from odd jobs and projects, including renovating the interior of the hunting lodge where they lived in Franconia. Though he'd never actually built a home before, he had a book, *Your Engineered House* by Rex Roberts, that broke down the process into an easy-to-follow plan.

He sketched a layout based on the blueprint in the book, eighteen by twenty feet, slightly longer than wide, with south-facing windows in the front. A shed roof rose from the back at an angle and extended past the face to provide an overhang for the front porch. Reverse board-and-batten construction would be used for the exterior siding, as Roberts suggested—meaning the inner wall studs made the seal beneath the exterior boards to save on wood. After the $2,000 for the land and other expenses, their $5,000 savings was dwindling quickly. Papa wished he could have cut and used the trees from the property, but there wasn't time to let the wood cure, so the lumber came from the local sawmill— cedar posts, planed pine boards, and two-by-fours. Regardless, they were able to keep the cost down to $680 to build the house we called home for the next ten years, at a time when the national average for a home in town was closer to $20,000.

Papa's tools consisted of a handsaw, hammer, level, measuring tape, and carpenter's square. On top of the foundation he laid the beams that supported the floor, then the corner and roof supports and wall studs. He nailed on the floorboards, roof, and walls, leaving breaks for windows. Rock wool insulation was unrolled between the studs, and black tar paper served for exterior roofing. The easy part was that there were no electrical wires or plumbing to worry about, no refrigerator, washer, dryer, toilet, bath, or other appliances to buy. Food would be stored in the root cellar, accessed by a trapdoor from the kitchen, and the bathroom was an A-frame outhouse located in the woods at the edge of the clearing.

As Papa worked on the house, Mama returned to Franconia with a trailer attached to the VW truck for the rest of their things. Noticeably pregnant, she managed to move the cast-iron cookstove onto the trailer with the help of friends. Next she herded the goats and chickens into the back of the VW and drove the seven hours to the farm. The chickens lived in a coop next to the camper, and the goats ran free. Jimi Hendrix, Janis Joplin, and the Monkees drifted in from the outside world on the battery-powered transistor radio as Mama and Papa cooked over a portable Coleman stove and showered with a plastic bag of water hung from a nail to warm in the sun. The camper was cramped and cluttered, but they kept up the illusion that they were on an expedition and it was base camp.

The first snow fell while Papa worked beneath the protection of the new roof. "We can't move in until it's done, otherwise we'll get used to it like this and never finish," he told Mama. The interior walls took shape, with planed pine boards nailed vertically from floor to ceiling over the insulation. To the front of the side door sat the wood cookstove, surrounded by an L-shaped counter with an embedded stainless steel sink, a ship's nautical water pump, and a water container below. A dining table made of varnished pine boards and crossed-log legs, with tree stumps for chairs, sat beneath the tall south-facing windows looking out under the overhanging roof. The far back corner walls were covered with bookshelves above built-in L-shaped benches that Mama would cover with maroon padded mats for a "sofa." In the corner behind the kitchen, a raised sleeping loft over closet storage formed the bedroom space. The only appliances were a galvanized grain mill clamped to the kitchen counter, the radio, and kerosene lanterns.

On a walk along the coast with the goats, Mama found a piece of driftwood that she carved and painted with their names, "Eliot and Sue Coleman," and nailed to a post where the rutted path to the house left the public dirt road. By December 1, a little over a month after they started, Papa declared the house complete. As anticipated, the four-hundred-square-foot space felt like a mansion after the cramped camper, and the accumulating snow made its comforts all the more welcome.

*   *   *

WHEN MAMA TOLD Helen Nearing, her new neighbor and mentor, that she was pregnant, she expected congratulations from the woman who was becoming an alternative—if opinionated—mother figure.

"You should have waited," Helen clucked instead. "One needs time and energy to make a foundation as a homesteader. Children will use all that time and energy." Mama recounted the incident to Papa, but passed it off by saying Helen probably didn't value the joys of childbearing because she was not herself a mother.

When the local doctor in Castine refused to do a home birth, Helen stepped up to suggest a midwife she knew named Eva Reich. The Reich home and laboratory, Orgonon, was located three hours west in Rangeley, Maine, but Eva lived with her husband on an organic farm in nearby Hancock. Eva's father, Wilhelm Reich, the noted psychiatrist, scientist, and former associate of Sigmund Freud, gained notoriety through his experiments with a natural energy that he called orgone, but was put on trial by the FDA in the 1950s for his unorthodox methods and his attempt to collect this energy for healing purposes. The government, in an amazing act of censorship, had Reich's orgone accumulators destroyed and many of his books burned, and Reich died soon after in prison. Eva later adapted her father's theories in her work with children, using what she called butterfly touch therapy as a way to heal traumatized or colicky infants, but in the 1960s she was simply part of the small network of midwives supportive of home birth at a time when the establishment frowned on it. Papa planned to call Eva from the Nearings' phone the minute Mama went into labor.

"Let's just hope she arrives in time," Papa said.

Four years earlier, when he was age twenty-six, a child of his own had been the furthest thing from Papa's mind as he approached the buffet in Franconia College's dining hall. A small college of three hundred students, it had a campus located on a ridge near Franconia Notch on the site of the once-grand Forest Hills Hotel, affectionately dubbed "the wedding cake." Athletics included the fringe pursuits of kayaking and rock climbing, and students were required to sign up for work programs—cleaning buildings, serving meals, washing dishes, and other daily tasks.

My mother, age twenty, was on meal duty that day. A slender sophomore in an embroidered Indian shirt, she had clear skin, square jaw, and hazel eyes set off by dark braids falling to her shoulders. Having dropped out of Lawrence University, where her parents had encouraged her to go, she'd decided instead to ski bum in Vermont at Mad River Glen. It was her first act of defiance, and she found reward in the carefree life of the mountains. Come summer she applied and was accepted to Franconia for fall, joining a community that shared her alternative inclinations. Behind the buffet, she glowed with newfound confidence that brought out her natural beauty. When she served Papa a scoop of mashed potatoes, their eyes met, and a spark of possibility ignited.

Mama's pupils widened in surprise, then contracted as if exposed to too much light. There was a confidence in Papa's blue eyes and quiet smile that made her heart beat more quickly and set off a sudden flutter in her stomach. Everyone was in love with the handsome new graduate-assistant Spanish teacher; his wiry athleticism and passion for whatever he was doing—for life— drew people to him. He also happened to be partial to petite brunettes.

"I'd like some more, please," Papa said to Mama, returning for seconds. When he returned for thirds, he invited her to go camping. Back then, teacher-student relationships were commonplace, but Mama told herself she wasn't about to become a cliché. She said she had a paper due. Papa found her wholesome yet shy manner intriguing. He asked again. Life reached out its hand, the bittersweet smell of fall in the air.

"Yes," Mama said.

MAMA'S WATER BROKE on the afternoon of April 9, and events unfolded according to plan—that is, until Eva's car got stuck in the mud. She had to walk the last mile to the homestead, worrying she wouldn't arrive in time. Mama was lying in the bed loft in darkness, the contractions rippling the bowl of her belly and clenching like fists between the bones of her hips. She breathed and sweated as Papa held her hand, assured by her confident grip. She'd been through birth before with the goats and knew it would happen on its own.

"Someone's here," Papa said as Eva, a middle-aged woman with mellowing Germanic features and short gray hair, bustled in and gave Mama a shot of natural sedative to help with the contractions, then walked down to the Nearings' to ask Scott to pull out her car. When she returned with Scott, he helped Papa boil water to sterilize the clamps and left them to wait. Around 1:30 a.m., after eight hours of labor, my slimy head crowned. Suddenly Eva was talking loudly to Papa. The umbilical cord was caught around my neck, and my face was turning blue. Eva quickly slipped a finger under and got the cord loose enough to cut. After the head, the rest of me slipped easily free, and I emerged sucking my thumb, apparently unperturbed that I'd almost strangled to death. Eva tied the rest of the cord into a knot, and Papa cut it from my belly button. A girl. They laid me on Mama's chest, and I immediately began to nurse.

Eva helped clean the loft but saved the placenta, suggesting

Mama eat some to replenish the blood and nutrients lost during birth and help contract the uterus. Mama was not offended because she knew the mother goats ate their placentas, too, so she tried it raw, remembering it as tasting like liver. Papa was amazed at how quickly her belly shrank back to normal—after a week of nursing, she was her regular slender self.

The name Melissa came from the book *Look to the Mountain*, for the pioneer woman who with her husband, Whit, settled in New Hampshire's North Country, near Mount Chocorua, in the mid-1700s. As teenagers expecting a child with no money to buy land in town, they traveled by birch-bark canoe to the wilderness, where they claimed their one hundred settlement acres, built a home, and lived off the land.

As it turned out, Helen's hesitance about children was not unwarranted. I arrived on the same day as a large delivery of strawberry plants, asparagus roots, and fruit trees that needed to be planted immediately, and one of the goats kidded a day later. The quiet of winter was over, and spring had arrived. Mama and Papa did the only thing they could—they embraced the challenge with all the energy and optimism of their youth.

AFTER PAPA CALLED family from the Bucks Harbor pay phone to announce my arrival, Mama's mother, father, and sister Marth came up to visit, driving from Lincoln, Massachusetts, to find life for the most part harmonious within the new pine cabin in the muddy clearing. Mama sat on the padded benches holding me in her lap, trying to act as if having a human baby at home was as normal as it was for a goat, but the harmony she worked so hard to foster began to unravel under the inquisition of her mother, Prill. Mama had called eight months earlier to say she was pregnant, and not to worry, but she was planning a home birth.

"Sue, dear, are you sure that's safe?" Prill asked, her voice taking on a familiar pinched tone.

"My brothers and I were born at home," my grandfather David said in the background.

"Shusshh." Prill motioned to David, holding her hand over the receiver. "*Your* father was a doctor."

In the 1960s, though we were only a century removed from a norm of home births, the old ways were branded just this side of witchcraft. To educate themselves, Mama and Papa read *Natural Childbirth* by Grantly Dick-Read, the British obstetrician who developed the modern concept of natural birthing. He believed that the social and emotional fear surrounding a hospital birth causes tension in a woman's body, making the natural process unnecessarily difficult. Not surprisingly, his theories were met with resistance from the medical community, accustomed as it was to using drugs and other methods Dick-Read deemed unnecessary.

Papa liked his in-laws and encouraged Mama to give them the benefit of the doubt. "You've got a legacy of Yankee and Puritan skepticism behind you," he said. "Not an easy thing to live with, but that's what makes you so tough." Three centuries earlier, Mama's ancestor, the pilgrim Henry Samson, left his home in Henlow, Bedfordshire, England, as a teenager to seek his fortune on the *Mayflower*, landing on Plymouth Rock in 1620 and celebrating America's first Thanksgiving the following year. Since that time, the family had become less adventurous and more Puritan. In one memorable incident, Mama's grandmother Nanna forbade Prill to elope with a handsome stranger from Kentucky. Nanna was domineering, "the Shark," the family would whisper in later years, and she was not about to lose her only daughter to a southern man.

"We need to keep the family together," Nanna told Prill with a hinting dismissal of Prill's father, who was asked to leave after being discovered in bed with the maid. Attractive and well liked, Prill found a husband closer to home, one of the four Lawrence brothers she knew from summering in Westport Point, Massachusetts, near Cape Cod. The son of a Boston doctor, David went to day school at Belmont Hill and on to Harvard like his three brothers, once going on a double date with JFK. He and his brothers especially loved to ski, often hiking up Mount Washington in spring to compete in the annual Inferno, a downhill race on the steeps of Tuckerman Ravine.

"My dear, they were adventurous boys," Prill would say. It was likely these hints of her father's adventurous spirit that Mama clung to in her own search for a fulfilling life, and found most appealing in Papa.

As a child growing up in Nyack, New York, Mama preferred the summer months when the family packed the car and headed for the guest cottage next to Nanna's house on Westport Point. In a style typical of the region, the weathered cedar-shake shingles of "the Wing" had faded in the salt air to a silvery gray that matched the stone walls of a once-thriving agricultural community. Mama loved the simpler life there, and the farms. What she didn't love was the weight of Nanna's often oppressive opinions, heavy on her family's shoulders. Prill and David were afraid to stand up to Nanna and did whatever she wished, suppressing their emotions with classic Yankee stoicism.

"I want to go to Putney," Mama implored, referring to a hippie boarding school in the mountains of Vermont that her uncle had attended, and she never forgave her parents when they said they couldn't afford it. They moved to the Boston suburb of Lincoln, where Mama attended high school and began to disappear. She was quiet and polite, but underneath there was something missing, some deep unmet expectation of happiness. She longed to spend more time sailing and skiing with her father, but his work as a bank vice president consumed him. Perhaps her expectations were too great, or perhaps her needs ran counter to what her family had to offer, but by the time she finished high school, she was already looking down alternative paths for fulfillment. When she met Papa, she glimpsed the possibility of a different kind of life, and she jumped for it.

MAMA'S JAW TIGHTENED as her family surrounded her, filling the small space of the house. She handed me to her mother, who sat down in the rocking chair where Mama liked to nurse me. When I arched my head back in my grandmother's arms, thinking it was time to nurse, Prill quickly handed me back to Mama. Prill had grown up during the transition from the discipline method of child rearing to what many termed the permissive methods of Dr. Spock. Her own parenting style had been a little of both, but in Mama's mind everything she did was wrong, even things like referring to bowel movements as "BMs" and pee as "tinkle."

Then as Mama lifted her shirt to nurse, my grandfather got up and left the room in discomfort. "I'd like to breast-feed our children," Mama had declared to Papa during her pregnancy, and he heartily agreed. In 1969, more than 75 percent of babies were fed commercial milk formulas. As a result of women's staying in the workforce in the wake of World War II and the well-financed marketing of formula companies, baby formula had become the norm and breast-feeding nearly taboo.

"The German chemist Justus von Liebig developed the first commercial milk formula," Papa explained to his in-laws. "He's also known as the father of the chemical fertilizer industry. That's what convinced me our children should be nursed." As in the garden, Papa wasn't about to trust a chemical substitute to take the place of nature. Though they may have been somewhat skeptical about Papa's passionate explanations, Prill and David were charmed by his enthusiasm and tried to ease into their role as grandparents. Mama, however, remained in a constant state of defense, unable to relax until her family packed up to return to Massachusetts.

THREE YEARS EARLIER in Franconia, it was a certain book that set my parents on this unexpected course of their lives together. Thinking of that book, I imagine it as an old genie's lamp waiting in that dimly lit health food store. Its magic was of the kind books possess when they come into our lives at the right moment to show us what we need to learn. As my parents opened its worn pages, their future was released.

Not long after they met, Papa told Mama he wanted to get a yogurt maker. Mama suggested a trip to Hatch's—she was looking for a grain mill to grind flour. In the 1960s, you couldn't easily buy whole wheat flour or real yogurt—you had to make it yourself—and Hatch's was one of only a few natural food stores in the southern New Hampshire–Vermont area where you could find these weird sorts of things.

"There are almonds and cashews in bulk," Mama said enthusiastically as they drove over to St. Johnsbury on a late fall day. "And coconut peanut butter, which is almost better than mixing tahini and honey. And an energy drink of tomato and lemon juice mixed with brewer's yeast and liver powder. What a boost!"

"Hot damn," Papa said.

Health food united Papa and Mama as much as, if not more than, their love of the outdoors. "How are the nuts and berries today?" more traditional friends liked to tease. Papa came to whole foods as an athlete needing to maximize his nutritional intake, but Mama's interest in healthy eating started as a way to keep her weight down. An aunt had given her *Let's Eat Right to Keep Fit* when she was a pudgy teenager, and she adopted the whole and raw foods advocated in the book to find the slender figure she would keep for the rest of her life.

Mama and Papa shared a growing anger when shopping at supermarkets filled with rows upon rows of packaged and canned processed foods, or when seeking something other than fast food on a road trip. Why did it have to be so hard to find good, healthy foods that nourished the body rather than depleting it? Before the industrial revolution and the world wars whole and fresh vegetables, meats, and grains had been more commonplace, but the factories and economic growth of the 1940s and '50s supported processed and canned food and the convenience of the supermarket. By the 1960s, bulk foods were all but outlawed in favor of prepared meals and mixes—"empty food," some called it. As one of Papa's favorite cartoons stated, in reference to the neutron bomb: "It's called the junk food bomb. It destroys populations while leaving profits intact."

Advertising had done its job—overworked women wanted to buy their food ready-made instead of slaving in the kitchen like their mothers. The problem was, no one yet knew the effects these "easy" foods would wreak on the health of the nation.

As Mama and Papa entered the white clapboard New England–style house at 8 Pine Street, a bell rang to alert the owners, who lived above the store. Hatch's was founded by former missionaries to India who had become missionaries of health food. Mama and Papa were greeted by the scents of candle wax and sage, and by the Hatches' son David, who wore a one-piece blue jumpsuit, his long hair pulled back in a shaggy ponytail. His wife, Carol, was breast-feeding her baby in a chair by the cash register.

"Welcome, welcome," David called, puttering nearby as they shopped.

There were bins of dried peas, kidney beans, lentils, brown rice, spices, and, of course, wheat groats to grind into flour and cultures to make yogurt. In the back of the store was also a lending library with books about natural living. Papa was drawn to one on healthy eating called *Faith, Love and Seaweed* by the father of Olympian swimmer Murray Rose about the diet and mindset that won the gold in 1960, and the less useful *Breatharianism*, about living on air. A month later they were back, not for the liver drink, which Papa found unpalatable, but for the bulk food and books.

"You've got to check out this one," David told them, pointing out Helen and Scott Nearing's *Living the Good Life: How to Live Simply and Sanely in a Troubled World*, the 1954 edition, with a print on the cover of a green wheelbarrow behind a row of maple trees. The pages were well worn.

"This is right on," Papa said, reading the book aloud to Mama back at the cabin they shared in Franconia. In *Living the Good Life*, the Nearings told the story of leaving New York City in 1932 to become homesteaders in Vermont—turning an old farm into their primary livelihood, building a stone house, maintaining an organic garden, and living off the sale of syrup from the maple grove on their property.

"We left the city with three objectives in mind," the Nearings wrote in their conversational but self-serious tone. The first was to live independent of the economy; the second, to improve health; and the third, to find liberation from the unethical trends in society. Ultimately, the Nearings sought to make a living "with our own hands." What Helen and Scott were talking about in *Living the Good Life* was not exactly revolutionary, except that in the 1950s and early '60s, it was. To give up your hard-earned place in the socioeconomic hierarchy and forgo modern conveniences was blasphemy; self-sufficiency was a threat to the status quo. But to Papa, the Nearings' book was far from a threat—homesteading sounded like the next great adventure.

I've climbed all the real mountains I want to climb, Papa thought to himself; here's a way to put those skills to use on a lifelong expedition, a mountain with no top. And Mama was eager to climb with him. They didn't want to be hippies in the traditional sense, having no interest in drugs or communes; rather, what appealed to them at the deepest level was the sentiment espoused by Henry David Thoreau over a century earlier, when he moved from the town of Concord to a rustic cabin on Walden Pond.

"I went to the woods because I wished to live deliberately," Thoreau explained. "To front only the essential facts of life, and see if I could not learn what it had to teach, and not, when I came to die, discover that I had not lived. I did not wish to live what was not life, living is so dear; nor did I wish to practice resignation, unless it was quite necessary. I wanted to live deep and suck out all the marrow of life, to live so sturdily and Spartan-like as to put to rout all that was not life."

They found that the idea of going back to the land was far from a new sentiment, and Americans, taken as we are by the romance of nature, seem to find the concept especially compelling. After Thoreau, the nature essayist John Burroughs left his job as a federal bank examiner in the 1880s to take up residence in the Hudson River Valley at a remote cabin called Slabsides, where he wrote about conservation and farmed in relative simplicity for the times. Then, at the height of the Great Depression, economist Dr. Ralph Borsodi began an experiment in "voluntary simplicity," a concept that led him to move from his native New York City to a farm in the countryside, as detailed in his 1933 book *Flight from the City*. *Living the Good Life* was now inspiring a new generation of discontented city dwellers, and soon the political climate and energy shortages of the 1970s would spark the coals of the back-to-the-land movement to flame.

FROM DECEMBER TO March, after they moved into the farmhouse and before I was born, my future parents lived "the good life," as defined by the Nearings, striving to follow the Nearing formula of four hours a day of bread labor, four hours of intellectual pursuits, and four hours of social time. In other words, divide the day between hands, head, and heart. Hands: chopping wood, making food, woodworking, sewing. Head: reading, learning to play the dulcimer. Heart: caring for each other, talking and laughing together.

The smells of wood smoke and simmering onions from soup filled the little house; the root cellar was stocked with vegetables they'd brought from their Franconia garden, as Mama planned for the birth of their first child and Papa prepared for the birth of the first garden. Mama sewed baby clothes and Papa made a wooden-handled box to carry his seeds, and a tool chest from leftover lumber, carving it with Scott's saying, "Work as well as you can and be kind."

They referred to *Living the Good Life* as their guide:

We would attempt to carry on this self-subsistent economy by the following steps:

1. Raising as much of our own food as local soil and climatic conditions would permit.
2. Bartering our products for those which we could not or did not produce.
3. Using wood for fuel and cutting it ourselves.
4. Putting up our own buildings with stone and wood from the place, doing the work ourselves.
5. Making such implements as sleds, drays, stone-boats, gravel screens, ladders.
6. Holding down to the barest minimum the number of implements, tools, gadgets and machines which we might buy from the assembly lines of big business.
7. If we had to have such machines for a few hours or days in a year (plough, tractor, rototiller, bull-dozer, chainsaw), we would rent or trade them from local people instead of buying and owning them.

"That list was our initial guideline," Papa told a visitor. On the Nearings' advice, they also developed a five-year plan to define their goals. "A plan is essential," Papa explained. "There are so many things to do that unless you follow a plan you may end up doing nothing except think about how much there is to be done. That first summer and autumn we planned to make a garden, build a little greenhouse in front of our living room windows, and dig another root cellar to complement the one we already had."

One of the many obstacles to self-sufficiency that winter was lack of firewood. The green wood Papa cut that fall needed at least six months to cure. "I'll be damned if I'm buying wood, of all things," Papa said. "We're surrounded by it." Each challenge, he began to realize, had a solution. While clearing more trees, he noticed that the thick dry branches at the bottoms of old fir and spruce trunks had up to fifty rings of growth. "It's such compact wood it makes for slow burning," he told Mama, pleased to find a temporary source for heat and cooking fuel that could be cut and used immediately.

The pulse of material needs began to slacken. The less they satisfied the urge to buy things, the more the craving—as with sugar, carbohydrates, and alcohol—began to wane. The drugs of the modern world were only a mirage of need easily forgotten in the absence of fulfillment. "I used to buy a new article of clothing when I was tired of wearing what I had even though it was no-where near worn out," Mama wrote in the journal she kept during those early years. "Now we try to have clothes we like and wear them until worn out (being patched over and over)."

"Use it up, wear it out, make do, or do without," was the home-steading adage, and it served them well.

When the Russian revolutionary classic *Dr. Zhivago* played at an Ellsworth theater, it alone merited emerging from hermit-age. Papa grew a Yuri mustache, and though Mama preferred him clean-shaven, she indulged his fantasies by sewing him col-larless Russian peasant shirts. They added the Russian "ski" to their names, which implied honor—Eliot-ski and Sue-ski, the dog Norm-ski, and one of the goats would be dubbed Goat-ski—imagining they were living the subsistence life that Dr. Zhivago and Tonya led at Varykino when the revolution forced them into hiding at a remote family estate.

PAPA HAD A picture book of European farms with rich ancient soil and gentle rolling hills that he'd look at in the evenings by the light of the kerosene lanterns.

"This one." He'd point out to Mama. "This is my favorite."

They dreamed of a patchwork of fertile beds spreading out

from the house in all directions, with careful paths and neat rows of plants. However, when they looked out the front windows that spring of my birth, the reality was tree stumps in all directions. Papa had cut as many trees as possible over the fall and winter, climbing up to saw off the branches for firewood, then felling the trunk and sawing it into logs to cure for next winter's wood. Once the snow melted, the carnage emerged, resembling the aftermath of a forest fire.

Living primarily on food grown or hunted yourself was a daunting concept in the supermarket 1960s and '70s, and for many back-to-the-landers, the biggest challenge. Added to our situation were the short growing season, thickly forested land, and poor soil.

"Whatcha growin'?" the Maine joke went, one farmer to another.

"Rocks," was the dry answer.

Despite the obstacles, the natural affinity Papa had found in his first garden at Franconia inspired and encouraged him to keep at it. As Mama nursed me in the rocking chair by the front windows, Papa declared war on the army of tree stumps with a pick, mattock, and handsaw. He'd heard from Scott that if you sawed the side roots and taproot from the center of a fir trunk, you could pull the whole thing out with your hands. He tried a small one, chopping the roots from the trunk with the mattock, then pushing it back with the pick to detach the taproot with the handsaw, and voilà! The stump came right out. Not all the trees were so easy. Some took hours to release. A friend of the Nearings told Papa he looked like Paul Bunyan, swinging his ax and wresting the trees from the earth with his bare hands.

"Ever thought of getting a chain saw?" the fellow asked innocently.

"We'd rather do without and work more slowly in peace," Papa replied in his affably militant manner. "A power saw is an unnerving noise. It pollutes in every way, the vibrations and the stench it makes."

"We prefer to use nature's lawn mowers," he added, pointing to the goats that ran free like a troupe of horned groundsmen, nibbling at the foliage, brambles, and trees to leave a nearly manicured, if a bit hoof-trodden and bark-chewn, landscape.

The sight of Papa tearing up stumps, struggling to grow food for our little family, assuaged Mama's old fears. He was so full of vitality, an athlete in his prime, it seemed nothing could stop him. She wanted to climb inside his arms and stay there always, but the twelve- to sixteen-hour workdays and his part-time job left little time for that. The next year we would sell vegetables at the farm stand for income, but that first year Papa worked odd jobs for Helen and Scott and other townsfolk for $2.50 an hour, to bring in cash on top of his work at our farm. Mama's day had multiple demands as well—hauling water for the pump sink in the kitchen, grinding grain with the hand grinder for baking bread, preparing meals, sewing and mending clothing, caring for me, and helping Papa while I napped.

"It was unremitting labor, the hardest time we had to go through," Papa would later admit in an interview with Stanley Mills, a visiting friend of the Nearings who published a quarterly hand-typed newsletter detailing our back-to-the-land exploits. "If you're going to homestead without private means you have to take it seriously," he explained. "It would have helped to have more money so that I could have given all my time to homesteading instead of taking outside work. Heaven knows, there was enough to do on our place. When winter comes, there's no going off to California. You have to stick it out and work much longer hours than the Nearing work formula suggests. We never had any doubts it was worth it, but at first we didn't realize self-sufficiency means nineteenth-century primitivism."

After the stumps on the half acre in front of the house were removed, Papa divided the area into twenty- by forty-foot plots, using a commonsense approach to small-scale agriculture. "We chose the size of the plots for their convenience," he told Stanley. "It's one fiftieth of an acre. Much information is available about needs and yields of land in terms of acres. In spreading lime, it's common knowledge that acid soil requires at least two tons of lime an acre. To find out how much a twenty by forty plot requires, simply divide two tons by fifty. This amounts to eighty pounds, and lime comes in eighty-pound bags. So one bag each plot." The lime served to decompose the vegetation and neutralize the acidity of the forest floor, thereby releasing the nitrogen that had been locked in by the acid and allowing for the growth of healthy soil bacteria. Next Papa tilled in compost and manure and staked out string in careful rows to transplant seedlings and seed the hardier crops.

Mama carried me on her chest or back with a cloth sling while she worked. After the gift boxes of Pampers from Mama's parents ran out, she put me in plastic panties over safety-pinned cloth diapers that she washed by hand in the ocean and hung to dry in the sun. Since we might be outdoors for hours at a time, she would augment the cloth diapers with the same dried peat moss we used for toilet paper. It's no wonder I would potty-train before the age of two. By midsummer I was able to hold my head up and roll around in the little playpen made from Mama's old purple poncho blanket draped over a wood frame. I can feel in my bones the chirp-cluck-brooding sounds of the chickens busying in the dust nearby, the smells of scythe-cut grass, freshly tilled earth, wet Normie-dog, and wood smoke from the cookstove as I lay on my back and babbled to the sky, grabbing my bare feet with my hands.

The garden was also finding its feet. The acre between the well and the house had, amazingly enough, become a rough version of Papa's imagined patchwork of garden plots with a network of trodden paths. The apple orchard grew as I did on the hill next to the garden, with saplings of varietals suited for the cooler climate: Northern Spy, russet, and Spy Gold. Come August, as Woodstock was giving voice to thousands of muddy festival-goers in New York State, we were celebrating a bounty of exceptionally large vegetables, including cabbages that literally weighed forty pounds. It wasn't until a couple years later that Papa learned that this abnormal growth was due to the release of all of the naturally occurring nitrogen that had been stored in the forest floor over the years. "The founders of the spiritual-ecological community of Findhorn in Scotland saw the forty-pound cabbages in their first garden as a spiritual sign, but it was most likely the same nitrogen release we saw," Papa explained, amused.

At the end of the long summer days, my parents fell to sleep exhausted, knowing they would be woken any number of times in the night by my crying before getting up at first light to start work again. Creating a living from the land with a newborn baby was indeed every bit as challenging as Helen had predicted. Each day was a swarm of obstacles. All they could do was stay focused on one task at a time and see it through to its resolution.

MY GRANDMOTHER SKATES arrived in September, joined by Papa's sister Lyn, her husband, Lucky Callen, and the four kids, Paige, Chip, Lindsay, and Hunter. They'd driven the nine hours north to find out for themselves "what the heck we were doing up in the woods of Maine." Papa's family was as modern as we were not, and upstanding citizens of one of New Jersey's oldest and wealthiest towns. The Callens lived in the updated house on Blackpoint Horseshoe in Rumson, where Papa grew up, while Skates had built her own modern home across the field by the river, with a dock where she liked to fish for snappers.

The year of my birth was the year of the first moon landing, Ted Kennedy's Chappaquiddick incident, the Stonewall riots, Charles Manson's murders, and the advent of no-fault divorce, signed into law—ironically enough—by a Republican governor named Ronald Reagan. In this Age of Aquarius the songs of Bob Dylan, the Grateful Dead, Joan Baez, and Crosby, Stills & Nash were giving voice to change. The turmoil brought on by hippies, radicals, and folksingers made Papa's family nervous. They were supportive of America, capitalism, and the status quo. More than that, they were staunch Republicans. Nixon, who had taken office that January, was their hero.

"Nixon," Skates said, "will return the world to equilibrium."

Skates's tall figure stood out in bright blues and whites against the browns and greens of the farm as she walked up the garden path to the house. She wore a striped shirt over wrinkle-free shorts with a perfect crease down the front, glasses hanging on a beaded cord that matched her blue eyes like Papa's and white hair styled in perfect short waves around her high forehead. Lyn and Lucky and the kids followed, a model WASP family of the 1960s, blond, fair-eyed, fresh-faced, and appropriately androgynous in pressed khakis and polos of light blues, yellows, and nautical stripes, their whites bright and unstained unlike our permanently dirty grays.

Skates often said Papa must have inherited his adventurous spirit from Thomas Coleman, the man at the root of the Coleman family tree, who left Wiltshire, England, on the *James* for the New

World in 1635. Thomas was awarded a land claim on Nantucket, where his son went on to marry Benjamin Franklin's aunt, and their son hunted whales from the harbor. As American settlers, they lived by necessity in the ways we would live by choice two centuries later—growing and hunting food, cooking and heating with wood or whale blubber, using an outhouse. Thanks to in-law Benjamin Franklin, as well as Thomas Edison and others, by the 1900s, Americans would have electricity, running water, telephones, and the automobile. Food would be bought at the store, vegetables grown commercially, cooking done on reliable gas or electric stoves. Life was good for Americans—the Roaring Twenties had arrived.

It was in this privileged time that my grandfather Eliot, nicknamed Skipper, undoubtedly for his love of boats, met Dorothea Morrell, a spirited girl from a fun-loving family in Morristown, New Jersey. She was a tomboy debutante with sporty tastes—skiing, fishing, hockey, and tennis. The nickname Skates came from the time she was playing hockey disguised as a boy for the Morristown pickup team and got knocked down, her hat falling off to expose curly, long blond hair. "A girl," someone on the other team yelled, "and she skates."

"Skipper was handsome, and a good athlete," Skates told us, athleticism garnering her highest esteem. His parents had moved from Long Island to the well-to-do suburb of Rumson, New Jersey, known for the oldest lawn tennis club in the country, a beautiful beach club, and easy access to Manhattan by train. When Skates and Skipper married, they set up house in the renovated boathouse of the Coleman estate on a tributary of the Navesink River. Aunt Lyn was born in 1936 and two years later, Eliot Warner Coleman Jr. came into the world at Morristown Memorial Hospital.

"He came out smiling," Skates claimed. She smiled, too, it was such a joy for her to have a son. We still joke that he was like her own little baby Jesus. There were so many pairs of knitted booties among the baby gifts, the nickname-prone family dubbed him "Boots," which later became "Bootsie," much to his chagrin. Boots was sent to private school at Rumson Country Day and then to prep school at St. Paul's in New Hampshire, where his cousins also went. He was a star cross-country runner and lacrosse player, though a mediocre student. Papa made close ties with friends and teachers, but was by spirit independent, even then preferring V8 to Coke. Though he was teased for it, he stood up for himself, to the point of once getting his nose broken in a fistfight in the dining hall.

"Attaboy, Boots," Skates likely said about the tiff. She ruled the home, children, and Skipper with a confident belligerence to any view outside her own. Skipper, who was slightly shorter than Skates's five feet eleven inches, was a quiet and gentlemanly husband, some said henpecked. He served in the navy and after the war commuted to Manhattan, where he worked as a stockbroker, making a decent living at it, though never enough to be rich. Instead they did what they should have known better than to do—spent the capital from his inheritance. Skates's sister and friends were all well-to-do, driving her to keep up with her tennis partners both on the court and off.

"Those were the years of the Hemingway model of adventure," Skates explained. She and Skipper passed on their love of sports and the outdoors to their children, teaching Boots and Lyn to fish and ski as soon as they could walk. They had a cruising boat, the *Here We R*, that they took out on summer weekends, and in winter they escaped to warm locales to fish or up to Uncle George's lodge in Stowe, Vermont, to ski. Papa began to

notice that when his parents were outdoors, they seemed hap-
pier and drank less, and he felt his own spirit lift and heart beat
more rigorously as he skied or climbed in the clear air of the
mountains.

"HELLO, BOOTSIE," SKATES and the Callens chorused when
Papa emerged from the farmhouse to greet them. Skates kissed
us all with her red-lipsticked bow-shaped mouth, smelling of soap
and something brighter than soap that made a shield around her,
separating her from the dirt and organic smells of the farm.

"That perfume is enough to take the paint off a car," Papa said
when she was out of hearing, wrinkling his nose about the smell,
and Mama laughed. To Skates, we must have seemed victims of
rural poverty, and boy, did *we* smell. Skates gave Papa a hard time
about needing to take a bath, and especially about us not eating
meat.

"You're too skinny. You need protein, working so hard out
here," she said. "Kids need protein too; are you sure it's okay for
Melissa?"

Papa was eloquent as always in his defense of vegetarianism,
explaining that humans had been vegetarians for centuries, and
animals had as much a right to live as we.

"Boots says he doesn't believe in killing animals," Skates said
pointedly to Lyn in reply to Papa's lecture. "Well, neither do I. I
have the butcher do it."

Everyone got a good laugh at that, and tensions eased, until
Papa yelled at the boys for playing with their cork gun in the
garden.

"No guns on my property!" Papa admonished.

"It's just a harmless toy." Lyn defended her children, but put
away the gun.

"Why does he have to be so self-righteous?" she complained to her mother when Papa was out of earshot.

"IF IT WEREN'T for that motorcycle accident," Skates liked to tell us, "your father would have gone on to become a respectable stockbroker like his own father." Skates also liked to say, as only a mother can, that with his sandy hair and chiseled features her son looked like a cross between Clint Eastwood, Robert Redford, and Paul Newman. His desire to be a farmer was beyond her upper-middle-class sensibilities. Pour her another Scotch, and she'd look over her glasses and tell you the neck injury made him crazy.

"Why else," she'd ask, "would a person with everything going for him move to the woods and live on a farm with no electricity, running water, or toilet?"

The accident happened during the spring Papa was considering enlisting in the army, on the verge as he was of flunking out of Williams College, the private liberal arts school in western Massachusetts that had also been attended by his father. Papa was on the cross-country running and ski teams and a fraternity brother at St. Anthony Hall. There he made two lifelong friends, Jan and Tony, who happened to own a pair of Triumph 150 motorbikes for riding the trails in the woods around campus. They were a handsome and athletic trio, skiing, mountaineering, and chasing women together, but Papa found himself lacking in commitment to his studies.

"There's a nice girl in Bennington," Papa told Tony one evening, it being customary for Williams boys to visit Bennington, Vermont, for the women's college and younger drinking age. "Let's ride your bike up there, find you a date, and take them out." After dinner it was decided that the girl, Muffy, would come back to Williams, and they climbed on the bike, Tony, Muffy, and

Papa in that order. They weren't going very fast along the winding backcountry route, but darkness obscured a boulder lying on the tarmac. The front wheel hit the obstacle, throwing the bike sideways and tossing Papa across the road into a signpost.

"He let go to save the girl," Tony said later. Muffy and Tony slid on the bike, which protected them from impact. In the aftermath, everyone was conscious, though Papa and Tony were soon in a lot of pain from road rash. As they waited for help, a party truck that some college guys had rigged up with couches and music in the back pulled up beside them. They didn't want Muffy to get in trouble, so she climbed aboard and glided away on one of those couches as an ambulance arrived to take the two boys to the hospital. (In a happy aside, Tony and Muffy would cross paths a couple years later and, while commiserating over the accident, fall in love—eventually getting married and having four children.)

"We lay on gurneys beside each other, while the nurses picked stones out of our behinds, trying to hide our groans as the pebbles plunked into a metal bucket," Tony recounted. Skates showed up at the hospital dressed for a party, pale hair coiffed, red-lipsticked, tall, and no-nonsense. She kept a cool head. On top of losing his front teeth, the doctors soon realized, Papa had ruptured a kidney and was bleeding internally. Then they found a cracked vertebra in his neck and immediately put him in a brace. At that point, the boys at the frat house began taking bets as to whether he'd make it or not.

In the final tally, Papa had a ruptured kidney, three splintered ribs, a broken arm, and a fractured neck. "It's only because he was in such good athletic shape that he survived," Tony claimed, relieved to have been spared the death of a friend. After the internal bleeding was stabilized and Papa's neck set in a brace, his life was no longer at risk, but he was immobilized and confined to the hospital for a month and a half to recover.

"I've never been very introspective," Papa told Tony. "But sitting in this damn hospital is making me look over the merchandise for the first time, and there's not much of note." He began to read anything he could get his hands on, from health books to tales of adventure. When Papa was finally released from the hospital, able to walk but still fragile, the doctor recommended he avoid school and physical activities for the rest of the year. Convalescing at home in Rumson, he began to see more clearly the depths of his father's quiet despair and the casual alcoholism of both his parents. Skipper and Skates smoked and drank as much as their friends, so they never worried it might have been too much, using alcohol to soothe some unnamed feeling of discontent created by the relative ease of their existence. The gnawing sedative made pale a world where Papa wished to find brightness and the grit of more difficult challenges. Skipper arranged an apprenticeship for Papa on the floor of the stock exchange in Manhattan, and a couple weeks later he received a Christmas bonus, a whole week's pay. Papa was dumbfounded at landing all that cash for such little effort.

"If I follow this path, all I'll ever make in life is money," he told his father, and to his surprise, his father agreed. "If you end up doing what I'm doing, you should have your head examined," Skipper remarked. That's when Papa's search for another way of life began in earnest. He didn't say outright that he was rejecting his parents' lifestyle, he just began to slip away.

"Oh, but he had everything going for him," Skates lamented.

Age twenty-one and fully recovered from his near-fatal motorcycle accident, Papa wanted to celebrate his luck. His love was outdoor sports, so he began to pursue that passion full-time, getting a summer job as a ski instructor in Chile. Any sport he heard about, he had to try—rock climbing, mountaineering, and white-water kayaking. His instinct was ahead of his time; back then, if you saw a kayak on a car, you likely knew the person. After finishing Williams, Papa received his master's in Spanish literature at Middlebury's program in Spain, then landed a job at Colorado Academy teaching Spanish and coaching the ski team. In summers he ran a whitewater kayak program near Aspen, helping kids build their own fiberglass kayaks. Teaching provided the perfect schedule to support his habits—during school vacations he could climb volcanoes in Mexico and summit Mount Logan or go on kayak trips down the great western rivers with his students.

"Bootsie's off on some expedition or other," Skates began to brag jovially to make up for the fact that he wasn't settling down to make a good living like her friends' sons. Soon he was offered the job at Franconia College, which seemed like a good place to continue his chosen lifestyle.

MY RELATIVES MIGHT have marveled as Mama milked the goats and sawed firewood with me on her back, carried water from the spring, and used the woodstove for cooking, baking, and canning, and were amazed when Papa showed off the root cellar stocked with the summer's bounty from the garden and talked of plans for clearing more land. But at the end of the day they were glad to retreat to a nearby ocean-side guesthouse with electricity, running water, and other modern comforts. The lodge was owned by Carolyn Robinson, who with her husband, Ed, wrote *The "Have More" Plan: A Little Land, a Lot of Living*, a bestselling do-it-yourself home-gardening book published ten years before *Living the Good Life*, and credited with launching an exodus of the middle class from the city to the suburbs after World War II.

Staying at the Robinsons' was the glorified good life. Skates could eat meat, drink Scotch, and have a bathroom at night, then come see us during the day. Visiting her son was an adventure, just the way Papa liked it, but she was nonetheless relieved at the end of the trip to return to her own, much safer world.

THE DAYS GREW short and cool as the endless light that had fueled us all summer lost minutes per day. Mama and Papa were busy as the squirrels, harvesting and putting away food. Some days Mama would sink under the weight of it all—the work of keeping life in order that never ended, the urgency to put away food to survive, and the burden of another being strapped to her body, nursing from her, needing her for everything.

Then there was the bucket of dirty cloth diapers, and no fresh ones. Dirty bowls in the sink and no clean ones, stains on her favorite shirt, a broken mason jar. Seaweed that needed to be hauled by the trailer load from the Nearing and Hoffman coves to cover the garden beds and provide potassium as it decomposed over the winter. Carrots and beets to be placed in sand in the root cellar, string beans to be canned in mason jars, winter squash to season on the patio, onions and garlic to braid and hang from the ceiling alongside spearmint, chamomile, and lemon verbena for tea and basil, rosemary, and thyme for seasoning. Meanwhile, Papa was occupied building a glass greenhouse on the front of the house to extend the growing season by bringing Skates's temperate climate in New Jersey nine hours north to Maine.

When I cried, the noise must have vibrated inside Mama's brain, sending an alert down each nerve ending in her body. An instinct in her bones responded to the sound, and she tried to soothe my cries with a mental checklist of generally successful actions. Nurse, change diaper, make sure I wasn't too hot or cold.

On bad days, when I cried about everything, whether she nursed or changed my diaper, the noise inside her brain was like a million mice gnawing away at the cords of her sanity.

If I could not be silenced, I imagine Mama set me down and covered her eyes with her hands for a moment, her forehead creasing. Behind her lids she saw her mother in the same gesture and her own mother's hands falling from her face to reveal the panic in her eyes. She felt the rise of anger paralyze her jaw. Instead of letting the anger strike out, she pushed it away as her mother had done. Anger was ugly, Papa would not approve. Her eyes went flat, and she "checked out," as she later came to call it. Sometimes she wouldn't come back for hours.

Papa began to wonder if Mama had a split personality. One minute she was the strongest woman he knew, as in childbirth. She'd sensed just what to do—he'd been the helpless one. Other times she got weepy and depressed for seemingly no reason. "Take some B," was his usual advice. From his reading, he suspected a vitamin deficiency as the cause of the moodiness, perhaps not enough vitamin B due to their vegetarian diet. Of vitamin B's many variations, B12—which assists in the normal functioning of the brain and nervous system—is not found in plants, leaving vegetarians deficient. The Nearings later admitted to getting B12 shots to supplement their diet, but did not widely discuss this fact, as it contradicted their claims of self-sufficiency. Later research has shown that the vegetarian diet is not as perfect as it then seemed, and may have indeed been responsible for Mama's mood swings as well as Papa's stress levels and eventual thyroid imbalance, an illness that would threaten the life they'd worked so hard to create.

Mama, however, generally resented Papa's attempts to fix her with vitamins, saying she had B-rich brewer's yeast coming out her ears, which was true, until her supplies ran out and she had no money to order it, or time to go to town.

"All I need is rest and more support from you," she countered, a tad hormonally, in Papa's opinion.

ON THE GOOD days it was hard to remember what the bad ones felt like. On the good days, the world was full of beauty. The weather cooled, the pace of the farm slowed down, and we tucked in for winter. There was time again to nurture ourselves. Mama woke in the mornings to the comfort of nursing, the hormone oxytocin relaxing her nerves as the milk relaxed mine. The drug of motherhood. The weight and shape of my body in her arms, the smell and smoothness of baby skin a balm for all sadnesses.

Papa came into the farmhouse followed by a gasp of cold air, the stomping of boots, and the skittering of Normie's paws on the wood floor.

"Wait till you see what happened to the blueberry field," he said, popping up the ladder to the loft bed, dressed in his warmest much-patched down jacket.

"What?" Mama asked, propping on one elbow to reveal her sleep-weary face and matted hair. Papa's blue eyes met her brown ones with a twinkle, the touch of premature gray in his hair a foil to the youthfulness of his mood.

"Get up, come see," he said, disappearing down the ladder. A thrill lit up her spine. It was cold even with the stove roaring, the thermometer recording lows of twenty below at night. Mama dressed herself warmly and put me in my snowsuit, setting me into the blue canvas and aluminum Gerry child backpack that had taken place of her sling and squatting to slide it onto her back. Outside the sun was bright against the cold air, the barren ground frozen. Papa had fetched a bushel basket for harvesting, and inside was a coil of twine.

"What's that for?" Mama asked.

"You'll see," he said. We followed him and Normie through the dormant garden, past the skeletal rose-hip hedge and the well pulley, up the lane by the orchard, and out to the sign Mama had carved with their names over a year ago. Across the main road, the expanse of the blueberry field opened up in maroon undulations to the sky.

"Look," Papa said. The low area in the center of the field had filled with water during recent rains and frozen with the sudden drop in nighttime temperatures to form an Olympic-size skating rink.

"Perfect black ice," Papa explained, running to slide across the smooth surface, mimicking skating strokes in his work boots. Like Skates, he'd played hockey growing up, once even competing at Madison Square Garden for a high school championship. Normie skittered on his paws, his legs splaying out of control, as Mama stood by the edge, watching Papa's joy, afraid to risk falling with me on her back.

"Here," Papa said, placing the bushel basket down on the ice. He pulled out the twine, fed it through one of the staves of the basket, tying the two ends in a knot to make a loop, then lifted me into the basket. I reached up with mittened hands, unsure at first, as the basket began to slide forward.

"See?" he said. He pulled a little faster, and Mama slid beside, clapping her hands and smiling to encourage me. The surface was black and smooth as opal beneath her feet, and the weight of her body disappeared as she ran-slid after us.

Norm gave up slipping on the ice to sit panting on his haunches, and Mama stopped to join him, pulling her camera with the rainbow strap from the case attached to the Gerry pack. I was flying in the basket across the pond behind Papa, my laughter coming in spurts. Papa looked back, grinning, his brown balaclava tipped up. The sun flashed in the blue, blue sky as Mama snapped a photo.

What joy it is to be alive, Mama thought, to have a handsome husband and a laughing young child. But as she felt the glow of happiness spread through her body, a voice inside couldn't help but whisper, *This joy will not last. Why should it now, when it never has before? Someday, this photo will be all that remains.*

She tucked the fear away and laughed into the sky.

CHAPTER TWO

Livelihood

OUR SECOND APRIL brought with it the welcome warmth of sunshine, the damp-cool smell of turned earth, the urgency of the world coming alive. From my bird's-eye view, I watch my young self playing with pinecones on the warm stones of the patio, barely one year old, big eyes under a cowlick of short brown hair, as Mama's and Papa's backs arch below, turning the soil of the garden. The first three years on Greenwood Farm, while physically demanding for Mama and Papa, were by comparison emotionally peaceful years for our small family.

If I hover close, I can feel the hazy shapes of brightness and color, the loneliness of hunger, and the sweet taste of fullness that made up my world. Around me the chickens fluffed and busied in the dust of the paths as Norm slept nearby, fur warmed and dog-smelling in the sun, paws twitching after dream rabbits. Across the yard, goats hooved the ground and rubbed their horns on the cedar posts of their fenced pen. We didn't know it, but we were all waiting. It was a feeling in the blood of impatience for spring.

As Mama and Papa turned the damp earth, two familiar brown birds alighted on the brush by the goat pen, fluffed their feathers, and sang out in perfect pitch, "Old-Sam-Pea-bo-dy, Peabody, Peabody, Peabody."

"The white-throated sparrows," Mama announced, looking up from her work.

"They're back," Papa acknowledged, resting on his fork handle for a minute to watch the sparrows hopping across the ground, searching for seeds, and rustling in the leaves. The arrival of the seasons was the one thing we could trust, and in their regularity we found our livelihood. Spring urged soil preparation, planting, and growth; summer brought the reward of ripening and harvesting; fall meant storage and preparation for winter. And if we were successful during the growing months, we could hibernate and rest in winter. Then spring returned, and the cycle commenced anew.

Soon the world was full of birds. They coursed the air like thoughts in the brain, twittering, singing, and building their nests. Red-breasted robins pulled at worms, blue jays jabbered, nuthatches walked upside down on tree trunks, woodpeckers rat-a-tat-tatted. There were pearly blackbirds, the flash of scarlet tanagers, bright finches. Crows and seagulls scavenged at the compost heaps, and flocks of swallows scattered in unison across the sky.

The presence of so many birds was a great comfort to Papa, despite their inclination for stealing seeds from the garden before they could germinate. Rachel Carson's *Silent Spring* had been published to much acclaim and controversy in 1962—its title alluding to John Keats's poem "La Belle Dame sans Merci" ("The sedge has wither'd from the lake, / And no birds sing"). In her groundbreaking work, Carson's research indicated that insecticides such as DDT were weakening the shells of birds, causing the offspring to die before hatching and threatening the extinction of peregrine falcons and the American icon, the bald eagle.

Used heavily since World War II as an agricultural pesticide, DDT was also, horrifyingly in retrospect, sprayed into wallpaper with the claim that it would protect children from mosquito-carried malaria. While studies have shown that DDT can cause infertility, miscarriage, and breast cancer in women exposed during youth, at the time Carson faced criticism and lawsuits from the chemical industry, especially Monsanto and American Cyanamid, which argued that DDT was safe, and that without it people would die from diseases like malaria. Nonetheless, the public outcry was such that the pesticide would be banned in the United States by 1972. Rachel Carson's message was so effective, perhaps, because birds represent freedom—the iconic bald eagle—and anything that threatens that freedom threatens us.

Papa saw the incident as yet another example of chemical companies defending their profits and letting the environment pay the price. He liked to quote a little poem by Ralph Hodgson:

> *I saw with open eyes*
> *Singing birds sweet*
> *Sold in the shops*
> *For the people to eat,*
> *Sold in the shops of*
> *Stupidity Street.*
>
> *I saw in vision*
> *The worm in the wheat,*

And in the shops nothing
For people to eat;
Nothing for sale in
Stupidity Street.

Papa was not alone in his concerns. The previous fall, the inaugural issue of *The Whole Earth Catalog* had put on its cover the first photo of Earth taken from space, giving humans a new perspective on the beautiful and surprisingly fragile orb of blue and green, and as a result, the first Earth Day, planned for that April 1970, would be celebrated by 20 million Americans across the country.

As Mama and Papa worked in the garden that spring, other news drifted in bits and snatches over the battery-powered radio that sat on the patio by the house: "One hundred thousand protesters march against the Vietnam War in Washington, D.C. . . . *Apollo 13* aborts mission to moon. . . . Four students at Kent State shot by national guardsmen during a protest over Cambodia." Then came the musical outcry of Simon and Garfunkel's "Bridge over Troubled Water," at number one on the charts, and Joni Mitchell's "Big Yellow Taxi," drifting across the airwaves:

Hey farmer, farmer
Put away that DDT now
Give me spots on my apples
But LEAVE me the birds and the bees
Please!

It wasn't until the weather report came on that Papa ran to the patio and turned up the volume, hoping temperatures would be warm enough to plant seedlings outside, and ultimately, put food on the table. While the songs and struggles of the outside world were hopeful, the requirements for survival in the woods were, by necessity, Papa's primary concern.

Or so it seemed at the time. Looking back, I see our isolated farm as the small dewdrop on the vast web, and Papa's individual goal to grow his own organic vegetables as part of a greater shift in the world, spreading like a chain reaction along the strands. Rachel Carson's concerns over chemical agriculture led in effect to Papa's desire to grow his own food, and his example and that of other organic pioneers would be followed by a trickle of oddballs, but a trickle that grew until, as the Y2K book *The Tipping Point* explains, it tipped, and today the word *organic* is mainstream.

Small drops, we see, like raindrops on stone, can eventually change the course of a river. These small forces, too, can change the path of a life.

STARTING SEEDLINGS WAS Papa's favorite part of the job, hopeful as it was to watch those tiny green leaves emerging from the brown potting soil.

"Come on up, little one," he'd say, patting his lap when I hung nearby. I'd climb into the hum of his concentrated excitement, my head under his chin and body in the cave of his arms as his callused hands tap-tap-tapped the card-size envelopes to drop seeds into the loamy potting mix. He'd spent the long winter poring over seed catalogs, settling on thirty-five crops best suited to our climate and soil and sending in order forms with creased dollar bills from under the couch for payment.

Papa shared with Mama from his reading: "Vegetables are similar to flowers, sending messages to our eyes that we should eat them, the way flowers send messages to the bees to pollinate them." The orange of carrots and squashes indicated beta-carotene for the eyes, the dark green of spinach held calcium for bones, and the reds of tomatoes meant lycopene for the heart.

Papa mixed extravagant potting soils from peat, compost, and soil with the care of someone preparing baby food. He whistled with contentment as he cut cedar logs to make into flats, or "borrowed" and modified Herrick's wooden blueberry boxes left in the field across the road. Soon, these flats filled with potting soil and germinating seeds covered every sunny window ledge, every counter, and all the floor space as well as the beds of the new greenhouse built onto the front of the house.

It didn't escape me that in spring Papa spent more time with his plants than with me. Perhaps that's why, once I could walk, I felt compelled to leave my perfect little footprints marching across his newly seeded flats on the floor. The smoothed soil was sand on the beach, calling out to my bare feet. This happened not once, resulting in a halfhearted scolding, but every spring until after Heidi was born, when I had a human sibling to compete with for attention.

Despite my meddling, the seedlings pushed through the soil, a V of tiny green leaves folding out from a white stem. Only the wooden stakes with Papa's scrawly or Mama's neat handwriting differentiated the kind of seed and date planted. They grew to distinguish themselves with the waxy double oval leaves of melons and squash, lacy carrotlike fennels, red crinkly lettuces, broccoli's thick, rounded heart leaves, the purple veins of eggplant, and hairy stems of tomatoes. We ate meals with an army of tomato plants that crept right up around our bowls, leaving their distinct cut-grass smell on our hands as we moved spoon to mouth.

"The average for this climate is one hundred and five frost-free days per year, leaving two hundred and sixty nights that might kill plants," Scott told Papa. So the tender tomatoes and melons were part of our family until after Memorial Day, or Decoration Day as it was called by old-timers, the date it was considered safe to plant outside.

TWO YEARS EARLIER it was another book from Hatch's, this one by Leonard Wickenden, that forever changed the way Papa understood agriculture. As a chemist in the 1940s, Wickenden set out to skeptically analyze the claims of the fledgling organi-culture—or natural farming—movement, but found that not only did chemical fertilizers deplete the soil, but vegetables tasted better when grown on healthy soil amended with organic matter and natural nutrients.

"Did you know there are billions of organisms in a teaspoon of healthy soil?" Papa asked Mama, his nose deep in the Wickenden book, the concept of a self-sufficient natural system opening the door to a new world. Conventional agriculture of the time ad-hered to the findings of the German chemist Justus von Liebig, the guy who developed commercial baby formula, who in the mid-1800s discovered that the chemical nitrogen was an essential soil nutrient that could be isolated and used to "feed" plants. He defined the law of the minimum, which stated that agricultural yield is proportional to the amount of the most limited nutri-ent. If the missing nutrient was supplied in chemical form, yields would increase until another nutrient became the minimum, and so on, resulting by the twentieth century in an economic bonanza for the chemical industry.

After the world wars, the companies that grew rich making bombs sought new markets. Agriculture was the perfect niche; small farms were giving way to large-scale commercial operations that had to sustain crops on overused land. Nitrogen, which had been used for bombs, could easily be dusted on the fields for fertilizer, and chemicals used for killing humans turned out to be perfect for killing pests. Pesticides and fertilizers became the new miracle. Soon the short collective memory had forgotten there was any other way. Wickenden, by contrast, argued for a return to the practices of feeding the soil with natural ingredients, rather than chemicals.

In the spring of 1967 Papa had bought a secondhand Troy-Bilt rototiller and set to work on a plot of land on the Franconia College property. He couldn't afford commercial fertilizers, but knew that those expensive products were just replicating the natural forms of nitrogen, phosphate, and potassium—N-P-K—that nourished the organisms in that teaspoon of healthy soil. He located free granite dust in the quarries of Barre, Vermont, for potassium and chicken manure for phosphate, and a local horse farm was more than happy to give him manure that he mixed with compost and bloodmeal to till into the soil for nitrogen.

"Even the old-timer farmers around Franconia were impressed with the success of our first garden," Papa told his students when they returned in the fall. As well as an abundance of delicious vegetables, he and Mama gained a deeper sense of satisfaction than they'd ever known before. They'd taken control of producing their food, and it had left them liberated—and well fed. They read books by one of the early natural-living gurus, J. I. Rodale, whose books and magazines advocated nutritional supplements and organic farming, and they soon gave up white sugar and flour, became vegetarians, got chickens, goats, and a horse, and began to dream of living on a farm for real.

That fall, a call came that shook Papa's foundations. As he was working in the garden after school, a student delivered an urgent message from Skates. Papa called his mother back from a school phone, hands still damp from the earth.

"Your father has passed on," Skates said over a crackly line. "A stroke."

Skipper had collapsed at age sixty-two while on a cruise in the Caribbean. Damn his bad diet and too much drink, was Papa's first thought. Mama found him in the hunting lodge, tears in his eyes for the first time since they'd met, but unable to express the depth of his sadness. His father had left too easily, a gentleman to the end. As he washed the dirt from his hands, Papa swore to himself he'd live a fuller life to make up for his father's short one. That meant staying healthy so an early death wouldn't strike him and his own family. Looking down at his hands, he realized that they were his most valuable tool in this quest.

ON THAT SECOND spring at Greenwood Farm, Papa planned to grow three times as many crops as the previous summer in order to sell vegetables for income, but the acidic, sandy soil needed help. "This area is unsuitable for agriculture," the Maine Soil Conservation Service report had stated in the first soil test.

"If you want to get me to do something, tell me it can't be done," Papa quipped, having seen firsthand in his Franconia garden that plants, like students, thrived with good nutrition and a supportive environment. That meant healthy soil and an enthusiastic gardener. He certainly had the enthusiasm, but what the soil needed was compost, and lots of it.

Papa was often out in his rubber boots with a pitchfork, the steam rising around him, as he turned the compost heaps to help the plant and food waste transform into "black gold," as he called it. The Nearing-style heaps surrounded the gardens like six-by-six-foot log cabins, built from saplings that Papa cut and stripped with an ax. At first the log house was very short, just eight logs stacked in a square on top of each other with ends sticking out, but as the heap grew bigger over the summer and fall with leaves, grass clippings, pulled weeds, dry pea vines, lettuce gone to seed, and scraps from cooking and leftovers, more logs were added, up and up until it was as tall as Papa. "The compost pile is another mouth to feed," he often said when adding dinner scraps to the bucket in the kitchen.

All the heaps needed were organic matter, air, water, and time—about six months—for everything to turn into black gold. If you were to stick a thermometer into the center, it might register temps upward of 150 degrees. Produced by the millions of tiny organisms that digested scraps into organic matter, the heat performed the secondary task of killing weed seeds that might germinate, unbidden, once the compost was spread in the garden. Earthworms also were key. Just as microorganisms consumed the organic matter, the earthworm in turn consumed the bacteria and microorganisms and left behind a condensed casting of nutrients. The only problem was, there wasn't enough time or compost to fortify the amount of ground Papa needed to cover.

Fortunately, Papa knew about another soil-enriching secret farmers had used for centuries: manure from horses bedded on straw. Horses were instant compost-producing machines. Their stomachs digested straw and grain and broke down the enzymes in a way similar to the decomposition process of the compost heap. When horseshit landed in the stall and mixed with bedding straw, it continued to decompose to create a mixture that when tilled into the earth could bring to life even the poorest soil, but over the years the symbiotic relationship between horse and man had been lost to the benefits of the automobile. Old-fashioned bedding straw was the key; sawdust, wood shavings, and other modern animal bedding products did not produce the same magic.

With some luck, Papa located a large straw-bedded stable in a neighboring town with owners tickled to give their manure to anyone who wanted to haul it away. Papa hitched the wagon to Skipper's old army jeep, often referred to as "Jeep" and later "Good Ole Jeepie" for its fortitude, and made trips back and forth with a pitchfork until there was a steaming brown mountain next to the garden. This he tilled into the soil with rock phosphate and limestone to help increase the pH to more desirable levels. And though he didn't have to, come summer Papa would compensate the stable owners by bringing them the delicious resulting vegetables.

Every morning Papa was back at it again, though even the lengthening days of spring proved too short. In the last of the light before going in for dinner, he spread the new garden plots with white rock powder over the compost and manure, so that when he returned in darkness it would catch the moonlight to guide the rototiller down the rows. The noise of the old red Troy-Bilt from Franconia growled into the silence of the dark woods and drifted out as far as the ocean. Though Papa wished he could turn the earth in silence with horse and plow like the original homesteaders, he knew the concession to the modern rototiller was necessary to attain his goals for the garden. But then, inevitably, the tiller conked out, and he was up all night in the woodshed with a kerosene lantern, trying to fix it.

"Son of a gun," he swore, lying on the dirt floor next to the tiller, hands greasy and oil smudges on his cheek. But as he worked to replace the broken belt, he felt a sense of peace settle in his chest.

He had all the time in the world. No one to answer to—except himself and his family. Nowhere he'd rather be than here.

"How many sons of a gun are lucky enough to have such problems?" he said aloud into the night, and then repeated the words under his breath like a mantra.

WHEN IT WAS time for my seedling siblings to make their way into the world, the flats were cut into cakelike squares of potting soil containing white cobwebby roots topped by a V of leaves. Papa gently lifted the squares and placed them into holes in the newly cultivated soil along straight rows marked by string. Once I was old enough, he let me tuck the earth in around them.

"There's nothing more hopeful than those rows of new plants," Papa said, looking back at the lines of green against brown. For the first couple weeks after planting, Papa listened anxiously to the weather for any signs of frost. Temperatures below freezing could quickly put an end to my new family. At the slightest risk, he and Mama dragged out sheets and blankets, newspapers and paper bags, anything they could lay hands on to protect the tender plants from freezing.

Soon enough the weather warmed and the garden exploded with growth. Come midsummer, when Papa climbed the tall blue spruce near the well with Mama's camera to capture the results, the plots marched across the acre in front of the house with the formation of a medieval army and its many varied regiments. As the Nearings recommended in *Living the Good Life*, the beds ran east-west in straight rows, with the low crops in one area, and permanent plants such as asparagus, rhubarb, berries, and herbs in another. Though Papa would soon surpass the Nearings with his passion and innovation in the garden, he used their practices as his initial guide. As in the Nearings' garden, our rows of pea vines were supported with tree branches, the beans with twelve-foot poles; cedar stakes marked the straight rows, the variety of plant noted on them in pencil.

"One of the most important secrets I learned from the Near-ings was succession planting," Papa claimed. Rather than the garden beginning in spring, producing in summer, and ending in fall, the Nearings succeeded in extending the short Maine grow-ing season by continually planting new crops. When the peas were done for the season in June or July, for instance, they were ripped out, fresh compost was spread, and the area was planted with a new crop. The pea vines were added to the compost pile, which would in turn be put back into the garden the following season.

Another successful habit adopted from the Nearings was their attention to detail, planning, and observation. They kept careful notes of what they did each year in the garden, such as which lettuces had grown well with what soil amendments and which ingredients worked best when making compost. Many of their discoveries came from chance observations that a less astute farmer might have missed, and from being in the right place at the right time. If something wasn't working, it was time for a new plan, and they were always thinking ahead, even putting in trees to create a windbreak they might not live to enjoy.

"Helen and Scott are the only octogenarians I know who are planning for ten years down the road," Papa often joked, but their steadfast and purposeful effort appealed to his still-young and im-petuous mind and provided him with a framework to achieve his goals. The Nearings would prove, like most mentors, to have clay feet, and their ideas fallible, but their achievements will always be an extraordinary example of the power of determination and effort.

"Just you watch," Scott liked to say about the unlikely force of water. "With continual effort it will find a way to the sea."

*   *   *

"LET'S VISIT THE Nearings," Papa had said to Mama two years earlier as they headed out in their VW truck with its built-in camper on a land-hunting trip around New England. They'd stopped at the Nearings' coastal Maine farm on Cape Rosier once before, to find that the *Living the Good Life* authors welcomed visitors, as long as you weren't afraid to help around the farm.

It was the summer of 1968, and Papa had just lost his job at Franconia College. That spring, Vietnam protesters at Columbia took over the administration and shut down the university, the musical *Hair* scandalized Broadway with full nudity, Johnson signed the Civil Rights Act of 1968, and Martin Luther King and Robert Kennedy were assassinated. For Mama and Papa and others, there was a feeling of powerlessness in the face of opposing forces and a longing for ground on which to stand.

The political climate at Franconia College was also in turmoil, tension building between the liberal faculty, including a card-carrying member of the Communist Party, and the conservative board. On April 5, the day after Martin Luther King was assassinated, an article ran in what *Time* dubbed the "archconservative" *Manchester Union Leader*. "Bare Debauchery at Franconia: Drugs, Liquor, Sex Rampant on Campus," it declared, effectively dwarfing the MLK story. Although the tales of sex and drugs at Franconia were said to be exaggerated, students certainly grew marijuana in the woods, and unmarried couples slept together on campus. The fallout was that Franconia's president was forced to resign, and many of the more vocal faculty members, including Papa, were let go or resigned in solidarity.

"To hell with them," Papa said. After the initial sting of loss, he felt a new freedom. They could do anything; now was the time to find land of their own. He had $5,000 in savings, which seemed like a lot of money at the time; the average national annual income was about $7,000. Following the Nearings' example, they sought a place they could afford to pay for in full—a perfect piece of land to start a farm and home.

"Everyone shares a kinship with the land," Papa wrote years later in his first book, *The New Organic Grower.* "No matter where we are in time and distance, the desire for the ideal country spot is very real. Whether the image comes from books, childhood experiences, or the depths of our souls, it has an indelible quality. The dream farm has fields here, an orchard there, a brook, and large trees near the perfect house, with the barns and outbuildings set off just so. The dream is effortless. The difficulty comes in trying to find such a place when you decide to buy one."

Beyond the tiny township of Harborside, the road narrowed to the width of the VW truck. Up and down hills they went, and around sharp turns. When the view opened out to the sea again, the road took a sharp dip before leveling to overlook a beautiful cove with a rock island in the middle. Across from that cove was a large mailbox with "Nearing" painted on it and a wooden placard with the greeting, "Forest Farm, help us live the good life, visitors 3–5 or by appointment," signed, "Helen & Scott." A sandy driveway led up through the woods past a stone-walled garden to an old clapboarded farmhouse connected to a barn by a wooden arch that they passed under to find a stone patio and table set with wooden bowls for lunch.

"Hello, hello, hello-e-o," came a lilting cheerio voice through the screen of the kitchen window. "Come in, come in, come in!"

Entering through the mudroom to a country kitchen with mottled pine floors and colorful cabinets, they found Helen standing over the stove, making soup. Small and energetic with short sandy hair, Helen possessed a hawklike quality in her face and movements, fierce, regal, and confident, but kindly, too. In her sixties, she wore a shapeless outfit over a trim figure, her age revealed only by a slight puffiness in the sun-weathered skin beneath her eyes and chin.

"Hello, hello," she said again, automatically almost, not seeming a bit perturbed to have strangers standing in her kitchen. "Where are you kiddos from?"

As Papa told her of their quest for land, Mama took in the small house. The counter and sink looked through mullioned windows to the patio. Across the room was the living area, consisting of a solid table with chairs and bountiful bookshelves, above which a large plaque read, "There is no religion higher than truth." They would later learn that this was the emblem of the Theosophical Society, and the quote was of the founder, Helena Petrovna Blavatsky.

"Scott-o's out in the garden," Helen said to Papa. "Why don't you tell him lunch's ready?"

Mama stayed with Helen, finding her the sort of alternative woman she wished she had for a mother. Born to what was described as an "eclectic and intellectual upper-middle-class family," Helen had grown up in the New York suburb of Ridgewood, New Jersey. The Knothes were Unitarians and members of the Theosophical Society, a nonsectarian group promoting the study of religion, philosophy, and science, and they were strict vegetarians, maintaining an organic garden on the property surrounding their rambling book-filled bungalow. Attractive, and wise for her youth, Helen practiced the violin, vegetarianism, and various alternative ideas promoted by the Theosophical Society, including reincarnation, palm reading, and dowsing with a rod to find water.

At age seventeen Helen first met Scott Nearing, twenty years her senior, but she was off to spend six years traveling and living abroad in Europe, India, Australia, and Amsterdam, where she met the Indian guru Krishnamurti, a spiritual leader recognized by the Theosophical Society. Krishnamurti felt an immediate connection to Helen and insisted she join the inner circle of people who traveled with him as he gave spiritual teachings. They maintained a mutually admiring, chaste relationship for a couple of years until a rumor that they were engaged to be married soured the relationship for the guru, who had taken vows of celibacy. Returning to the States without a clear path before her, Helen, now a self-possessed twenty-four-year-old, invited Scott to speak at a Unitarian church meeting. Separated from his first wife, Scott asked Helen a number of questions about her travels, then invited her to go for a drive in the country. He proved to be fun-loving, impulsive, and a believer in fairies.

"I thought, What kind of a guy is this?" Helen said. "I was going with four or five fellows at the time, but I was taken with his integrity, his purpose in life. Even those who disagreed with him responded to his warmth."

Soon enough she fell in love.

SCOTT WAS IN the stone-walled garden, hoeing the cabbage patch in rubber boots, sleeveless work shirt, and knee-length shorts that hung from old red suspenders. With his high forehead topped by thinning white hair, he looked closer to his eighty-four years than Helen did to her sixty-four, but only because the lines of his skin were so deeply creased into his tan face.

"If he had any more wrinkles, you'd have to roll him out to see what he looked like," the joke went. Others used the comparison to an apple that had been in the root cellar all winter, the skin leathery and mapped with lines.

"I've been sent to tell you it's lunchtime," Papa told him, feeling an easy comfort in the warmth and peace of the walled garden. When Scott looked up in greeting, the lines of his face softened from forehead to cheeks as he smiled, revealing a strong and handsome bone structure beneath.

"Hello, son," he said. "Grab a hoe and help me finish."

Born nearly a century earlier in the rural Pennsylvania town of Morris Run, Scott saw the first telephone, flush toilet, and electric lights come to town during his childhood. After attending the University of Pennsylvania, he received a graduate degree in business and became secretary of the Pennsylvania Child Labor Committee, fighting against big businesses for child labor laws. Despite some successes, he decided instead to become an economics and sociology professor at Penn, where he wrote pamphlets and books on child labor, women's issues, wage and income, racial and social change, and eventually war.

In 1915 Penn's trustees decided not to renew Scott's contract, as many were uncomfortable with his antiwar views, and a year later he was let go from the University of Toledo for the same reasons. Options narrowing, Scott joined the Socialist Party in 1917 and took a post at the Rand School of Social Science in New York City, where he became a radical in earnest. It was there he wrote a pamphlet called *The Great Madness*, which argued that capitalism and big business, hand in hand with the government, encouraged and profited from war, using it to protect and further investments "in the name of liberty." Scott was arrested and put on trial along with the Socialist Party, charged with attempting to obstruct the draft under the Espionage Act, a piece of legislation similar to today's Patriot Act. In a very public and controversial trial Scott defended himself and was acquitted of the charges, but his career was in ruins.

"Thus began my education at the College of Hard Knocks," he

liked to say. He traveled abroad and in 1927, after visiting China and Russia, put in an application for membership in the Communist Party. This was before the age of McCarthyism, when the U.S. Communist Party was gaining numbers—opposed as it was to the threat of fascism. It was the volatile time later portrayed in Warren Beatty's 1981 movie *Reds*, in which an aged Scott would appear as one of the real-life "witnesses." Scott eventually resigned from the party when a pamphlet of his was rejected because it didn't align with Leninist thinking. The party was angered enough not to accept his resignation, instead expelling Scott for his individualism.

It would be individualism, and his union with Helen in 1928, that defined the rest of his life. In Helen, he found a woman who was both a helper and an equal. Though their relationship was at first tempered by the age difference, they formed a remarkable liaison. The conservative world of the Great Depression settled in on them, leaving Scott few outlets for his views, as the media was controlled by the very forces of financial power he sought to expose. Helen and Scott chose instead to shrug the weight of public life from their shoulders and move to an abandoned farm in Vermont in 1932 to start their rural experiment. Thirteen years later, on Scott's sixty-second birthday, August 6, 1945, President Truman gave the order to drop the first atom bomb on Hiroshima.

"Your government is no longer mine," Scott wrote to the president in objection. Then in 1952, when Vermont became popular with skiers and city vacationers, the Nearings picked up and moved even farther away from New York, to Maine.

Working next to him in the garden, Papa admired the palpable strength of Scott's character and was encouraged by the fact that a man who'd been fired from his teaching posts by a conservative society had gone on to lead a full life of his own choosing. Now, with an unpopular war being waged in Vietnam, the Nearings' example was inspiring increasing numbers of back-to-the-landers. In Papa's eyes, Scott had won.

Joining Helen and Mama on the stone patio, they talked over carved wooden bowls of vegetable soup topped with freshly chopped parsley. In Mama's memory it was the most delicious soup she'd ever tasted—to this day, the smell of parsley brings back that charmed afternoon.

Back at Franconia in August, Mama, while waitressing at a restaurant called Lovett's, found herself running to the bathroom with nausea after delivering food to diners. She thought her period was late because she hadn't been eating much, but soon it was confirmed that she was pregnant, due in April. Her heart danced a jig. For the past year, something in her body had been telling her it was time for a child. Papa was also thrilled, but at twenty-nine years of age, with a twenty-three-year-old wife, he felt ever more strongly the need to provide a home and income for his growing family. During the July visit to the Nearings', the older couple had mentioned owning a hundred-some acres on Cape Rosier, though Papa hadn't dared to think they would sell. As the cool weather of fall began to close in, he decided to write and ask. A week later, they received that postcard from Helen offering them the sixty acres.

"I'm afraid to believe it's for real," Mama said, as they drove up in the VW to look at the land. Back in the Nearings' kitchen, Helen and Scott asked what they could afford to put down. Papa estimated about $2,000, leaving enough reserves from their $5,000 in savings to build a house and live until they could start making money. Divide $2,000 by sixty acres, and the Nearings offered them a price of a little over $33 per acre, the amount the Nearings had paid when they bought the land almost twenty years earlier.

"Most important to pay as you go," Scott said, referring to his lifelong economic philosophy of never going into debt. He also said he didn't like to make income without doing work to earn it, which meant it was morally offensive to him to raise the cost of the land simply because it'd appreciated over the years. Helen piped in to say she'd seen in the lines of their palms that they'd be good neighbors. So with a handshake, it was settled—Papa would bring the $2,000 in cash when he returned.

It was not the dream farm Papa had in his mind's eye during the search, lacking as it did cultivated fields and a pond. But none of that mattered; it was their ground on which to stand, unbeholden to a mortgage or bank, and it was up to them to make it into the dream.

As I TOTTERED and babbled after the chickens, Mama finished carving and painting her masterpiece, a large sign for the end of our driveway with the words "The Vegetable Garden" in big letters over a painted outline of a wheelbarrow full of a cornucopia of vegetables. She planted a bed of marigolds and snapdragons beneath it. Our farm stand was ready for business. At first it was only a few baskets of this or that next to a chalkboard with names and prices. With Mama's help, the random customers could select for themselves the lettuce or tomatoes of their choice.

Soon word got out, and the trickle of customers wandering down the grassy lane began to increase. They'd heard about the flavorful tomatoes that Papa pronounced "to-mah-toes," "because you say ahhhh when you taste them." The carrots were so sweet, they would eventually be dubbed "candy carrots" by an appreciative child. There were butterhead lettuces that held the beautiful formation of enormous roses, and cabbages the size of basketballs. "I've never cared for spinach until yours," a customer said of Papa's large and especially tasty leaves. Even Helen and Scott were impressed.

"It wasn't until the second summer of 1970 that I really began to understand gardening," Papa told Stanley Mills, the friend of the Nearings who wrote the quarterly newsletter about us. "That winter was when I read Sir Albert Howard's classic, *An Agricultural Testament*, in which Howard claims that if plants are healthy there is no role for insects. The role of insects with plants is like the role of wolves with deer and caribou: to eliminate the unhealthy and unfit. The sicker, the weaker the plants, the more appealing they are to insects. After two years of following Rodale, I began to see how things really are. After this we began experimenting with the soil. With Rodale I was working in a system akin to Ptolemaic astronomy, with Sir Albert Howard I hit on Copernicus. The results speak for themselves."

For most modern farmers of the time, when the pests arrived, it was time not to think about building up the soil but to get out the pesticides and kill the enemy. And no wonder—the farmers were being marketed to by formerly war-based companies.

"Gardening books published prior to nineteen-forty were mostly organic; those after nineteen-forty were mostly chemical," Papa explained to Stanley. "Nineteen-forty seems to be the transition between organic and chemical practices, a kind of continental divide."

In 1971, a certain loud-talking, strong-opinioned Dr. Earl Butz was making himself known as President Nixon's new secretary of agriculture. He planned to encourage commercial farmers to plant commodity crops "from fencerow to fencerow" using pesticides and chemical fertilizers, in order to revitalize agriculture and cut costs, as well as to help out his friends in the chemical industry. His motivation was to feed the world on cheap corn, but small farmers were unable to compete, and this situation led to a counterculture movement to save the small farm and restore less invasive farming methods. Therein organic agriculture began to find its voice.

Papa's future theory of plant-positive farming, for which he would gain renown, was based on Sir Albert's claim that "the health of soil, plant, animal and man is one and indivisible." Instead of adhering to the mainstream concept of pests as a negative and using the alternative methods of pest control advocated by J. I. Rodale, Papa saw that simply creating fertile soil made the plants happy, and happy plants did not attract pests.

The secret, Sir Albert believed, was to leave the land better than you found it. That meant putting more nutrients and organic matter—in the form of compost and manure—back into the soil than you harvested from it. "The law of return," Howard called it. The concern with chemical fertilizers was that the nitrogen, phosphorus, and potassium—or N-P-K—were used directly by the plant and didn't provide food for the soil. It became a vicious cycle similar to a drug addiction, leaving the victim unable to function without drugs. Sir Albert felt it was more productive to feed the soil for future growth. This age-old concept was far from revolutionary, but its discovery was, for Papa, a revelation. As long as we fed the garden, it promised, the garden would feed us. And because it seemed like such old-fashioned common sense, Papa had little idea that it was on the forefront of what would become an organic agriculture revolution.

The dragons along the path took the form of Butz-style ag extension agents who were quick to say ideas about compost and manure were full of shit. Despite their dismissal, further reading in books such as *The Living Soil* by Lady Eve Balfour left Papa confident that the natural sources of N-P-K were far better over the long term than the chemical versions. The only catch was that the old ways required trial and error and a good dose of patience to get the balance just right.

When Papa succeeded, people said it was the best lettuce they'd ever tasted. When he didn't, the pests were just as happy to eat the unhappy plants and leave us with cabbages full of holes, or in one infamous case, slugs in the lettuce that we sold to Jonathan's, a fancy restaurant in town—resulting in one very unhappy diner and chef. Though we sometimes had pithy celery, extra-bitter radicchio, or aphids and worms in the corn, Papa believed that with enough attention and trial and error he could figure out the problem and solve the imbalance organically.

"Gardening skill is something of a mystical thing," Papa told Stanley for the newsletter, his thinking influenced, perhaps, by Helen's Theosophical leanings. "In the garden, I empathize. As much as anything, I feel what needs to be done. That's why it occurs to me that in another incarnation I must have been a gardener because working in the garden is just heaven for me, just right. It's what I know I should be doing."

Soon enough, Papa's successes in the garden, and the sharing of these findings with others, would become far more vital to him than the less compelling—by comparison—demands of homesteading. While Mama relished the myriad tasks of the good life, Papa had found his true vocation in farming.

CHAPTER THREE

Sustenance

FALL ARRIVED WITH its honey light and cool evenings, and the maple leaves brightened to match the reds and yellows of ripe apples. It was time to put away the bounty of the warm months for fortitude during the cold ones, as humans had done for centuries.

"Drove by the Holbrook orchard today," Papa announced as he came in the door, just back from a trip to town in the jeep. "The apples are ready."

"Time to go foraging?" Mama smiled from the stove, where she was busy canning vegetables. She reveled in the spark in Papa's blue eyes, the backward sweep of his silver-tinged hair, and the wiry strength of his body, so utilitarian in form. His simple excitement over ripe apples ignited in her the love she felt deep in her soul for their life together. At its essence, theirs was as simple a relationship as that, united by this passion for their lifestyle, for good food, and for their mission of self-sufficiency. Food, from its procurement to its enjoyment, was the force that held them together.

"We'll get apples tonight," Papa said, and Mama's eyes brightened in return.

EVEN DURING THE first winter in the woods, before I was born, there was more than enough to eat. The root cellar was stocked with vegetables that Mama brought from their Franconia garden—carrots, potatoes, beets. Onions and garlic were braided together with the dry stems into chains to hang in the kitchen. They had the goats for milk, which Mama made into yogurt and cheese. The chickens provided eggs, and Mama sprouted alfalfa sprouts in mason jars topped with cheesecloth for salads. Not only did they find the vegetarian diet suited to their sensibilities, but it made their limited food choices simpler, and they enjoyed the shared commitment with their neighbors.

"We don't eat anything that wiggles," Helen liked to say.

She'd show fishhooks to visitors, lures with three-pronged hooks on them. "Would you want to bite this?" she'd ask, brandishing the hook at them. "Then why would you want a fish to do the same?"

"I became a vegetarian because life is as valid for other creatures as it is for humans," Scott wrote of his decision. "As a vegetarian I do the least possible harm to the least numbers of other living entities. Recognizing that all forms of life are worthy of respect, I disturb the life process as little as I can."

Papa's hesitance to harm animals came partially from a childhood memory of killing a squirrel with a BB gun and the feeling of regret over the surprising weight of the limp body in his hands. "When you have animals, you see their individuality and name them accordingly," Papa told a visitor, adopting a dose of Scott's self-righteousness. "How can you eat cranky old Tom or winsome young Will? We prefer not to. To provide milk and cheese we have goats, such attractive creatures. We feel perfectly healthy and vigorous as vegetarians. We feel good about it. Good in body and spirit. I'm perfectly sure the reason we get through the work we do is because of the excellent fresh vegetables and fruit we eat."

As I later found out, I was probably the only child in America in the 1970s who actually ate my vegetables. Little did I know that my peers across the country were hiding peas and carrots in napkins or milk cups, sitting cross-armed refusing to eat, and otherwise disparaging anything that came from a plant.

"Kids are smart, they know a shoddy knockoff," Papa said. "Not only don't the supermarket vegetables taste good, they didn't have the nutritional value of vegetables grown and picked from your own garden."

Learning from his enthusiasm, I would come to know each month of spring, summer, and fall by what it produced. May meant Jerusalem artichokes boiled and covered with butter like a new potato but tasting crisper and fresher—tasting of spring. Asparagus poked from the earth in stiff tufted spears to be snapped off and steamed to an even brighter green, making our pee smell of wet money.

June brought snap peas, lettuces, spinach, spring onions, and wild edibles, including dandelion greens, purslane, nasturtium flowers, sorrel, and the succulent sea grass found along the beach. July saw yellow summer squash, zucchini, purple and white cabbage, string beans, and tomatoes that had been started in the greenhouse. August produced more tomatoes than we knew what to do with and everything else—new potatoes, shell beans, bell peppers, celery, cucumbers, kohlrabi, turnips, parsnips, cauliflower, and broccoli. September and October were a bounty of melons, pumpkins, winter squash, garlic, and onions.

Fruits were also magically spaced across the summer by Mother Nature to make sure each month provided something for dessert. May was rhubarb, which we sautéed with honey to make a threaded tart-sweet pink mush that we ate over yogurt. June was strawberries; July, raspberries; August, wild and cultivated blueberries and blackberries. Late September, of course, was apples.

UNDER COVER OF darkness, Mama and Papa drove to the old Holbrook orchard and wildlife sanctuary, Jeep's headlights off so as not to wake the sanctuary ranger, and me, age one and a half, nodding out in the back. Giddy in the shared adventure, they imagined themselves members of the French resistance in dark clothing, pillaging the orchards of the aristocracy.

Putting away enough food to get through the thin months of winter was a challenge we couldn't afford to shirk. It was a simple equation: if we didn't save enough food and money from summer, we would go hungry in winter. The obstacles were many. Canning seals didn't hold, chipmunks ate apples stored in the woodshed, and vegetables rotted if the root cellar got too damp, but Mama and Papa held to the fact that humans had been surviving the winter for centuries without the conveniences of refrigerators and supermarkets. They were further encouraged by the Nearings' words in *Continuing the Good Life*:

We can be and we are largely self-sufficient in food. Self-sufficient means that we can feed ourselves. During half a century of gardening there has never been a time when we have lacked a supply of organically grown produce. This food comes directly from the garden for a large part of the year. During the late fall, winter and early spring we have three additional sources of supply.

1. It may come from the sun-heated greenhouse where we grow lettuces, parsley, radishes, leeks, kale, spinach.
2. It may come from our root cellar where apples, potatoes, carrots, beets, rutabagas and other root vegetables are stored in bins of autumn leaves.
3. It may come from our stock of bottled soups and juices and applesauce which we put away during periods of surplus production and use when the garden is in deep freeze.

"The Nearings never mentioned stealing from abandoned orchards," Mama joked.

"We're obviously more resourceful." Papa smiled, parking on the edge of the sanctuary's dirt road. It wasn't that the apples belonged to someone, they told themselves—the orchard had long ago been abandoned by the original owners—but they knew the ranger would object.

The orchard distinguished itself from the forest by the bent and gnarled stature of trees possessing the dignity of Scott's aged yet sturdy frame. Papa climbed the bunioned trunks of Northern Spys and Baldwins to shake the branches, apples hailing down with thuds onto the grass below as Mama followed to collect them into burlap bags. She paused now and then and bit into a fruit, savoring its crispness as she watched Papa swing down from a tree, land solidly on his feet, and head for another, the pale light of the waxing moon catching the youthfulness of his features. By the time the moon was high, they carried their bounty of apple-lumped bags to the jeep and placed them around my sleeping body. Whooping like Indians once they passed the darkened houses of town, headlights off in the moonlight, they returned home to put their loot in the root cellar. Bounty was where you found it.

"It's amazing what we can store in the root cellar," Papa explained to anyone who would listen. We had a small cellar under the trapdoor in the kitchen floor and another built like an underground cabin in the rise above the garden. For the most part, the cellars maintained a thirty-seven-degree temperature in winter and low fifties in summer. Those bags of apples could last for months. The same for brassicas like cabbages and brussels sprouts. Potatoes, turnips, celeriac, carrots, and other root vegetables were stored upright in sand or in buckets. If left too long, they grew masses of white roots and eventually turned to stinky mush, but by that time we usually had early crops growing in the greenhouse.

As Papa did in the garden, Mama was constantly planning ahead for our food storage, preparing now in order to feast later. She used her Foley food mill to transform boiled apples into golden jars of applesauce, some with raspberries, blackberries, and blueberries added for a taste sweet as pie. She carefully canned the overabundance of late-summer vegetables with boiling water in mason jars sealed with canning lids. Her favorite concoction was a mix of tomatoes with basil, oregano, onion, garlic, zucchini, and cauliflower that could later be made directly into a hearty winter soup. She also dried apple and carrot slices, blueberries, beans, peas, and corn on the cob in the wood oven on low heat, as they'd read that drying best preserved a food's nutrient value.

This was all long before Martha Stewart became a household name, though today's homemaking maven has admitted to being inspired by the Nearings. Back then, Mama was doing the kinds of housework many women believed they'd left behind with their virginity in the 1960s. Rather than resenting the work, she found solace in the repetitive nature of what were already becoming the lost arts of the kitchen.

For fruit juices she poured boiling water into mason jars with wild raspberries and honey to make raspberry juice, called "shrub" by the Nearings, and the same for rose hips from our hedge, their orange fruits floating like lobster buoys at the top of the jar. Come cold and flu season, the jars of raspberries and rose hips were worth more than gold for their vitamin C content.

Helen was known to have a soft spot for exotics like avocados, bananas, and Florida oranges, which she had shipped to Maine, but as they didn't support the self-sufficiency stance, these were conveniently not mentioned in their books. When we could afford it, we'd go in on an order of those Temple oranges from Vero Beach, and if there was enough money, a case of peaches to boil and store in mason jars as well. By first snow, the apples, brassicas, and root vegetables in the root cellar were surrounded by shelves lined with as many as four hundred colorful jars of preserved vegetables and fruits.

"Those peaches are as bright as summer sunshine when I shine my flashlight into the dark root cellar on a cold day," Mama told Helen. "And the oranges look like jewels from some exotic land."

If he needed a hit of vitamin C, Papa would climb down into the cellar under the kitchen, unscrew a mason lid with a creak and a pop, tip the jar back, and drink from it right then and there.

The raspberry-and-honey-flavored water was tantalizingly sweet to his sugar-free tastebuds, and at the bottom was the prize, a thick pulp of berries that colored his lips red as they slid into his mouth.

"You've been into the berries," Mama would scold, but she couldn't get too mad because she, too, snuck them like that.

DESPITE THE IMPORTANCE that food held in our lives, or perhaps because of it, Mama and Papa sometimes fasted during holidays, as the Nearings did, when the rest of America was "glutting," as Helen called it. Practiced over the centuries for religious and political reasons, fasting in moderation is thought to benefit health and slow the aging process. For my parents, it was cleansing and helped ease the burden on our winter stores of food. They drank only water and tea or juices made from carrots, beet, wheatgrass, and apples. One of Mama's favorite inventions was a grater and cheesecloth that she used in place of an electric juicer.

Mama loved fasting and the light-headed euphoria that set in after the first day or so of hunger, her mind free to wander more endorphin-laced paths. There was a sense of control in it for her that went deeper than the political and health stance of the Nearings. Somewhere along the way, the endorphins produced by hunger became an addiction for Mama equal to any drug. For Papa, hard labor had a similar effect. As with alcohol or drugs, the high of fasting and the grit of a good day's work momentarily eased a troubled mind. While the material addictions of the outside world had given way to purer ones, the effect was the same. As with alcohol, Mama often became spacey from fasting, a side effect of initial low blood sugar that made the simplest tasks exceedingly difficult. Little details such as fixing my dinner didn't matter so much anymore. I would try to communicate important things to her in my rudimentary language, how hungry I was, for example, but she wouldn't really hear me.

"Uh-huh," she said as she busied herself making her fruit and vegetable juices with her grater and cheesecloth. "Uh-huh, uh-huh, yup, sure."

Fasting became another way, really, of checking out.

FOOD FOR MAMA was equal to love, and, though she might withhold it when fasting, she usually meted it out to Papa and me straight from her heart. The preparing, cooking, and storing of food made up the pulse of her days. I'd wake in the mornings to the sound of Mama grinding grain. Clamped to the kitchen counter, that steel mill from Hatch's was her magic tool, transforming inedible whole grains into vital ingredients as she stood beside it, hair pulled back, working the crank. The groats went in a funnel in the top, to be ground by opposing metal wheels attached to the crank, and depending on the setting, meal or flour streamed or puffed from the spout into a bowl.

To supplement the food from the greenhouse, root cellar, and stores of mason jars, the fourth component of our food supply, also not mentioned in the Nearings' books, was the ordering of bulk nonlocal foods. We went in with the Nearings on orders from the organic supplier Walnut Acres: twenty-pound bags of oats, wheat groats, and sunflower and sesame seeds, plus five-gallon metal containers of oil, nut butters, maple syrup, and honey. Most important to our diet were the whole grains, which had not been processed to remove the fiber and nutrients, so had to be ground by hand instead.

For breakfast, Mama often made hot cereals—twelve-grain, Irish oatmeal, or cornmeal, all ground with the mill and served with butter and maple syrup. Lunch might make use of the leftover cornmeal for corn dodgers with baked beans. For dinner, the organic Durham winter wheat groats were ground for bread to go with her famous vegetable soups, served with salads from the garden or greenhouse.

Once I was old enough, I'd come and wait expectantly by the stove as the smells of baking bread filled the house. The cookstove was our most important possession, without which we would either starve or freeze to death. To my young imagination it looked like a black animal with four stout legs under a square body, a flat top with lids that opened to the fire, and one long tail of a chimney that curved through the wall to puff smoke outside. It had three mouths, a small one to make little fires for cooking, a bigger one for overnight fires, and the biggest of all for the oven, with white enamel around a temperature dial ranging from "cool" to "very hot" and the brand name, "Kalamazoo." When the bread was done, Mama opened the oven door and the loaves came out golden brown and steaming, to be placed on the counter to cool.

"Warm bread will give you a tummy ache," Mama said, if only to protect the bread, moving it out of reach of my small hands. That didn't stop my stomach or me, as I grew older, from indulging in the delight of warm bread and butter melting in the mouth.

Our staple was a yeast-free flatbread called a chapati, which Mama learned to make from David Hatch, who learned in India. Mama let me help mix the flour from the grain mill with water and salt to make a pliable dough, then kneaded it to bring out the gluten and let it set for an hour before making round golf balls of dough that she flattened with a rolling pin into thin, but not too thin, pancakes. She prepared the cookstove ahead so there was a bed of hot red coals in the firebox, and heated a greaseless twelve-by-sixteen-inch cast-iron skillet to sear both sides of the chapati and trap the steam inside. The chapati was then placed on a bent clothes hanger over hot coals inside the firebox, where it would blow up into a steamy balloon. Once it was removed from the flame, the air in the middle was released and the balloon flattened to form a perfect tortilla-like vehicle, warm or cold, for whatever you chose to put on or inside it.

Papa liked to make himself sandwiches by filling a chapati with alfalfa sprouts, sliced tomatoes, handmade mayo, arugula or basil, and grated cheese for the perfect quick lunch or snack. For dessert he'd take another chapati and spread honey and butter with coconut peanut butter from Walnut Acres or tahini made from finely ground sesame seeds and, depending on the season, fresh strawberries, blueberries, raspberries, or grated apple and cinnamon. This became officially known as the "Pa-wich."

"Mmm, mmm, mmm, Pa-wiches," I'd sing, rubbing my belly.

"Not bad for a boy," Papa always said of his culinary creations.

He made "bacon" by frying strips of nori seaweed in oil to form a crisp and salty treat. And on Thanksgiving he and Mama amused themselves by creating a "turkey" out of a large butternut squash filled with traditional stuffing and potatoes attached to it with toothpicks for drumsticks.

Our other staple was goats' milk, which we drank raw or was heated by Mama with Irish moss and honey to make a custard-like dish called junket, or blancmange. I loved to find junket cooling in small bowls on the shelves by the window. "Don't touch," Mama said from the stove, but when she wasn't looking I'd tip one up to my lips and let the warm sweet curd slip down my throat to settle comfortingly in my tummy.

Goats' milk was also used to make yogurt with the help of cultures mail-ordered from France. Mama sterilized the milk by heating it to 160 degrees to kill the bacteria, then mixed it with the culture and poured it into quart canning jars with lids. These sat in a large pot of warm water on bricks on the far back burner of the cookstove for about six hours or more, depending on how tart she wanted it. When the yogurt was cultured, she submerged the jars in cold water in the root cellar, and it would stay fresh for days. Yogurt was especially recommended by a doctor friend of the Nearings, who said it would help provide the B12 vitamins missing in our vegetarian diet.

"Scott-o absolutely *loved* my yogurt. Did you see him wolf it down?" Mama bragged to Papa after the Nearings joined us for lunch one day. "And Helen asked to borrow my corn dodgers recipe." The recipe, which consisted of adding salt and oil to corn-meal mush, forming the mixture into patties, and baking these on a cookie sheet until firm and slightly crunchy, later turned up in Helen's anticookbook *Simple Food for the Good Life*.

"I was not born a cook," Helen often said, but during summer there were many visiting and helping mouths to feed, and feed them she must, so she came up with quick and nourishing, if sometimes unpalatable, solutions. Her secret was that she had a captive audience—there was nowhere else to eat out on the cape, and when you're hard-worked and fresh-air hungry, pretty much anything tastes good. Helen's other secret was that her ingredients from the garden were fresh, and of top quality—like those in the parsley-laden vegetable soup of Mama and Papa's first visit.

Across the country in California, a French-trained chef named Alice Waters was opening, in 1971, what would become the well-known Chez Panisse restaurant, founded on these very principles of freshness that Alice had learned in France. Fresh local food was not political at that time; it simply tasted best.

Names grew up around Helen's less inspired and more utilitarian creations—Horse Chow for oats and raisins with oil and lemon juice, Carrot Croakers for a cookie made out of leftover carrot pulp from the juicer, Scott's Emulsion for boiled wheat berries, honey, and peanut butter "where the eater does the work, not the cook," as Helen quipped, and Miracle Mush for grated carrot, beet, apple, and nuts. There were always large wooden bowls of popcorn drizzled with melted butter for a snack, and Helen was known to drop handfuls into people's soup bowls for extra fiber, whether they wanted it or not. These names and combinations didn't exactly make the mouth water, but they provided the body with the necessary nutrition and fortitude for hard work.

"A meal is best when eaten with your feet under your own table," Scott liked to say over lunch, the philosophical feeding him as well as the physical. Papa often quoted another of Scott's sayings, "Health insurance is served on the table with every meal." As Papa saw it, good food was the secret to longevity and well-being that would save him from the early death of his father. The healthily aging Nearings were living proof that a simple diet was the key. But as it would turn out, the formula for health is not one-size-fits-all.

As with organic farming, health is more about individual trial and error, and my family would soon have its share of both. Yogurt alone could not make up for the B vitamins lacking in our vegetarian diet. Not being a nutritionist, I know only one thing for sure: that our high-carb diet often caused bouts of "the farts," a condition that Papa denied, Mama relished, and I liked to laugh about, especially when one struck while I was seated on Mama's lap for a bedtime story.

STILL, EVEN IN the clutches of winter, when we should have been wasting away for lack of something fresh, Papa, like a garden elf, cut calcium-rich kale from the glass cold frames and dug parsnips and carrots buried and insulated by snow in the garden. Then, passing through the low door to the greenhouse on the front of the house, he added salad greens to the basket, ever amazed that the hardy greens and root vegetables germinated before daylight savings in October could survive the cold with such simple protection. He brought his offerings inside to Mama and laid them in her capable hands.

"This meal is fit for royalty," Papa said enthusiastically to Mama and me over the dinner of baked sweet parsnips and onions with steamed kale, brown rice, and a fresh salad. His eyes sparkled in the lamplight. "Who knew we could eat from the garden like this in December in Maine?"

I see now that what also made the meal so delicious was that, despite the appearance of bounty, we were always on the edge of not having enough. And if our food supplies fell short, our "health insurance policy" was at risk. If either Mama or Papa were to become ill, there would be expensive doctor bills to pay, and the vital work to produce more food would fall behind.

That my parents had chosen this lifestyle over an easier one wouldn't matter in the moment when the goats had eaten the spring lettuce, there was nothing left in the root cellar, the drinking water was muddy with runoff, and there was no money under the couch for gas to get to town—not to mention that Jeep's registration had expired, and we had no savings account, trust fund, or health insurance policy, no house in town to fall back on. We were living the way much of the world actually lives. On the other hand, we didn't have phone, water, or electrical bills; health insurance premiums; or a mortgage, a car payment, or any other monthly payment, for that matter. No one could come to shut off our utilities and take away our home.

Mama nodded at Papa over the dinner table and smiled, salad

dressing shining on her lips. When eating a good meal, with our feet under our own table, we felt that we were, indeed, royalty.

"And applesauce for dessert," Mama said with a wink.

I hover close here because I understand that our survival lay in that exchange, and in the precarious balance of Mama's and Papa's emotional investment in our lifestyle. To succeed at this life, they had to constantly feed their vision of it, or it would wither and die.

CHAPTER FOUR

Seclusion

BY CHRISTMAS DAY the ground was covered in thirty inches of snow, a few crystals still suspended in the air out the front windows. Papa brought in a spindly-branched fir tree, and Mama and I decorated it by threading strings of popcorn interspersed with shriveled red hawthorn berries.

"It helps to think of Christmas as in ancient times, of bringing light to the dark of the year," Mama said.

Those darkening days of December filled us with the urge to hibernate like the animals. Hands turned clumsy, pulses sluggish, and we moved as slowly as the pale red-and-black-spotted ladybugs that clung to the interior walls of the farmhouse. It was the time to turn inward for strength to combat the blues Papa said came with lack of light and vitamin D.

The darkest stretch was from Papa's birthday on December 15 to Mama's birthday on February 7, the shortest day being the winter solstice, a week after Papa's birthday, when the radio reported less than eight hours of light. We followed the sun's progress across the sky like a baby following his mother's face, willing her to stay nearby. As early as four in the afternoon, Papa would light the kerosene lanterns with a poof of flame, turning down the knob of the fancy one until its cheesecloth wick glowed a winter blue. It whistled like wind in the trees and filled the little farmhouse with a steady glow as the last of the moths pounded the windowpanes, drawn like us to the light.

Mama wrapped our gifts in newspaper, tied with garden twine. Other gifts came by mail wrapped in silver and gold foil and colorful paper with big bows and notes that said "From Skates" and "From Grandma and Grandpa." Papa grinned his elfin smile that evening as he took down hand-knitted stockings and I tore through the wrappings like any child. My favorite gift was a painted wooden Russian doll Helen and Scott had brought back from a recent trip to Russia. Inside it was an identical-shaped doll, and so on, until at the very center was the solid smallest doll. The shells lay around me empty and broken open, but the baby fit into the space of my closed hand, a comforting shape inside.

"That one is the heart," Mama said, her own feeling tender during the dark of the year. "Let's put it back in to be safe."

"People give us too much," she wrote later in her journal, overwhelmed by the material bounty. "Decided to fast (me apples and simple raw protein, Eliot tea, water, Liss mostly milk)."

The solitude and simple rhythms of the homesteading life suited Mama's spirit well, but as it turned out, the winter of 1971 was the peak of our quiet years, as spring would bring a visit from the *Wall Street Journal* that would change our lives in unforeseen ways.

PAPA WOKE IN the darkness before sunrise, stoked the stove, dressed, and went out. A short saw and ax were all he needed. Already he'd made good progress on the back field, climbing the trees and sawing off branches to use as firewood, then toppling the bare trunks and sectioning them into stove-size lengths to cure and chop for firewood. "Heating with wood warms you three times," the saying went. "Cutting, stacking, and burning."

Cold pinched the inside of Papa's nose as the first rays of sun bloomed behind the darkened points of fir and spruce surrounding the snow-covered clearing. The air was still, waiting for the day to begin, smoke rising in a column straight up from the chimneystack without a breeze to shift it. Those early mornings reminded Papa of the lonely snow-covered mountaintops from his mountaineering days, but as he warmed from work he was reinforced in his belief that a mountain with no top was far preferable. Rather than the glory of the peak, he found his salvation in the warmth that came with the constant effort of the climb, and the accompanying adrenaline that erased all sorrow.

"To travel hopefully is better than to arrive, and the true success is to labor," Scott often quoted, from Robert Louis Stevenson.

When Mama woke to find Papa gone, she left me sleeping and ventured to the outhouse, the snow brilliant white underfoot, each step squeaking like Styrofoam when opening and closing the root cellar door. The air sang with electricity, and sun sparked the snow into a field of diamonds. She scanned the back field for Papa and, spotting him in a tree, let out a yodel, the Swiss mountaineering call Helen had taught them for communicating in the woods.

"Yo-del-lay-he-who!" She paused a beat as the echo returned

from the forest. "Eh-he-who . . ." Then came Papa's reply: "Yo-del-lay-he-he-whooo!" The call bounced around the sparkling bowl of the farm, making Mama's sluggish blood surge to life better than any fire. She wanted this moment to last forever, but deep down knew its impermanence was what made it so beautiful. It was on days like this that Mama would gasp as the sun broke through the clouds at just the right moment, the trees shuddering with meaning, or when the Christmas cactus on the windowsill bloomed before her eyes. In those moments it seemed that the fulfillment she sought in nature had presented itself, attainable and real. But then the sun would pass, the trees still, the flower close, and nothing remained; even the searching was forgotten after such a moment. The physical world could not provide the depth of love she craved.

WHEN MAMA AND Papa went on their first date together, camping amid the bright foliage of the White Mountains, Papa was both gentlemanly and boyish, leaving Mama flattered by his attention and amazed at her luck. He in turn was taken by her natural beauty, shy manner, and adventurous spirit, and glad to find a woman who shared his love of the outdoors but didn't expect a big diamond or bank account.

"I'll teach you to paddle and roll a whitewater kayak," Papa suggested for their next date, and Mama felt a rebellious thrill. This meant tipping the kayak and its occupant over, as often happens accidentally in whitewater, then snapping the hips to flip it back upright, thereby saving the kayaker from a wet exit in wild waters. Being trapped beneath a boat in a murky creek was not most women's idea of a good time, but Mama loved the challenge. She was able to relax underwater, thanks to summers on the ocean in Westport, and after a few wet exits she was rolling, much to Papa's admiration.

After school let out, Papa packed the car for Colorado to teach kayaking at the Colorado Rocky Mountain School, as he'd done in previous summers, and Mama was overjoyed when he invited her to join him. Before they left on June 16, 1966, they invited some friends to dinner and halfway through the meal they asked the friends to be witnesses and went and got married, just like that, by the justice of the peace in the Littleton, New Hampshire, courthouse. They then hit the road in Papa's old rust-colored Pontiac station wagon loaded with kayaks to drive straight through to Colorado. At a gas stop near Buffalo, they called their parents.

"I got married," Mama told Grandma, the feeling of a high dive in her chest. Prill was speechless, possibly thinking of her own inability to run away with that long-ago Kentucky suitor. Mama hung up with a heavy face, but Papa tried to cheer her. "Just think how relieved your father is not to have to host and pay for an expensive wedding," he joked. Then Papa called Skates, who asked if Sue was pregnant. When he said no, Skates was profuse in her disappointment at not being invited to the wedding of her only son, *and* not even getting a grandchild out of the deal. "Don't take it personally," he said. "I'm just doing my own thing." The big white wedding was another tradition he was happy to shed.

"To hell with it," Papa said as they hit the road. "This is our life now."

Spending the summer building kayaks and taking students down the Colorado and Green rivers, Papa once worried he had gotten Mama in over her head when they hit a section of rapids and she flipped over. He looked back upriver from his own kayak, helpless to do anything as she floated upside down toward some rocks that would surely ruin the fiberglass hull and might knock her unconscious. But when he looked again, she was back upright—she had rolled and steered clear of the rocks.

"Way to go!" he yelled, pumping his paddle in the air. There was one cool woman.

Upon returning to Franconia in the fall, Papa noticed an old hunting lodge on the school property, surrounded by open fields and forest, and asked the school if they could fix it up and live there. It was run-down, the outside covered in black tar paper, but he set to work creating a new interior of white pine walls with a sleeping loft and built-in bookshelves that he would emulate when building the cabin in Maine.

"I have a surprise for you," Papa told Mama when she returned from class one day. He led her into the woods, where he'd built an A-frame with the obligatory quarter moon in the door.

"Our very first outhouse."

"So romantic." Mama laughed.

Mama took Papa's rock-climbing class and studied Russian. They hiked and skied under the protective gaze of the Old Man in the Mountain, a rock profile that once perched on a cliff near Franconia Notch, and read *Dr. Zhivago* to each other. Mama tried her hand at pottery and became a fixture in the pottery studio, making cups and bowls for the cabin. You could say it was an alternative education; her pottery class even led a revolt against the administration. It was the 1960s, after all, and her spirit was coming alive in the atmosphere of freedom and self-expression.

"I finally feel a bit good at things," she said. In Papa, Mama had found a kindred spirit to ease her old loneliness.

"IT'S ON SUSIE'S birthday that you can feel the light returning," Papa liked to say, which of course made Mama smile. Mama's birthday arrived on February 7, and with it the lengthening days, if not warmth. They celebrated with the Nearings, and again on Helen's birthday two weeks later on February 23. "Had an excellent birthday party for Helen—food was superb and we all enjoyed ourselves through and through," Mama wrote. "Scott looks very well."

Soon after, Helen and Scott left for Europe on a lecture tour to promote their books. When the Nearings traveled in the winters, they paid Mama to reply to their mail, fill book orders, and look after their house. The money was welcome, and the work kept her occupied. The mail was often spread out on the table, letters lots, bills not many, as Mama sorted it into piles and I played in the low winter sun streaming through the south-facing windows. Most of the letters were from people who had read *Living the Good Life* and wanted to visit or had already visited during summer.

"We were so encouraged by our tour of your farm," one said. "Now we're looking for land to start our own homestead."

Mama read this again and again; people were fleeing to the woods. Another thing she noticed was that some of the envelopes were unsealed, the glue appearing to have been steamed open and then unsuccessfully resealed or taped. Helen had said not to worry about it—Dot Crockett was tampering with the mail. The Harborside postmistress, the Nearings believed, read their correspondence to keep tabs on what were thought to be their Communist activities. It was no secret that Scott had been a member of both the Socialist and the Communist parties. Some even knew he'd written that letter to President Truman stating, "Your country is no longer mine."

"Commies," the more conservative locals muttered about the Nearings. "Pinko lefties."

"Choose your enemies carefully," Scott liked to say, "for you will become more like them than anyone else."

We now know it was President Truman who set in motion the National Security Agency, or NSA, to keep tabs on citizens in ways very similar to what we deemed the Soviet Union's evil KGB. One of the jobs of the NSA was to systematically intercept and monitor the phone, mail, and telegram communications of millions of regular Americans. During the 1970s, these efforts were focused on citizens identified as "unreliable," such as civil rights leaders, antiwar protesters, teachers, and union leaders, as well as some politicians and church officials. It would later be acknowledged in the 1975 Rockefeller Commission and Church Committee investigations that the Nearings and many of their friends were on this short list of "unreliable" citizens. Scott believed this was because anyone who championed human rights in favor of the free acquisition of wealth was a threat to capitalism—and hence the government—which he saw as banking in the back pocket of big business.

"When we left the city, we sought to provide, by example, an alternative," Scott said. In his view, this disengagement was also threatening to the government because people living outside of society could no longer be controlled. Dot Crockett, it seemed, was a means of keeping tabs.

Trips to the post office were darkened by a childhood intuition that Dot Crockett might cook me for dinner. The post office was located in an annex attached to an old mustard yellow farmhouse on the main road in the quiet hamlet of Harborside. We'd enter a small room with dusty wooden floors, a wall of individual brass-plated PO boxes, and a teller's window that dominated the back wall, with a ledge that was just a little too high, so Mama had to reach up in order to hand through the outgoing packages. The imposing figure of Dot Crockett blocked the light of the window, her cropped hair musty and uncombed, her equally dark eyes rimmed by glasses. If she spoke to Mama at all, it was to criticize something about the mail, or the way in which it was packaged, in a voice leathery and raspy from smoking.

"This package's not taped right, you'll have to redo it."

"Only books can go book class."

"Wrong zip code."

One time the postmistress actually slammed the window shut when she saw Mama coming with a larger than usual stack of packages.

"Some people are easily threatened," Papa said, when Mama told him about the incident. "Work as well as you can and be kind," he added, quoting Scott's favorite saying.

THERE WAS ONE small store on Cape Rosier, Perry's Store, located in a white New Englander on the road near the turn to Dog Island. Perry had a gas pump out front, and a selection of packaged and marked-up processed foods lined the dusty shelves of the dim interior. We usually drove the half hour to Blue Hill, or forty-five minutes to Ellsworth, where we could find a wider range of products for less, but every so often Papa stopped at Perry's Store in a pinch to pick up batteries or buy gas.

"A-yuh," Perry responded to Papa's hello.

Most of the locals on Cape Rosier had lived in the area for generations. The previous generation might have survived without electricity and flushing toilets, but this one had fought (and paid money) to get electrical and phone wires brought to their remote roads. Why in the hell someone would want to live without these luxuries now was beyond them.

"Queer folk," they said, referring to us. "Hippies."

"You mean the rabbit food eat-ahs?" Perry would joke when visitors asked at the store for directions to the Nearings. Native Mainers spoke in what you might call a dialect of the Kennedy Boston accent. *A*'s had become *r*'s, and *r*'s had become *a*'s. *Melissa* was "Melisser." The combination of *e* or *o* with *r* sounded more like *a* and *h*. *Mainer* was "Maine-ah," *neighbor* was "neighbah," and *lobster* was "lobstah." "You can't get they-ah from hey-ah," went the famous saying. Other common Maineisms were "A-yuh" for *yes*, and "Mothah," as an affectionate name for one's wife. Children, or friends of any age for that matter, were called "dee-ah," meaning *dear*. The word *farming* sounded more like "famine," as Brooklin neighbor and *Charlotte's Web* author E. B. White pointed out in his essay "Maine Speech," and *bastard*, pronounced "bayster," was often coupled with *ole*, for just about anything. "He's an ole bayster, they say, when they pull an eel out of a trap."

Perry viewed Papa, as he did the Nearings, with a mixture of curiosity, humor, and suspicion. There was no getting around it, the fact that we were "from away" immediately labeled us as "not likely to last the wintah." Now that the Nearings had lasted nearly twenty winters, they were at least acknowledged as being in existence as residents, even if they did sometimes disappear during the cold months, which was regarded as highly suspect and bordering on the category of "summah folk." Summer folk had long been populating second homes along the Maine coast as a hot-weather escape from the cities, and their numbers increased dramatically with the easy access provided by the automobile in the 1920s, though they were generally ignored, unless, of course, they were buying something.

Papa had respect for the locals and treated them accordingly. As he was paying for gas that day, he mentioned to Perry that he now had a daughter who'd been born in Maine—perhaps that counted for something?

"Elyut," Perry said. "You know how the saying goes. If a cat has kittens in the oven, you don't call 'em biscuits."

OTHER LOCALS WEREN'T so affable. A fellow named Percy, who sometimes worked as Carolyn Robinson's gardener, thought himself a more able farmer than the "city folk" living on the cape. He took it as an affront that the Nearings, and soon Papa, were recognized and written about for their gardening expertise. In retribution, Percy was known to leave piles of tacks on the final section of road leading to our land, with the intention of causing a flat tire, usually in the most inopportune of situations.

Papa was towing a trailer of manure back from his favorite horse farm when he found himself stranded at dusk by such a flat. Not having a spare, he unhitched the jeep from the trailer and left it by the side of the road, returning the next day with a patch kit. He removed the offending tack and mended the leak, only to find that the trailer's other tire had been slashed in the night by a vindictive knife.

"Sacre bleu!" Papa swore, borrowing the French Canadian curse used by the locals. At that time of winter, nearly spring, we were down to the bottom of the money stash under the couch, and a new tire was more than Papa could afford. He swore again, this time in English, and then did the only thing he could do—he went and got a job pruning a neighbor's trees for a few days until he had enough cash to buy a tire and bring the much-needed manure back to the farm.

"How many bastards are this lucky?" he reminded himself with a laugh as he finally patched the second tire. "How many ole bay-sters," he repeated in Maine-speak, "are this goddamn lucky?"

*   *   *

IN APRIL THE white-throated sparrows called out their arrival,
the ground thawed, and spring was off and growing again. By
that third year, we'd fully succumbed to the seasons. We felt the
changes in our blood and waited anxiously as the mud began to
grow things. The first blooms were white, as if to match the melting snow. Pale pussy willows proliferated in barren thickets, and
snow blue clumps of bluets dusted damp grassy areas. Soon an
abundance of pink blossoms exploded across the orchard, their
round petals falling like a late snowstorm and accumulating on
the ground in drifts.

"Most beautiful day we have had in weeks," Mama noted in
her journal. "Still eating apples stored since last fall in the root
cellar. They remain crisp and juicy: Northern Spies and Golden
Russets."

As the white flowers faded, everything turned green. Grass
thickened to a vibrant carpet as clumps of chives returned to
the herb garden, where they'd been planted the previous year.
Segmented stems of horsetails sprang from low, damp areas, and
green tongues of wild lily of the valley caught the light around the
edges. Spruce and fir branches put forth electric green bristles,
and baby fiddleheads brightened to an edible chartreuse that
Mama snapped off and brought home to sauté with butter for
lunch.

While Papa seeded flats with me in his lap and readied the
farm for planting, Mama carried water from the drinking spring,
milked the goats, cooked meals, and sewed or mended clothes
on her foot-powered treadle Singer sewing machine. She brought
out cotton shirts from storage, put away sweaters, washed the
windows, swept, dusted, and mopped the floors. Spring cleaning
helped get the winter doldrums out of her mind, too.

"I used to be a troubled person—not able to find myself nor find a way of life that suited me," Mama wrote on April 9, thinking back to her difficult adolescence. "I believe I grew up in a fear of life setting and this I somehow think drains creative energies (anti-life being negative leading to destructive energy). Then I came here, found homesteading and made myself well."

Papa was in the garden tilling, spreading compost, and transplanting as I trundled after him in my favorite red-checkered Marna coat, as I called it, handmade by Mama's sister, Aunt Marth, of a blanket "borrowed" from the ski lift at Mad River Glen. The once-poor soil was now rich and dark brown from compost when Papa dug into it with a trowel to transplant seedlings. We put our noses close to inhale the fresh scent of spring.

"That's the smell of possibility," Papa said.

Mama watched us through the front windows as she sat with her journal, hoping to capture her feelings of contentment and well-being. "Realized for the first time in my life that I am truly happy," she added to her previous post. "Happy to be with Eliot and to have had Melissa and to be living here with the Nearings as neighbors. My life has become meaningful after years of confusion and chaos."

WE RECEIVED THE message from the *Wall Street Journal* on a rainy day in May of 1971. The newspaper my grandfather Skipper read as he rode the train to his job as a stockbroker in New York City wanted to do a story on us. Mama's initial thrill turned to apprehension.

"This is exactly the type of thing we wanted to escape," she said. Papa nodded, but his thoughts were elsewhere. The article could be used, he thought, to spread the word about a better way of living. Furthermore, his *Wall Street Journal*–reading family and friends in New Jersey thought he was a financially destitute hippie. A story in their paper of choice might prove otherwise. It could show that material wealth was not the only wealth.

The reporter, David Gumpert, might as well have been covering a story in a third-world country. A staff writer at the Boston office, he'd been captivated by an article about us in the *Maine Times* and proposed a story on this new interest in going "back to the land." Sales of the 1970 edition of *Living the Good Life* had reached nearly 50,000 copies, compared to only 10,000 for the previous edition, and *The Whole Earth Catalog* and Rodale's *Prevention* magazine were giving voice to this growing subculture of environmentalists, natural foodies, and organic farming advocates. The problem was, there was no easy way to get ahold of us. Gumpert finally succeeded in contacting Papa through Bucks Harbor Market's phone, and left the city to enter our world for three days, sleeping in the guest camper/soon-to-be goat house and following us through our workday. He had lived only in Chicago, New York, and Boston, so our lifestyle was an especially exotic contrast to his own. Quiet and easy to talk to, the young reporter adapted without complaint to the difficulties of using the outhouse and eating our vegetarian food, though he secretly thought the goat's milk tasted of the barn-yard, and it sent him to the outhouse with the runs.

"All I want to express to the world via the newspaper is this," Mama told him. "We are a family of human beings trying to live a happy, healthy and fruitful existence in a world where it is difficult to do so. Our goal is not to prove anything, but is mainly to survive as decently as possible."

While Mama wanted to protect her privacy, feeling the dirt under her fingernails and patches on her clothes illuminated in the glare of self-consciousness, Papa took advantage of the opportunity to share our way of life.

"I'm working sixteen hours a day for survival," Papa told Gumpert. "This isn't any game I'm playing. If I don't grow enough, it's that much less to eat this winter. But we find, every passing day, we're just so happy here."

Mama was less encouraged. "The reporter from Boston has left and I realize how difficult it is to express our way of life to those who live so differently," she wrote in her journal. "I realize now that the experience with the reporter was an unfortunate one. He was like an intrusion, making me feel uneasy and paranoid the three days he was here."

The article and a picture of my two-year-old face hit the front page on Tuesday, July 13, 1971, and despite Mama's fears, it turned out to be a favorable profile.

"When Sue and Eliot Coleman sit down to eat in their tiny one-room house, they use tree stumps instead of chairs," the story began. "When they need drinking water, Sue walks a quarter of a mile through the woods to a freshwater brook and hauls back two big containers hanging from a yoke over her shoulders. And when the Colemans want to read at night, they light kerosene lanterns. The young couple—Sue is 26, Eliot 31—aren't the forgotten victims of rural poverty or some natural disaster. They live as they do out of choice. . . . With their two-year-old daughter, Melissa, Sue and Eliot are trying to escape America's consumer economy and live in the wilderness much as the country's pioneers did."

Our serve-yourself farm stand was soon crowded with summer folk on a treasure hunt to find us on the winding roads of the Blue Hill Peninsula. No one could believe we were surviving on less than $2,000 a year, as reported.

"Eliot and Sue still retain some ties to the money economy," Gumpert wrote, tailoring the story to his financial audience. "During the spring and summer Eliot does gardening and other odd jobs for local residents three or four mornings a week, for which he is paid $2 to $2.50 an hour. Sue also has done some part-time secretarial work. Together, they were able to earn about $1,400 last year. They earned another $350 from the sale of surplus vegetables from their garden—mostly peas and lettuce—to neighbors and tourists, for a total income of $1,750. The remaining $250 they spent came from the last of the savings they had when they moved to Maine. . . . The Colemans are among a tiny but apparently growing number of young couples, often from middle-class families, who are taking up the pioneering life, or 'homesteading' as it's often called."

A friend of Papa's from prep school was working in New York in publishing at the time. "Well, I'll be damned, Eliot's gone and put his finger on the zeitgeist," Ian said when he picked up the paper that day. The article, it turned out, was a messenger of change, as more and more people became interested in a simpler way of life—people who would seek us out in droves during the coming energy crisis. Soon, the isolation of the woods would be anything but.

CHAPTER FIVE

Companions

THE ONE THING I yearned for those first years was a baby sister or brother, and by the fall of 1971, it looked like my wish might come true.

"All is well on Greenwood Farm," Mama wrote in her journal on October 27, 1971. "Apple storage almost completed; canning completed (over 300 quarts); cabbage in; apples being dried; cheese making started (with rennet and sour cream to activate); and still eating fresh strawberries from the garden!

"It seems I'm pregnant, due May 28, 1972."

Then on November 2: "I made seven wheels of goat cheese weighing two–four pounds each. Some had cumin and caraway seed, and some were plain. All were rubbed with sesame oil and salt to form a rind and then scraped and bathed with vinegar and salt to keep mold down."

Mama didn't mention the miscarriage. She'd found a four-leaf clover a couple days before it happened, always a sign of good luck, so she told herself that maybe it was the right thing; perhaps the baby was not healthy enough. She'd been working so hard, it was likely she didn't have enough nutrients left over for the baby to form correctly. But none of those thoughts mattered to her body. It was in mourning. All that blood, gone now.

"I feel very alienated to most women in town," Mama wrote. "Here I am a woman at the peak of reproduction and child bearing and cannot talk about it to anyone."

I must have felt her sadness, and my own. I really wanted a friend. Mama read me a story about a fledgling bird that fell from its nest and went around asking the other animals, "Are you my mother?" I was like that bird, but I went around asking, "Will you be my friend?"

"BE MY FRIENDS?" I asked the chickens. They clucked and nodded.

We had about a dozen hens and one rooster. The rooster had a red wattle on his head like a wound and liked to crew and strut his iridescent tail feathers. Some of the hens were pale beige, some speckled brown and white, one brownish, others black. They taught me to roll in the dust to get clean. Brownie was my favorite, friendly and gossipy. She told me she would always be my friend.

We collected eggs from the coop and the secret places where the grass was matted by the shape of the hens' bodies. Most eggs were tan and perfectly shaped, like magic stones with speckles and rough bumps in the shell, but the bantams' were pale blue, like robins' eggs. When I held a blue egg in the palms of my cupped hands, it felt so hard and strong, like nothing could break it, but I knew that the littlest drop or bump would turn it into a sticky mess of slippery clear bled into by yellow yolk. The shattered egg was nothing so strong after all.

Every once in a while a fox would get one of the hens.

"I guess the fox needs to eat, too," Papa said, but it sure made him mad. As replacement, we'd let some of the eggs hatch, and I'd thrill to find the chicks lying under the mother like feathered eggs.

At first Mama and Papa loved having fresh eggs. "Look at the difference in color between our yolks and the pale store-bought ones," Papa said to Mama. "Ours are a rich orange. Makes you think how much better your human eggs must be, eating a good diet, compared to the eggs of other women eating junk."

"Maybe I miscarried because I wasn't getting enough vitamin E," Mama said in reply. She kept hidden the fear that the hard work might have also been the cause. She didn't want Papa to think she couldn't hack it.

The Nearings didn't eat eggs and didn't believe in keeping animals of any kind, and after a while Mama and Papa began to wonder if it was good to eat eggs, not only because the Nearings disapproved but also because the chickens were more mouths to feed in the lean months of winter. Then one day, just like that, Papa packed up the chickens into crates and gave them away.

Later when I thought of the chickens, one of those rare pale blue eggs rose up into my throat. The chickens had been part of our family, and the egg in my throat was the feeling of something missing. It was hard and smooth and heavy, but also so fragile it might break and make me cry. It was the feeling of growing out of a favorite shirt, milk spilled on the floor, the last bit of honey in the jar, falling apple blossoms. It was the lump in the throat behind everything beautiful in life.

NORM HAD BEEN missing all morning. We looked out the front windows for him, the sky hanging low and gray over the dormant earth of the garden. There had been little snow that winter of 1972, and what had fallen so far had not stayed on the ground. Normie's brown-black coat usually blended into the colors of the earth as he did his morning rounds of his territory, sniffing to find what animals had visited in the night and lifting his leg to pee and let them know whose farm this really was.

"I'll go give a holler for him," Mama said, putting on her wool coat and hat with earflaps.

"Hope he didn't get into a porcupine," Papa mumbled.

When he wasn't guarding the compost heaps from squirrels and coons, Norman the Normal Dog, as he'd been dubbed by Papa's college fraternity brothers, was often getting into some kind of trouble or other. Chasing Puss-o, Helen's Maine coon cat, onto roofs and trees. Getting sprayed by a skunk and stinking up the whole house so Mama had to wash him in tomato juice. Worst of all for Normie was getting into a porcupine. He couldn't resist the lumbering animals that poked about the woods and looked so much easier to catch than a raccoon. But when he pounced at them, the wiry gray-white hair stood up on end like armor and the quills seemed to shoot out, hooking barbs into the soft flesh of his mouth and tongue. He'd yelp and skitter away, tail between his legs, his head a pincushion of hurt. "Son of a gun, not again," Papa would say. I cried, too, as Norm whined and squirmed while Papa pulled out the quills with a pair of pliers.

After the chickens left, Normie had taken their place as my

best friend. I liked to nap with him on the padded benches, fitting my head in the soft hollow where his leg haunch and stomach met and waking from common dreams of chasing rabbits in summer, he whining and leg-twitching in his sleep.

"He fell in the dry well hole," Mama said when she came back from looking for Norm.

She settled him on the couch, his back legs limp and dragging behind. He looked at me with his dark eyes and tried to lick my face.

"Poor old guy," Mama said, hugging him to her chest. "Your legs are giving out on you."

"Poor ole Norm," I said, patting his fur.

"Time for an extra-special diet," Mama said, heading for the kitchen. "Grated carrots and olive oil have resurrected him many times before. I'll add some herbs and raw veggies mixed with cooked millet, cod liver oil, brewer's yeast, and lots of garlic."

From the couch, Normie-dog rolled over and groaned.

WITH NORMIE OUT of commission, I turned to books.

"Books," Papa often said, "are the truest of friends." Papa sat at a long table in the dusky great room of the local library. He had a stack in front of him and was writing into a notepad as columns of light from the windows cut tunnels through the dust and made the curved parts of his ears glow.

"Papa, read me books . . . ," I said, but Mama gave me a look under heavy brows.

"Shush." She pressed her finger to her lips. "Whisper."

"Sss," I repeated huskily, pressing my finger to my nose. "Whispure."

Mama tried not to smile.

"Papa is doing research," she told me softly. "He needs to concen-trate."

Mama took my hand, and we walked down the rows of grown-up books to the children's section. The books surrounded us like wrapped presents. It was only by opening them that you could find out if they held anything special. I picked out the ones I wanted and we sat at a table with the stack in front of us, just like Papa.

"This one," I said, choosing one with a picture of a green island surrounded by blue sea on the cover.

When Mama opened the book and started to read, the story reached out and took my hand; it told me I was not alone in the world. In a good story, the characters were telling a secret that you knew was true because you remembered it from somewhere deep inside.

"The cat looked underwater and saw that the island was connected to the earth . . . ," Mama read. My scalp tickled from the hair rising up. All the islands around our home were connected, too. If someone swallowed the sea, like in one of my other books, we could walk out on the land between the islands. So the island was connected to the land, but it liked to have the sea there to keep it separate from the rest of the world.

Just like us.

"HAD A WONDERFUL sauna and supper with Dick, Susan and Carl and kids and work crew for their boat," Mama wrote in her journal. Dick and his wife, Mary, moved from Connecticut to Brooksville to semi-retire, followed by their son Carl, whom Papa met when he was working for extra cash as a carpenter to restore the schooner *Nathaniel Bowditch* in Bucks Harbor. Best of all for me, Carl and his wife, Susan, had two kids, Jennifer and Nigel, who was my age and would become a playmate.

Not only was it a rare treat to meet like-minded folks with

kids, but Mary, who was of Swedish descent, shared with us some interesting traditions from Scandinavian culture. Dick and Mary had a Swedish-inspired wood-fired sauna in their house on Horseshoe Cove and invited us to join them on Sunday nights. We all piled into the cedar-planked room and sat naked on the wooden benches until we couldn't bear the heat anymore, then ran out and jumped in the ocean to cool off. It was supposed to be great for cleansing the blood, and certainly left us cleaner and better smelling than our small metal bathtub at home, which we filled with water heated on the stove.

Mary also gave me an illustrated book called *The Tomten* about a Scandinavian gnome with a long white beard and red pointed hat who lived on farms and took care of the people and animals. Susan told Mama that in the Swedish tradition the Tomten brought gifts for children and animals, like an ongoing Santa Claus. Mama and Papa began to do the same for me.

"Someone I know was born three years ago today," Papa said one morning, lifting me up and bouncing me on his knee on the stool by the bookshelf. I'd been standing nearby as he read, eyeing to get into the sphere of his attention.

"On this day, you came out of your mama's belly over there in the loft and started nursing," he said, eyes alight. "Not many kids can say that about their birth."

When he lifted me up, I felt the shape of my own body within his arms and the tickle of his unshaven cheeks. He smelled of damp earth from working in the greenhouse.

"Why don't you go check outside and see what the Tomten brought for your birthday," Papa said.

"Tomten?" I looked into his eyes. His face was serious, but there was a sparkle in the blue and a smile hiding beneath the stubble on his cheeks. He looked over at Mama by the sink and winked.

"Outside the door," Papa said. "I saw it when I came in."

I hopped off Papa's lap and ran to the door, reaching up on tiptoes to slide the handle. If I could ever see the Tomten, with his red cap and long beard, I wanted to ask him to be my friend. And just maybe, I hoped, he might bring me a doll with real hair. I opened the door to damp spring air and a yard spotted with remnants of snow. No Tomten. No doll. My eyes trailed back to the house. There by the doorstep was a little pair of sinew-and-wood snowshoes with bindings just the size for my feet.

"Bring them in, quickly, and close the door," Mama said. Papa helped me lay the snowshoes out and put my feet into the bindings so I could clomp around on the floor. All of our snowshoes were the old-fashioned kind, made by Indians, woven from the sinew and tendons of animals around an oval wooden frame. The snow was gone now, but next winter I could go on treks with Mama and Papa on the snowy paths, and in a couple years I would snowshoe the half-mile path down to the Nearings' to catch the school bus.

"The Tomten is pretty smart," Papa said. "He knows what we need out here in the woods."

"Most important for making this homesteading experience work, is having needs precede wants," Mama wrote in her journal that evening.

MAMA WHOOSHED IN the door one morning, her cheeks and nose flushed red.

"Goatski is having a kid," she said. Every morning Mama went to the goat pen behind the house to milk and feed the goats. She liked to get creative about their food as she did with Norm, adding oats or wheat groats to their chow, and fresh carrots and seaweed in summer. The goats didn't seem to mind like Norm did.

"Does eat oats and mares eat oats and little lambs eat ivy," Mama liked to sing. "A kid'll eat ivy, too, wouldn't you?"

"No!" I chimed.

"Goat's milk is the best kind of milk for you to drink," she told me. "It's easier for kids to digest." Some people wrinkled their noses about the taste, but I didn't know any differently.

Mama taught herself to milk her first goat in Franconia. She held an old waterlogged how-to-milk book her father had given her in one hand and practiced squeezing the heavy finger-shaped teats with the other. After a few tries the milk squirted out in hot, hard streams to make a lonely patter into the stainless steel bucket. Her hands and arms got cramps at first, but once she got the hang of it, calluses built up on her palms and she could get a pail in ten minutes. The milk squirting into the liquid of a full bucket made a satisfying *cheeeeet* sound. Once the females gave birth, we could get milk out of them for nearly a year. We'd keep or sell the baby girls, but the boys were in less demand.

Papa looked up from his bowl of oats. "Let's hope it's not a billy."

Papa didn't like to talk about how to get rid of the billy goats. We needed only one billy, who got to visit with the female goats when they were in heat. Brutus was big and black and a little scary as he stood in the doorway of the old camper with eyes glowing out of the darkness, or sometimes snorting and stamping around his pen like the bull in my book *The Story of Ferdinand* after he got stung by a bee.

"I'm going back out to make sure Goatski does okay," Mama told Papa. She felt a bond with goats during birth; she'd been there, too.

"I want to come," I said.

"Okay, bundle up."

The air steamed from the goats' nostrils and they stamped their tulip hooves in the mud at our approach. Ma-Goat's udders swayed back and forth when she trotted up to the fence, her own pregnant belly hanging like a water balloon from the knobby ridge of her spine, knees bulbous under the weight. The goats were my friends, but they were complicated. Their eyes were not warm and gentle like Norm's but urgent and impatient, swirled marbles with the distinct black bar of the iris in the middle. Once their needs were met, they became playful, rubbing their pointy-ridged horns on the cedar fence posts and butting at each other, but never becoming exactly cuddly.

"Give them this," Mama said, handing me a head of lettuce she'd brought from the greenhouse. "Make sure everyone gets some, but stay outside the fence."

Barley's square teeth snapped out of her delicate mouth at the leaves. Through the opening of the door, I could see Goatski lying on a nest of hay in the shed, her body heaving and lurching as Mama squatted beside her.

"Here it comes," Mama said. Soon I heard the bleating of a baby goat as Mama helped pull it free of the birth sac.

"Oh, shit," she muttered. "It's a boy."

We left the kid to nurse and went in to tell Papa.

"Better to get it over with," he said as he put on his coat.

"I want to come," I begged, sensing a disturbance in Papa's mood.

"Not this time," Mama replied, her lips firm.

Papa, I imagine, tried not to let his feelings get wrapped up in it as he headed to the goat shed. The billy had short black hair in cowlicky curls like a child's, legs long and gangly, hooves still soft. He must have bleated and searched Papa's hand for a teat as Papa put him in the burlap sack filled with cast-off rocks from the garden and tied it tightly. The oak-staved rainwater barrels sat under the eaves of the farmhouse to catch the runoff and in early spring grew a dark skin of ice overnight. Papa punched the crust through with an ax and dropped the burlap bag into the water, forcing himself to stand next to the barrel and make sure it ended quickly. The bubbles rose furious and opaque in the dark water as broken shards of ice tapped against themselves. When the bubbles slowed and stopped, he reached in to grab the bag, the cold water stinging his hands. It always seemed so much heavier coming out. He would bury it in the apple orchard with the others. Papa was glad to get away from the house and put effort into digging hard and fast into the thawing ground until his blood flowed again and his mind drifted to a calmer place. Still, he knew he'd feel a heaviness in his chest for days afterward.

"The reality of this way of life is that you have got to keep at it even when you don't feel like it," Mama wrote in her journal to ease her mind while Papa was outside. "Otherwise you won't make it. It's no life for dabblers. You've got to dig it wholeheartedly, for if you don't, you just simply won't be happy nor successful at what you do."

THE TRIALS OF the colder months were forgotten as the cape exploded in flowers. Lupine came at the tail end of May, their fronds of purple-blue pea shapes rising from the concentric-leaved clumps covering hillsides along the roads. Yellow dandelions exploded into seeded tufts that floated on the breeze and gave way to the taller but sparser cover of yellow buttercups. Our rose-hip bushes, planted the spring I was born, blossomed with pink heart-shaped petals, bumblebees dipping into the pollen-filled centers.

On walks in the woods, Mama always kept an eye out for the rare pink lady's slipper among the white bunchberry dogwood, wild lily of the valley, and starflowers carpeting the forest floor. The delicate pouch hung from a single stem and leaf, regal in its solitary beauty against the tangle of the forest.

"It looks like a scrotum," a visitor said once, and Mama blushed as if she'd been caught looking at his.

There were other flowers showing up, too, "flower children," Mama joked. The Nearings' farm was overrun with students attending a seminar on how to homestead. They came in one-week shifts, and stayed in rental houses four miles down the single-lane road in the town of Harborside. Scott taught them to transplant lettuce and make compost, and then put them right to work doing whatever he needed done.

"It's paid labor of the best kind because the laborers are the ones paying $100 a week," Papa noted in amusement.

Whenever I saw Scott's hunched and lined figure, often pushing a wheelbarrow, my young imagination was reminded of the A. A. Milne poem "Jonathan Jo," which Mama often read to me.

Jonathan Jo
Has a mouth like an "O"
And a wheelbarrow full of surprises.

Every Monday night, people gathered after dinner on the lawn in front of the Nearings' house to listen to Scott talk about social, political, and agrarian issues. These gatherings became known as Monday Night Meetings and were open to all. Monday nights also meant potential young friends; even though the guests were mostly grown-ups, there was always the chance that a child or two might be brought along. After work we'd throw buckets of water from the well over our heads to wash up before Papa carried me down the path on his shoulders. Apprentices and visitors hung around on the back patio, talking and playing music. From my shoulder perch, I scanned the crowd for small persons, and if there were any, we'd chase each other around the wide lawn until it was time to "pay attention." We all sat in a circle around Scott holding court in his chair as he talked in his low melodious voice, the vowels bumping and rolling over each other like stones in a riverbed. Popcorn was served in large wooden bowls, and the question-and-answer period evolved into lengthy discussions into the summer evening.

Once, when Helen interrupted Scott during a particularly long ramble, he cut her off by saying, "Quiet, woman." The younger onlookers were scandalized, but it didn't faze Helen. Though they were progressive in their teachings, the Nearings' marriage was rooted in an earlier era.

While Monday night was Scott's domain, Sunday night was Helen's music night, when she played classical records on the phonograph. Though Helen no longer practiced the violin with regularity, sometimes there'd be a live concert. We all sat on the floor of the Nearings' long living room, me in the V of Mama's legs, the room full of smells from a potluck and the sweat on the skin of the people gathered in the warm summer evening. Arranged before the fieldstone fireplace was not your traditional quartet, certainly, but one pulled together by Helen to take advantage of the talents in attendance.

Helen played a recorder or her violin. There might have been a lady with a dulcimer, similar to a violin but with a longer hourglass shape, that lay flat on her lap, three strings plucked by her fingertips to produce a folksy dulcy sound, or a Middle Eastern oud, a tear-shaped guitar with multiple strings over wood rosette, and perhaps someone with a hammered dulcimer, a trapezoid on legs topped with strings struck by small mallets to make tinny reverberating sounds. Whatever the odd combination, on Sunday nights at the Nearings', music connected us to the world.

Papa said he'd learn to play an instrument if he wasn't genetically tone-deaf, like Skates. The joke was that Skates couldn't even sing in the shower. During his *Dr. Zhivago* phase, Papa fancied taking up the balalaika, but it mostly just hung on the wall. Mama had more of a natural gift for music. She tried to teach herself to play the dulcimer in the evenings, but claimed she didn't have the time to get good at it. If Mama and Papa were to have musical themes the way Zhivago and Lara did, Papa's would be the boogie-woogie on the piano, the popular bluesy dance music from the 1930s and '40s with an upbeat rhythm and funky beat that made you want to get up and, well, boogie.

Mama's theme song would have to be "Simple Gifts," a hymn composed in the Shaker community of Alfred, Maine, in the mid-1800s and made popular by Aaron Copland in the 1940s. Mama loved to sing it as she worked or walked the paths in the woods.

> *'Tis the gift to be simple, 'tis the gift to be free,*
> *'Tis the gift to come down where we ought to be,*
> *And when we find ourselves in the place just right,*
> *'Twill be in the valley of love and delight.*
> *When true simplicity is gain'd,*
> *To bow and to bend we shan't be asham'd,*
> *To turn, turn will be our delight,*
> *Till by turning, turning we come round right.*

Music, I was learning, both came from the outside world and was uniquely our own. As I sat with Mama at the Nearings' concert, drifting off on the river of sound, a familiar tune rose from the melody of strange instruments, and a friendly woman began to sing along beside us:

> *Oh Susanna, don't you cry for me.*
> *I come from Alabama with a banjo on my knee.*

WHILE MOST OF the flower children at the Nearings' came and went, there was one cheerful face we began to see week after week. Susan showed up for a session and proved proficient at following Scott's directions, so they asked her to stay the season and help run the summer workshops. Susan's path to Cape Rosier was similar to that of Mama and Papa—she'd also found a copy of *Living the Good Life* at a health food store. She heard the Nearings were offering weeklong seminars, and decided to drive from Maryland to Maine to participate.

She had a cherubic smiling face and long brown hair in thick braids with a short line of bangs across her forehead. At twenty years old, she was about as excited to be alive as anyone we knew. Her bright eyes always seemed to be either slightly surprised or on the verge of laughter, and her musical voice could be heard exclaiming at the size of the zucchini in the garden in an extended "Ohhhhhh!" or singing along the forest paths. Susan's laugh of ringing bells filled the Nearings' patio at lunch as everyone gathered around her like bees to honey.

Susan was not alone in her desire to learn how to farm organically. The summer before, a large event held at Thomas Point Beach in Brunswick, Maine, brought together experts on organic gardening and farming with Scott and Helen as guest speakers. From that meeting, the Maine Organic Farmers and Gardeners

Association, MOFGA, was started to bring small farmers together through local chapters, potluck suppers, and garden tours.
MOFGA soon sponsored a no-spray register, a campaign focus-
ing on the hazards of pesticide drift, an organic certification program, and an apprenticeship program. Soon there would be many
more workers like Susan looking to us for training.

"We work in the gardens—planting, harvesting, building stone
walls—and cook our meals from the food we grow," Susan told
her mother. "I'm in heaven!"

"A FARMER'S FOOTSTEPS are the best fertilizer," Papa told me
as I rode on his shoulders while he walked around the garden at
the end of the summer day, keeping tabs on the crops. My legs
fit snugly between his jaw and shoulders, hands clasping his ears
or across his forehead, his silvery hair tossing back under my chin
as he held my feet with his callused hands.

"You can do anything you set your mind to, little one," he said.
"Look what we've done with this farm."

We gazed out over the neat plots of vigorously growing plants.
It was hard to imagine it had been forest only a few years earlier.
Papa's seemingly superhuman feats were bringing more and more
reporters to our farm to take pictures and talk with him about
the innovations he was making in his garden. Other people, it
turned out, were eager to learn from him. He'd decided to follow
the Nearings' example and raise money for education and research, starting an organization called the Small Farm Research
Association to provide a network of small farmers with the latest
information about organic gardening.

"Don't we have enough on our plate?" Mama asked, wary of
the undertaking, complicating as it might the simple pleasures
of homesteading. But Papa's nature needed a challenge—he'd

figured out how to homestead, and now he sought to take on agriculture. His goal that year was to be able to live off the summer sales of vegetables and the income from the research association so he could focus on the farm without taking outside jobs.

"Members receive copies of all our publications and are entitled to our agricultural advisory service," he explained in the introduction to members. "All questions and letters will be answered on the basis of the best and most comprehensive information available." A sponsoring membership was $20 per year; other memberships were "whatever you can afford."

"Nothing is impossible," Papa said, dreaming to himself, as we continued our rounds of the garden.

"But I can't fly," I'd giggle, coming up with games to lengthen our time together.

"You're flying right now," he said, tipping me this way and that, and suddenly I was. When you looked at it through Papa's eyes, anything really was possible.

Papa knew it would take tremendous effort to make the farm profitable, but since the *Wall Street Journal* article, visitors wanted to stay and learn, and he realized the extra hands could help him meet his goals. Like the Nearings, he would teach the apprentices to garden and then put them to work building a new farm stand for the growing vegetable business. The problem was where to lodge all the eager workers. The Nearings didn't like the expense of putting up helpers at the rental houses in Harborside, and sought to provide a better option.

Recently, they'd decided to sell a section of land to a young couple named Keith and Jean. The couple met in high school biology class in Ohio; both were from working-class families, Keith a tall, square-jawed football player, Jean a bookish type with long hair and glasses. After graduation, Keith spent two tours in Vietnam, and out of sorts with the world after combat, he began to talk about living off the land. They'd read *Living the Good Life*, and like Mama and Papa, took a land-hunting trip in their VW bus and stopped to visit the Nearings. Seeing potential in the young couple—and the lines of their hands—Helen offered them a deal similar to ours on the thirty acres that lay between us and the Nearing farm.

In the summer of 1972, the Nearings and Papa made a deal with Keith to section off three acres between our two properties for a campground, and the Nearings financed the building of tent platforms and a cook shack. Visitors set up tents to work for us, the Nearings, or Keith and Jean, walking up and down the path in the woods between the three homesteads. Lunch and garden produce were provided in exchange for work, and there'd often be a potluck at Monday Night Meetings. Music, the smell of wood smoke, and voices talking and singing, drifted from the campground in the evenings. From my perch on Papa's shoulders I could see the fire pit glowing in the dusk and knew that soon the chords of a guitar would join the stars twinkling above.

Screaming in delight, I held tight to Papa's ears and tightened the grip of my legs around his neck as he flew me across the farm and home for dinner. "Your father has the confidence of a natural athlete," Skates always told us in that complimentary way reserved for the most important attribute a person could have. It was a confidence you couldn't help but love. The problem for me was that the more people came to our farm, the more competition I had for his attention. When they came, I forgot why I'd wanted friends so badly in the first place. Mama agreed; she wished everyone would leave us alone.

*   *   *

"WENT FOR THE most refreshing swim today—best I've had all summer," Mama wrote on September 27, 1972. "We are trying to get back to normal after a busy hard-working summer. It's great to be six months pregnant and enjoy all of our usual pleasures thoroughly."

As well as the friends in the campground, it seemed I would also get that sibling I'd dreamed of for so long. The birth would be at a hospital this time because Eva, the midwife who'd delivered me, wasn't available. Papa considered doing the delivery himself, as Mama's grandfather had done for his children, but decided against it when the hospital agreed to a natural birth and to allow Papa in the room, requests that were rarely granted at the time. The fact that her mother was so enthusiastic about a hospital birth made Mama, who preferred to have the baby at home, even madder, though she eased her stance after her father suffered his first heart attack that fall, relieved as she was at his recovery and not wanting to add to his stresses.

"I'll only stay the required twelve hours," she stated. "Then I want to come straight home with the baby." Papa knew better than to argue with a very large pregnant woman.

Our new neighbor Jean was fascinated to hear of my home birth and Mama's resistance to the hospital. Products of midwestern upbringings and recent military service, Keith and Jean were trying to navigate the strange world to which they now belonged. It wasn't until after they moved up that the Nearings discovered, much to their not always silent disapproval, that Keith and Jean were "carcass eaters," as Helen and Scott called nonvegetarians.

The arrival of our new neighbors is perfect timing, Mama thought to herself, despite their carnivorous inclinations. Or maybe Helen planned it that way. Mama had explained to Helen that she wouldn't be able to do the book work come winter with the new baby, and Papa had been too busy with his own plans to help Scott as much as he used to. They would have to forgo the money earned from the Nearings with the hope that they could make it at the farm stand the next summer. The Nearings needed a new couple to do their bidding, and planning to be away that winter again, they offered discounted land; then Helen asked Keith and Jean to take care of their house and do the paperwork as Mama had done.

THE CAMPGROUND WAS clearing out for the winter, but one hearty soul remained. Brett, a marine biology major with fine carpentry skills, had visited the Nearings with his girlfriend on bicycles the summer before. They'd ridden across the country from Ohio, stayed for a couple weeks to work for the Nearings, and then biked home. During his short stay, Helen asked Brett to bring up our mail—the Nearings' mailbox being, at that time, the farthest the postman would deliver. Papa noted Brett's quiet manner and solid frame, square face with heavy brows, long ponytail, and professed skill with carpentry, and invited him to work for us. Brett had returned in May, clearing stumps to expand the back field, doing small construction projects, and living out of his VW bus in the campground with Susan and the other apprentices. That fall, Brett stayed on for a job finishing restorations on the *Nathaniel Bowditch* in Bucks Harbor.

"The doors of the bus keep freezing shut at night from the moisture of my breathing," he told Papa one morning. "I had to break a window to get out."

"What we need is a cabin," Papa said. He suggested that Brett put his carpentry skills to work building himself a place to stay. The Nearings put up some cash, and Brett scavenged pine boards for the 250-square-foot interior while tearing down a house in Harborside. He used driftwood he found on the beach for the porch and covered the A-frame roof in sheets of cast-off galvanized steel. But by the time the cabin was completed, Brett had to leave it behind, having accepted an invitation to sail down the coast on the *Nathaniel Bowditch.*

Meanwhile Susan, the Nearings' star apprentice, was looking for a place to stay that fall, and took up residence in the new abode. One of the visitors passing through caught her notice. A recent Dartmouth College grad, David had a long brown Walt Whitman beard and sparkling blue eyes. His quiet and methodical soul was immediately drawn to the playfulness of Susan's carefree spirit. Little did they know at the time that they would eventually marry and have kids; they are still together, farming organically, to this day. David slept on the porch of the cabin, and they talked late into the night. When it got too cold for camping, he invited Susan to work with him on a farm near Hanover, New Hampshire, for the winter, and they made plans to return to the cape the following summer and help manage our growing workforce.

PAPA WAS BUSY building that December, too, finishing an addition to the farmhouse so we would have room for our growing family. As the cold of December closed around us, he spent the short days and into the night adding a twenty-by-eighteen-foot room behind the house.

"You need to take it easy," Mama said, already in bed with third-trimester fatigue, when he came in from pounding nails in the dark.

"I have to get the roof up before the snow," he replied, eyes closing the minute he lay down. Once the roof was up, he said he was pushing hard to finish before the baby came, but Mama thought there was more to it than that. When Papa was tired, he became more obsessive about work. It was as if overworking set off an alarm in his mind telling him he needed to work more. Instead of taking care of himself, he pushed harder.

"I've always had an extra gear I can count on when things get tough," Papa explained to Mama over breakfast, trying to ease her fears. During his years as a mountaineer, when the climb seemed the hardest and he wanted to give up, something in his body said, "Don't stop now or you'll die," and the adrenaline kicked in and carried him through to safety.

"It seems you've shifted into that gear permanently," Mama replied.

Mama worried about Papa as she worried about her father and his heart. While Grandpa was sensitive to life, its stresses taking their toll on his health, Papa had seemed the opposite of that, so vital and invincible, but now Papa, too, was weakening, showing signs of being human. Sometimes Mama's fears were not a problem to be solved, but simply an emotion that needed release. If they weren't, her fears ballooned inside and became bigger than all else. Mama longed to relax into Papa's arms, slip into the cave created by the touch of skin on skin. When Papa resisted her need, she tried to hold on more tightly, but already he was slipping away from her grasp. Putting on his coat. Going to work.

"Wait, Eliot," she called. When he turned back, his eyes were hard, and words failed her. She didn't know how to ask for what she needed. He didn't know how to listen to her silences. He went out the door, and the back of his head disappeared into the day.

Snow fell in tiny pricks against Papa's cheek, and the cold nipped his fingers as he rolled the tar paper onto the new roof. His heart seemed to beat too quickly in his chest, and he had a cold he couldn't kick, despite gallons of rose-hip and raspberry juice. Even his old mantra, "How many son of a guns are this lucky?" held little comfort.

He tried to make sense of things in his mind. Health insurance, he believed, was on the table at every meal. In other words, the best way to deal with illness was to invest in prevention—eating a good diet that kept the body healthy. As with plants, Papa believed that if you became sick, it meant your body wasn't getting what it needed. He'd read up on vitamins and minerals, learning which foods were highest in A, B, C, D, and minerals like calcium, magnesium, and zinc. He drank rose-hip juice for vitamin C, ate garlic and echinacea to build immunity, used peppermint and lemon balm tea to soothe the stomach, and used chamomile to calm the nerves, but perhaps all this wasn't enough.

He knew that if B vitamins were lacking, it caused mood swings and other imbalances, but it seemed the bigger problem was stress, and there wasn't much he could see to do about it. He never thought to question the vegetarian diet espoused by the Nearings. By Christmas, the roof and walls of the new addition had to be finished so he could break through the back wall of the house, creating a door to the new bedroom. And just in time.

CHAPTER SIX

Water

EACH DROP OF water, we're told, has existed in its myriad forms since the beginning of time on this planet. And water, as Scott liked to say, always finds a way to return to itself. It travels from cloud to mist to rain to ponds, lakes, streams, rivers, and, finally, to the sea. From this water we are born.

At 1:35 a.m. on January 1, after six hours of easy labor at home and a final hour and a half of hard pushing at the hospital, Mama gasped as her second child slipped from its waters into the world. Papa roused a cheer, having supported her from first contraction through the last hard strains of labor, but there seemed to be a problem with the baby. Mama looked down to see a gray parcel—a baby's shape, but not quite a baby, the head and shapes of arms and legs covered in a translucent gray membrane.

"En caul," Dr. Brownlow said, unperturbed. The term was a reference to Hamlet, shortened in medical terminology from "enshrouded in a caul," to refer to a baby born in the amniotic sac.

"Your waters didn't break," he explained, proceeding to remove what is sometimes called "the bag of waters" from around the child. Heidi emerged pink and perfect to gasp her first breaths of air, and become the first Maine baby of 1973.

A caul, I now know from research, is uncommon, appearing in fewer than one in a thousand births. Due to the rarity and strange appearance of the sac, legends have built up over the centuries, the most common being that a baby born en caul will never drown. As a result, cauls were once collected and preserved at birth and sold to sailors, who believed it would protect them from drowning at sea.

Upon weighing in at six pounds thirteen ounces, the baby was immediately placed on Mama's breast to nurse, as Mama had requested, and the small mouth began to suckle instinctively. While at the hospital, Mama tried to imagine she was at home. She had asked that Dr. Brownlow give her no medication or episiotomy, no silver nitrate after the birth. Instead she drank one quart of raspberry leaf tea during labor and one immediately after. Papa even worked up his nerve to delicately tell the nurse that they'd like to take home the placenta. Dr. Brownlow was skeptical about these requests, but admitted it was one of the easiest births he'd attended.

Twelve hours later, as planned, Mama was ready to go home. Papa bundled mother and child into the jeep, wrapping them in blankets against the drafts. They tried to think up a girl's name over the roar of the engine. Mama was so sure the child was a boy, due to differences in the pregnancy, including more morning sickness and carrying lower, that all they'd prepared were boys'

names. Leif, after Leif Ericson, Starbuck after Coleman ances-
tors. David for Mama's father. They even flirted with Eliot the
Third, but dismissed the tradition of giving a son the father's
name, as Papa had been given his. Not until two days later did
they decide on Heidi, a nickname for Adelheid from the book
Heidi, about the orphan girl who finds a home and many adventures with her grandfather on a remote mountainside in the Swiss
Alps.

It makes sense we'd have a girl, Papa thought to himself. Based
on something he read and the amount of stress he'd been under
that year, he theorized that the gender of a child was determined
by which partner was under more stress during conception. If the
man was more stressed, the child would be a girl; if the woman
was more stressed, it would be a boy. This was nature's way of
looking out for us, he reasoned; either the man needed more females around to nurture him, or the woman needed more males
around to take care of the hard work. It was one of Papa's less
enlightened theories, but at the time it made sense—he was certainly stressed, and perhaps something in him was also disap-
pointed not to have a son.

They fetched me from the Nearings' house, where they'd left
me with Keith and Jean, and let me hold the tiny sleeping parcel
in my arms. I felt a mixture of fear and then tenderness when she
mewed and began to fuss. Mama took the bundle back and lifted
her shirt to nurse. Another feeling came suddenly and inexplica-
bly. Mine! I hovered next to Mama and clung to her arm.

"Mama," I said, "Mia," which was what I used to call nursing
when I was little.

"You're a big girl now," Papa said. "Mama needs all the milk for
the baby."

I felt the blue egg rise from my belly. It didn't come all the way up to my throat, but it didn't go back down either. It lingered somewhere near my heart for a while.

"When will she be ready to play?" I pouted.

"Not yet, but we'll get you a doll so you have your own baby to worry about," Papa suggested. That evening while Heidi was sleeping, I was glad to go alone with Mama to milk the goats, as I had the night before. "I gave birth and didn't even miss a milking, just like the she-goats do," Mama bragged to Papa when she returned still high on postpartum hormones, with the full bucket.

THOUGH IT WAS not as exciting as I imagined it would be, I finally had a new sibling. Sadly, around that same time, an old friend was on his way out. Norman the Normal Dog spent most of the day on the padded benches, his back legs useless, moaning when he moved.

"It isn't right to make him live in pain," Papa said. "We'll have to put the old guy to sleep."

It didn't sound so bad, to go to sleep, but I started to cry at the thought of Norm lying there still, his nose quiet on his paws.

"Papa, why does he have to go to sleep?" I sobbed.

"He's really tired," Papa said, his eyes as hard as they were about the billy goats.

Norm knew. He whimpered and licked my hand when we made him comfortable in a blanket. Papa wrapped it around Norm and lifted him in his arms to take him to the vet in the jeep. The bundle seemed so little.

"Don't take him away," I cried.

"Norm will come back to rest in the orchard with the billy goats," Mama said, her nose reddening. I flopped down on the couch where the hairy imprint of Normie's body in the cushion was still warm and dog-smelling and cried until I, too, felt like sleeping.

"Lissie, come rest with me and Heidi," Mama called.

"No," I sobbed. I didn't want to go to sleep and not wake up. Whenever I thought of Norm "sleeping" in the orchard, the old lump rose again to my throat.

BEFORE WE KNEW it, the days lengthened and Papa was out in his rubber boots, turning the compost with a pitchfork and starting seedlings in the greenhouse.

"Know what?" I said to Papa. I'd just gotten in trouble for walking in his flats and hoped to make amends by helping to transplant seedlings.

"What's that, kiddo?" Papa asked in his easy garden voice. My favorite thing in the world was to talk with Papa while helping him in the garden. There was something peaceful about his energy when he was working in the soil, and he spoke directly to me, making me feel like the smartest kid on earth. Even the toughest concepts made sense when Papa explained them because he let me figure them out for myself.

"Plants grow in compost and then turn back into compost when they die," I said.

"Yup, that's the magic of Mother Nature." Papa nodded. "Dead plants turn into new plants."

I thought about it for a little bit as Papa made dark wet circles with the watering can around the transplants.

"Papa," I said. "What happens to dogs and people when they die?"

"They turn back into dirt, too," Papa said. "They get buried in the ground and decompose."

"So do dead people turn into new people?"

"Nobody knows for sure about reincarnation," Papa said. "But if you pay attention to Mother Nature, it would make an awful lot of sense."

SKATES'S GARDENER, BILL, drove her up to visit her new granddaughter. They came from a world where the Paris Peace Accords in January of 1973 had brought an end to left-wing protests over U.S. involvement in Vietnam, while the Supreme Court decision in *Roe v. Wade* the same month had initiated right-wing anger over legalized abortion. Skates stayed, as usual, at the guesthouse at Carolyn Robinson's and came over to the farm during the day, bringing store-bought gifts like animal crackers in a colorful box with a red string handle that I coveted so much it made me cry.

"What's wrong, dear?" Skates asked.

"Skates," I said between sniffles, eyeing the animal graphics marching around the box, "we don't eat dead animals."

I was elated when Mama said not to worry, they weren't real animals, and I could eat them. "Just this once," she added, explaining patiently to Skates, "It might not be meat, but we don't eat processed foods with white flour and white sugar, either. They aren't good for you."

I was normally the staunchest follower of these edicts, labeling people who ate meat as "other people," the kind of people who lived in cities. When asked what I thought about cities, my reply was certain. "Bad," I said.

"Poor Lissie will probably marry a butcher and move to Manhattan," Papa joked, realizing our militant stance on diet had created in me a conflicted desire for what I couldn't have.

"WHITE-THROAT IS BACK!" Mama wrote on April 19.

The mist settled over the farm, smelling of salt and wood smoke from the cookstove, as crows and seagulls circled and called above the thawing compost heaps. These scents and sounds of spring made my toes and ears tingle as if they were growing as fast as the seedlings on the windowsills. I wanted to take handfuls of earth and put it in my mouth the way Heidi would soon do, leaving a dark mustache around her lips.

Mama was both comforted and alarmed by the speedy growth of both of her offspring. Children made time rush by like a river in spring, swollen with runoff—you'd look back, and a year was gone. The feeling of my four-year-old body when Mama lifted me on her lap seemed suddenly alien to her, so much heavier than only a few weeks earlier. There was a solidity to me now, legs and arms long and skinny, only my child's belly protruding. Just yesterday, it seemed, I'd been the size of Heidi.

"You have to keep them growing just as fast as they can." Mama copied this quote from Lester Hazell's *Commonsense Childbirth* into her journal. "Plant them when the temperature is right for maximum growth, have the soil fertile, and water them when they need it. A vegetable that stops growing for any reason is in trouble. The same is true of children."

"Last night I realized how total Heidi's dependence and helplessness has been when she for the first time ooched over to me to nurse," Mama added, when Heidi was nearly five months old. "I felt she knew I was there and she could come to me instead of me picking her up when she cried. A big step!"

I had ideas of my own about the small creature that was my sister, who now took the portion of Mama's energy and attention formerly belonging to me. Papa was busy as ever with his seedlings, and now Mama, too, had a seedling of her own. As with my plant siblings, Heidi had succeeded me as the center of the universe, so it seemed only natural that this new sprout should be put up for sale in the farm stand like the others. One morning while Mama was cooking lunch I occupied myself by wrapping a roll of the green twist ties used for bunching vegetables around Heidi's tender little body as she slept, fastening the paper-covered wire snugly at her neck.

"Oh!" Mama exclaimed when she found us, her face not a bit as pleased as I'd imagined. "Not so tight around the neck!"

The terrible clutching in Mama's chest at the fragility of her children, the fear that they could so easily perish, played seesaw with the unbidden postpartum feelings of exasperation during which she wished we would, in fact, perish and just leave her in peace. She'd struggled with the baby blues after my birth and was again navigating the ups and downs that can come with the hormonal readjustment.

"Yesterday it touched me deeply to see a young visitor's concern and love for her baby," she wrote. "Sometimes it moves me so much, I fear getting too closely involved, thinking it might break my heart."

Papa always said he admired Mama's strength during childbirth but found her a different person in the aftermath, weepy and prone to depression. Deep down, perhaps, Papa also missed the strength and devotion of his helpmate.

"I fear Eliot is working too hard again this year," Mama wrote. "He looks tired and like he really needs rest."

And then she crossed out her June 7 entry in a moment of frustrated rebellion:

"I have got to remember that my main and most important job is keeping the home together, doing the chores, kitchen work, washing our clothes, keeping Heidi and Liss happy, milking and caring for the goats, and in my spare time cutting firewood."

I wonder now if one source of Papa's stress began as early as when I came along, adding the extra work to the homesteading lifestyle that Helen had so aptly predicted. As long as Mama was carrying her formidable half, Papa had superhuman strength for his. But when the balance began to tip after the birth of a child, when Mama's side of the seesaw sank lower, nearly touching the ground, he had to use his extra gear to get it back in balance. Mama's alliance shifted, too. We became her primary focus as she struggled with the challenges of being a postpartum nursing mother—leaving less energy for Papa.

PAPA WAS WORKING twofold in order to reach his goal of turning a profit at the farm stand that summer. The projected income of $3,200 seemed an incredible sum, almost $1,000 more than last summer's earnings, but one that would finally support our family for the year. Due to Mama's reduced role, he began to rely all the more heavily on the help of apprentices, Susan and David, Brett, and anyone else he could find. With this help the new farm stand was completed, featuring a cedar-shingled hip roof and tiered shelves covered in wet pebbles to keep the displays of harvested vegetables moist and fresh for customers.

Mama was still counted on for her creative arrangements of carrots in sunbursts of orange, and beets, yellow squash, cauliflower, and lettuces coaxed into colorful landscapes. Braided onions and garlic hung from the rafters alongside herbs and dried flowers. She also printed up recipes to give customers ideas for preparing vegetables in new ways, including a yellow squash dish that was a farm lunch favorite:

Combine in a large skillet three sliced large yellow summer squash, ⅓ cup chopped celery, one finely grated onion, one finely chopped clove of garlic, two tablespoons oil, two tablespoons chopped parsley, one tablespoon honey, ½ teaspoon oregano and ½ teaspoon salt. Bring to a boil, reduce heat and cook covered for 15 minutes or until squash is tender. Sprinkle with one tablespoon flour until liquid thickens and serve sprinkled with ¼ cup sunflower seeds.

I was even given a job—selling potted flowers—and wore the patchwork apron Mama had made me the year before to match hers. Taking on Mama's knack for display, I picked dahlias, marigolds, and snapdragons from the garden and stuck them into the pots that weren't blooming yet so they looked more attractive to the customers.

Thanks to free advertising from another article in the *Wall Street Journal*, the stand was drawing ever more summer folk from the surrounding towns of Blue Hill, Bar Harbor, Deer Isle, and beyond, and Papa saw in this success our financial security, albeit at the expense of our privacy.

"We're almost over the hump," Papa told David Gumpert when the reporter returned to do the follow-up article on us, exactly two years after the first. Gumpert's original article had been so popular with readers—generating record numbers of letters—that the editors decided to send him back to check on our progress. "The idea was that the first five years would see the farm supporting us. I think we'll do it," Papa said. The second article noted we'd grossed $2,400 from the farm stand the previous year, up from $350 in 1971, and made significant additions in farmable acreage and buildings such as the woodshed (which cost $100 to build), root cellar, house addition ($300), and new farm stand.

"All of these changes, within the context of the Colemans' existence, are vast," Gumpert wrote, "but they haven't been accomplished without the attendant headaches and sacrifices—one of these sacrifices has been abandoning from time to time the homesteader's aim of shunning modern technology. Eliot, for example, finally decided that pulling all of the tree stumps out of his land by hand was too time-consuming, and last summer he hired the owner of a back hoe to pull out the stumps at a cost of $25."

"It was like the jolly green giant had come in to help me make the garden," Papa was quoted as saying.

"Sue and Eliot have discovered that the dramatic increase in vegetable sales has brought them the headaches that go along with any small business," Gumpert wrote. "So fast have they grown, Eliot says, that 'pretty soon it's going to be g-r-o-a-n.'" These headaches included the loss of garden time to tending the busy stand and the occasional spying customer looking in the windows of the farmhouse.

"They wanted to see how the freaks live, I suppose," Mama told Gumpert. She had afterward installed a "Private" sign on the front door to deter such curiosity in the future.

"I feel in a way I've blown it here and I've let the place get too big," Papa said in a moment of reflection. As much as he wanted to meet his goals for self-sufficiency, he was aware that the compromises were many. "I sometimes think that maybe I'd like to pick up in ten years and go someplace else and be even more self-sufficient."

"THE RIGHT ATTITUDE for summer is to work for enjoyment, not for money, even if it means not earning enough for winter," Mama wrote in her journal in opposition to the craziness of summer. "With money one's goals become greedy (if you succeed) and angry (if you don't)."

We kept our money in a black metal money box that opened like a treasure chest; a key was tied to the handle with a piece of string so you could lock or unlock the lid. The metal handle hung with a comforting weight in my hand as I carried the box from the house to the farm stand in the morning. At the end of the day, I would bring the box back, feeling its weight heavier on my fingers from all the cash the customers gave us. Once I stopped in the privacy of what we called the Enchanted Asparagus Forest, with its overgrown wispy branches reaching taller than Papa, and opened the box with the little key. The half shelf on the top was full of coin compartments—pennies at one end, then nickels, dimes, quarters, and silver dollars. The paper money sat under the coin shelf, bills rising up in piles of ones, fives, tens, and twenties. For some reason, I felt compelled to slip out one of the twenties and look at the pictures on it. It made a crisp and important sound when I folded it neatly and put it in my pocket.

Mama noticed we were short that evening. She always checked the receipts against the earnings, leaving some bills for change and putting the rest under the couch.

"Where could that twenty dollars have gone?" she said to Papa. I was the only option. At first I denied taking it, but finally I confessed and handed over the bill.

"Lissie, you don't need that money for anything," Mama scolded.

"I just wanted it," I replied, chin dipped in apology. I must have sensed deep down that the value of money was greater to us than Mama and Papa were willing to admit.

THAT OCTOBER, AS the world economy reeled from the 1973 oil embargo, Helen and Scott remained unperturbed, planning construction of their final stone home overlooking the cove. When Papa went down to look at the site, he found Scott bent over with age, methodically sawing down the smaller fir trees one by one with a handsaw to open up a path that would later become the driveway.

"Get a chain saw, man," Papa wanted to say, his recent success at the farm stand bringing with it a certain impatience for the confines of homesteading. But there was no teaching Scott new tricks at the age of ninety.

By the close of business at the end of September, the farm stand had grossed $3,600 in vegetable sales from one and a quarter acres of cultivated land. Thanks in part to all the extra hands working the farm, and despite the dry weather, the 1973 earnings beat Papa's projections by $400. It made little difference that the national average annual income of $12,000 was three times that. He'd finally made enough to support our family of four for the year without taking outside jobs.

This success was nothing to rest on; Papa was already seeking the next challenge. Financial goals met, he wanted to pursue the dream that everyone could know the taste of delicious vegetables grown in their own garden, or on a small farm. A photographer from Rodale's *Organic Gardening* magazine had recently taken a handsome photo for the December cover of Papa at Hoffman's Cove, harvesting seaweed for mulch. Papa's hope was that more press like that could inspire people to grow their own food organically. He mentioned this aspiration to Scott as he helped him clear trees.

Despite his old-fashioned ways, Scott surprised Papa by offering to give the Small Farm Research Association a grant to do research and visit organic farms in Europe and bring back successful organic techniques. Papa thanked Scott for the Nearings' generosity and kindness, and felt ever more the responsibility to live up to their confidence. But when Papa told Mama of the offer, she felt a heaviness in her stomach. She was continuing to lose him, and their homesteading dream, to new goals.

* * *

LIKE THOREAU DURING his hermitage at Walden, we did on occasion leave our remote cabin in the woods to eat at more civilized tables, and Christmas was generally the time to pay homage to our relatives. That winter, our first stop was Mama's family in Westport, Massachusetts, for Nanna's eightieth birthday party, where I enchanted relatives by saying to Nanna, "I know why we call you Great-Grandma. Because you're so GREAT."

"The innocence of children," Mama thought to herself, her family nudging in her the long-ago anxieties of her own childhood. The next stop, a five-hour drive from Westport in the bumpy old jeep, was Rumson, New Jersey, where Papa, too, would wrestle with his family's opinions, but at least the energy crisis was lending some validity to his chosen way of life. Rumson was buzzing about the oil embargo that was driving up oil and gas prices and causing rationing, resulting in lines at the gas station. The accompanying stock market crash had also taken a bite out of Skates's already slim investment portfolio. For the first time in years, Papa felt almost smug at the dinner table as his sister and mother complained about the hopeless state of the world's energy problems, not to mention the ban on Christmas lights.

"We simply prefer to do without such things," Papa noted.

"Say please and thank you, and don't hold your fork overhand," Skates admonished me in reply, trying to tame her grandchildren at the very least, her hair freshly coiffed in perfect white curls for our visit.

"Smile for the picture," she said when I got it right, wanting to capture our every move, but I was in an antiphoto phase, scowling and turning my head away.

"Bootsie, if you just came to see me more," Skates said, "I could teach your children some manners."

To this day I have a fear of incorrectly setting the table, which I would inevitably do at Skates's house, lacking training in placing the shiny silver knives, spoons, and forks in the correct order around linen napkins, china plates, and crystal glasses. At home all we had were our carved wooden spoons and bowls. Thankfully, I didn't yet have to attend the dreaded tennis lessons of later summers, when I'd show up at Skates's private club in my not-white whites and socks pulled uncoolly to my knees, trying to pretend I hit yellow balls with a webbed racket every day of my life at the oldest manicured grass club in the nation.

At Skates's house everything was, "Careful, fragile!" as Mama always said. There were Skipper's decorative navy swords on the walls, and wooden, glass, and ceramic birds of all kinds, flying, perching, and calling to our young hands—but, we soon found out, as easily broken as the white sofas and carpets were quickly stained.

My favorite, and also least favorite, things about visiting Skates were the bowls of nuts. They didn't come in a shell like ones at home that we had to crack open with a metal cracker. Skates's nuts were ready to eat, from china dishes shaped like fishes and silver bowls with lids and miniature spoons. There were large meaty Brazil nuts, round sweet macadamias that Mama loved, skinless peanuts. My favorites were the salted cashews and sugary pecans, the trick being to chew a pecan and a cashew on each side of the mouth and then mix them together, sweet and salty, on the tongue. When the nut bowls got empty, I knew Skates kept more in the bar, with its rows of sparkly glasses on mirrored shelves and many bottles for mixing grown-up drinks.

"Lissie!" Mama said, finding me deep in the bar cabinet. "No more nuts. They'll give you bad dreams. Come on, it's time for bed."

As I lay in one of the guest rooms all to myself, sick from nuts, I felt giddy with the thrill of the beautiful things at Skates's house. The downy toilet paper, the Q-tips that Skates said were for cleaning only the outer parts, *not* the inside, of your ears, the soft white-white towels monogrammed with her initials, the electric orange juicer, the dishwasher and trash compactor, the stationery and pens on her desk printed with her name, Mrs. Eliot W. Coleman.

That night I never wanted to eat another nut again, but the next day I knew I would want more. Tomorrow the nuts would taste good again. Fancy things were like that, too. After a couple days, the allure of Skates's possessions would wane, but the next time I came back to visit, after a year of not having them, they would be exciting again.

A FEW WEEKS after Heidi's first birthday in January, our neighbors Jean and Keith had their first child, Becca. On the way down the path in the woods to the Nearings', I'd stop to check and see if she was old enough to play. It was on one of those visits, on a snowy February afternoon, that I found yet another friend. Jean was nursing Becca and Keith was sitting at the table by the front window, cutting up a butternut squash, when we saw a young stranger walking up the path from the Nearings' in the gray afternoon light.

"Hi, I'm Kent," the sandy-haired boy said when Keith let him in. "I'm looking for Eliot Coleman."

We learned that Kent had heard about us from Doc Brainard, a professor at Springfield College, where Kent was a freshman. Kent read *Living the Good Life* and mentioned to Doc that he wanted to go work for the Nearings, but Doc, who owned a summer home in nearby Brooksville, told him he'd heard the

Coleman farm was becoming the hipper place to go. Kent wrote a letter to Papa saying he was an eighteen-year-old student interested in farming and wanted to apprentice.

"You're welcome to come," Papa wrote back. "But you should know farming's no picnic."

The warning didn't deter Kent, who decided to borrow his brother's car and drive up to Maine during a winter break from school. He got stuck in a snowdrift on the hill just before the Nearings' house, and the winter caretakers directed him up the path in the woods. At first he thought Keith and Jean's was his destination.

Wow, this is so cool, he thought to himself, seeing bearded Keith carving up the squash through the window. A secret world of hippies in the woods. It was quite a contrast to his life at Springfield College, where he was a clean-cut student on the gymnastics team.

"This is Eliot's daughter, Melissa," Keith said. "She can show you the way."

Dusk was falling as I led him up the trodden snowy path, feeling highly self-important leading this enthusiastic visitor to my home. My feet knew the turns by memory as the darkness of the forest closed around us in silence. When we emerged into the campground, I turned to see Kent right behind me, eyes shining. I explained where the gardens lay under the snow as he followed me down the back road to the house, the windows glowing with lantern light.

Over dinner in wooden bowls, we drew Kent into our world—Mama's vegetable soup, the warm cabin, Papa's intellectual enthusiasm for gardening, Heidi toddling around, me showing off my dress-ups. After dinner, Papa took Kent out to the log cabin, where Susan and David happened to be staying for a short visit.

"More cool hippies!" Kent thought when David answered the door with his long beard and Susan welcomed him with her trilling laugh from the loft above. David set Kent up in a sleeping bag on the floor and returned to the loft, where he proceeded to read aloud to Susan from *Moby-Dick* in a sonorous, slightly nasal voice. As he drifted off to sleep, Kent thought he'd arrived in heaven.

The next day, David helped dig the VW out of the drift, and Kent went back to Springfield, hatching a plan to get out of summer gymnastics camp and return to become a hippie farm apprentice in the woods of Maine.

"It was a psychedelic trip without the drugs," Kent told his friends at school.

"YEOWH! YIP. WERH!"

That was the sound Papa made when he jumped into the icy ocean below our friends Mary and Dick's house. Papa's pale body had steamed through the darkness, down the hill to the water, and disappeared into a hole in the ice before quickly popping back up yipping. He climbed from the dark water and onto the icy shore, grabbing for his towel, then ran up the steps to the deck with wet hair stuck to his head, bright eyes, and red skin.

"Yeowh," he said, and tickled me just for fun. More people were coming out of the sauna onto the deck, and steaming naked bodies rose all around me. The sauna made us hot enough to stand outside in the winter with no clothes, and everyone was excited, running to dip in the ocean and coming alive from the heat and the cold water. Inside a wall of windows I could see Mama with Heidi and Mary and Dick's grandchildren—my friend Nigel and his older sister Jennifer—sitting in the room next to the sauna. When we got cold, we went back into the sauna, where the air was warm and sweaty like a mitten and the cedar walls smelled of the trees on the path to our drinking spring. There were two rows of benches, the high one for hot-hot and the low one for medium-hot. Papa was on the hot one, talking in French to a petite woman with long brown hair. He spoke Spanish fluently but French not as well, and she was laughing at his accent, her breasts sweating in the dark heat.

Between Papa and the Frenchwoman, the heat, the thrill of so many people, and the kids to play with, it was hard for me to think. I wanted to watch everyone jump in the water, to stay in the sauna, to play with the kids, to eat. My head hurt with the choices. I got up and ran out of the sauna to the deck.

"At Mary and Dick's, a porch is called a deck," is what I wanted to tell Mama, running toward the glass door, where I could see her inside the light. Suddenly I was on my back, my forehead pounding, the bright orbs of goats' eyes exploding in my head. When I opened my own eyes, a circle of penises and noses hung over me.

"She ran into the glass window," someone said.

"Get a flashlight and shine it into her eyes," someone called.

"You'll have a bump," Papa said, bending over and touching my forehead with his warm hand. "Can you hear me?"

I nodded. Someone was shining a flashlight in my eyes, so I closed them.

"Should we take her to a doctor?" a voice asked.

"She'll be fine," Papa said. "I don't need a doctor to tell me that."

He carried me inside to look in my eyes in the light. Then Mama picked me up, holding me instead of Heidi for a change, and pretty soon I felt okay.

"I'm hungry," I said, and soon everyone walked over to the main house to eat. Nigel came and looked at my bump, coming close with his green eyes, ski-jump nose, and thick, sandy-haired bowl cut.

"You thought the window was a door."

"So."

"Ha. Ha."

"Shuddup."

By the time we headed home in the jeep, everyone had forgotten about my accident.

"These saunas get better every time," Papa said, humming to himself.

"Yes," Mama said.

"*Plus qu'hier et moins que demain*," Papa said. "More than yesterday and less than tomorrow."

"I do know that much French," Mama said. Her voice was little.

I drifted to sleep on the drive, my body spent from the heat of the sauna and collision with the window. When the jeep growled to a stop, there was the safe embrace of Papa's arms lifting me onto his chest. As he carried me across the farm to the house, my eyes opened to see the stars wheeling overhead—Orion's Belt, the Seven Sisters, the Big Dipper, Cassiopeia, the thick band of the Milky Way—so bright against the darkness as the waning moon melted into a lump of butter in the black pan of sky.

AGAIN THE SNOW melted, and the waters rose up from the earth.

"I'm going to hire a backhoe to dig an irrigation pond," Papa announced to Mama one morning, employing the short tone he used to hide discomfort. The summer before there'd been a nasty dry spell, forcing Papa and apprentices to carry water from the well to irrigate the gardens. Even the bicycle-powered water pump and healthy young apprentices were no match for the lack of rain, with helpers pedaling furiously for only a small return in water. If not for convincing the local volunteer fire truck to come irrigate the fields, we'd have lost our biggest moneymaking crop, the sweet corn, to drought.

"People who say, 'I would like to buy a farm,' usually have in mind land rather than water," the Nearings wrote in *Continuing the Good Life*. "Yet land without water is all but useless. Whether they are thinking of themselves and their family, their farm live-stock, their growing crops or their own hour-to-hour and day-to-day needs, they must include water among their basic necessaries. In homesteading the two prime requisites are enough land and an abundance of unpolluted water."

Most of our water came from the stone-lined well below the house that Helen guided Papa to dig that first spring via her mystical skill with the dowsing rod. Finding water, Papa had learned, was one thing; managing it was another. When he was building the well, the stones that held in the earthen walls loosened and fell out with muddy splashes until he conceded to using Helen's cement to stabilize them. Once completed, the well had a home-made well sweep for fetching water that the Nearings had seen used abroad. It looked like a giant fishing pole braced on a stand, with another smoothed cedar pole hanging down like the fishing line and a hook for attaching the bucket. You'd pull the pole down and it would push the bucket into the water while at the same time lifting a rock weight attached to the fishing-rod end. When the bucket was full, the weight of the rock as it sank back would lift the heavy bucket from the depths of the well.

Papa also learned from the Nearings how to make a wooden yoke that fit over the shoulders, with cords hanging down on each side and hooks for buckets. When you shouldered the yoke, it took the weight off your arms, making it easier to carry the heavy five-gallon buckets of water.

Mama looked like an ox in her yoke, with Heidi on her back, as I followed her the quarter mile to a spring in the woods to fill the containers for the sailboat-style hand pump used in the kitchen sink. We used about a bucket of water a day, so every two days the containers needed refilling. Whenever anyone offered help, Mama refused, saying she enjoyed the task. The spring flowed silent and pure down from the "mountain" behind the farm to the ocean, passing through what we called our "enchanted swamp," and gurgling into a pool formed by a fallen and mossy cedar log that curved from one sphagnum bank to the other. We paused a moment to stare at our reflections in the crystal face of the pool before Mama lowered her bucket in and pulled up quickly.

"Dammit," she'd said more than once last summer. The spring got so low that the bucket hit the bottom, sending a swirl of organic matter through the water. She waited for the specks to settle so she could fill the second bucket and then, turning our backs on the disruption, we headed up the path. Mama's shoulders were heavy with the weight of Heidi and the buckets on the yoke, her head bent down to watch the path for roots.

Not long after that it had rained, and the gardens were for the most part saved, but Papa wanted to prevent such a close call from recurring this summer.

"I have to focus on the garden," Papa said, justifying it to himself as much as Mama. "The backhoe can do in one day what it would take me all year to dig myself."

The Nearings had a pond with a stream running out to the edge of their garden for ease of irrigation, and local legend was that Scott had dug the pond by hand, a legend that was for the most part true, though he'd certainly had helpers. It never occurred to Scott to get a machine to dig his pond for him; it was what needed to be done and he did it, wheelbarrow load by wheelbarrow load—15,000 total, by Helen's estimation. It took nearly three years to get it to a good size. Papa used to say he would dig a pond himself, like Scott, but that was no longer an option; he needed water by summer.

"I don't blame you," Mama said. "It's too much work."

"Yeah," he said, and they were both quiet. Something about the silence said they were both thinking they were getting a little soft.

Soon enough it was confirmed: the backhoe was coming. I got as excited about the backhoe as we did about the UPS man—both were in the category of "things that came from the outside world." When the backhoe rolled off the trailer in the customer parking lot, Papa directed it to the mossy area in the stand of cedar trees at the base of the garden. The driver put the claw under the trees to pull them out of the ground, then dug up the earth in mucky scoops and put the soil on a new patch of garden. We watched with wonder as the machine did in minutes what it would have taken Papa months to accomplish, the water rising to fill the hole as if it were dug in sand at the beach.

The pond was muddy at first but eventually became that rusty tea black—the color of rainwater in the barrels where the billy goats were drowned. That pond would be our salvation, bringing water to the dry months of summer. And for a few short years it, too, became a friendly place where Heidi and I liked to play.

CHAPTER SEVEN

Tribe

FROM THE TIME Heidi was old enough to walk and at last a real companion, age one and a half to my five, I took responsibility for her education in survival. Barefoot training began as soon as the snow melted. She ran after me down the damp sawdust paths of the garden, the tilled soil of the beds, the cool indent of the wooded paths, the packed-pebble ruts of the back road. We worked ourselves up to the gravel of the main road, limping like cripples, "Ouch, ouch, oh, ooh," knees bent, swaying side-to-side to take the weight off, our heads bent to watch for sharp rocks that dug into tender arches and filled us with quickly passing thoughts of putting shoes back on.

"Where are your shoes?" Mama was always asking whenever we had to go to town. Heidi and I looked at each other with empty stares, trying to remember the last time we'd seen them. Most likely they were growing daisies.

By the time the first strawberries were ripe, the soles of our feet had hardened into a thicker type of skin, like a callus. Tan mixed with dirt—hobbit feet. Now we could go anywhere. We walked on the hot tar roads in town, lost-shoe shoeless, on the rocks along the edge of the ocean, and on the prickly-needled forest floor of the mountain.

"Walking barefoot is like getting a whole-body massage every day," Davora, one of the Nearings' helpers, told us. Mama was sitting on the grass with her foot in Davora's lap as Davora pressed on her heel. Davora was into reflexology, which she said was an ancient Chinese belief that the bottom of the foot is a map of the body. She had a chart in her book that showed the foot divided into different colored regions relating to specific organs.

"The Achilles tendon is for the reproductive glands," she told Mama, and they smiled at each other and giggled.

Naked started as soon as the air was warm enough to get freckles. At first just shirts came off, revealing bellies white and rounded, arms skinny with a few permanent freckles that quickly multiplied on shoulders and noses and cheeks.

"Freckle face," I said to Heidi.

"You."

"No, you."

"You."

Soon the pants came off, left where we stepped out of them, as if a person had just vanished. Our legs were skinny and straight, with knobby knees, and the hairs on them made fine curves that glinted blond in the sun, not like Mama's, which were dark on her calves.

"It's because I shaved as a teenager," she complained. "The hair always grows back thicker."

Heidi and I loved that our skin was smooth and continuous all over, without rough patches of hair under the arms and between the legs like grown-ups. Pretty soon we didn't even get dressed in the mornings. Our whole bodies brown and freckly, we wandered the gardens, eating things that were ripe, bending our knees to pee when we had to pee. We relished without embarrassment the thrilling shiver through the body when we were peeing and the deeply satisfying release of pooping.

"Not in the garden!" Papa yelled. He got especially mad if we pooped near the pick-your-own strawberries. "The kids are shitting all over the place," he complained to Mama one day. "This has got to stop."

"Put on your clothes," Mama shouted after us, but Heidi and I didn't listen. We ran off to hide in the Enchanted Asparagus Forest or graze through the rows of snap peas, reveling in the curve of our bellies and the knot of our belly buttons, the single line between our legs, the smooth round peaches of our buttocks. The shapes of our footprints in the dust.

MAMA EMERGED FROM the farmhouse, hair pulled back under a bandanna, and set a stack of wooden bowls on a picnic table shaded by the ash tree. Hearing the slam of the screen, Heidi and I came running bare-bodied from the woods, the heat of the day warm on top of the head. I reached the house first and pulled a little cord by the door to make the lunch bell chime out across the clearing.

"Luunnccchhh," a voice called in reply.

"La-uuuunch," Papa echoed from somewhere.

Susan unfolded out of a crouch in the lettuce patch, where she was weeding in one of the peaked rice-picker hats Helen had brought back from China, her short bangs made sweaty by the band above her vibrant blue eyes. She and David were in charge of the handful of full-time apprentices that summer, overseeing the daily tasks of harvesting vegetables and running the stand, which was a steady success, with a record of nearly one hundred people on busy days and lots of cars in the parking lot.

"Lissie Lissie bo bissie, fi fie fo fissie," Susan said whenever she saw me coming, her voice bubbling up from some deep well of joy. "Banana-nana, bo bissie. Lissie!" I thought this was the coolest thing.

"Say Heidi, say Heidi," I begged.

"Heidi Heidi do didi, fi fie fo fidi, banana-nana do didi. Heidi," Susan unwittingly chimed, and I collapsed in laughter because we called the cloth diapers—which Heidi hated to wear as much as I had—didis.

"Heidi-didi," I sang, "Heidi didi, diaper breath," which of course made her pout.

Kent, the young gymnast from Springfield College, left off tending the farm stand, and David leaned his pick against the stump he was extracting, pulling back his long ponytail. Sweat shone on their tan backs as they came to the farmhouse like bees to a flower, the stone patio edged by the full bloom of daylilies panting their tongues in the dappled light under the ash tree.

Papa followed, carrying something as he did, never making a trip across the farm without accomplishing a task at the same time. He was so skinny that summer, his cut-off shorts bunched around his waist with an old belt to keep them from falling down. His eyes seemed bluer than ever, almost too blue, popping from his lean face. Sometimes he moved so quickly you couldn't quite get a fix on him, the backward toss of his short silver hair lending the impression of constant motion. He talked fast like that, too, about all the things that needed to get done. There was less time lately for shoulder rides, and what remained was shared with Heidi.

"Papa, Papa," Heidi called, running to him, screaming in delight as he lifted her up in his arms, her sparkle of blue eyes meeting his. We all loved him like that.

"Double piggyback," I begged him, and he acquiesced because it was lunchtime, getting down on all fours so I could climb onto his back and Heidi onto mine.

"Giddyup, Papa," we cheered around the yard, until he tumbled us off to get food.

Mama brought out the soup pot with two hands, elbows up, skin dewy from the steam, the air filling with the smell of sautéed onions, herbs, and vegetables. "Watch out, watch out, hot!" Next came a large wooden bowl of salad dressed with olive oil, vinegar, and sesame seeds, followed by a basket of raw carrots scrubbed bright orange.

Kent smiled at Mama with his carefree grin as she tucked back wisps of hair framing her face. He saw Mama as the beautiful earth mother who fed and sustained him with her delicious lunches. She smiled back at Kent with a shrug and her shy laugh, though it was not, I knew, her private in-the-house laugh, with its ascending throaty oh, oh, ohs and occasional snort when she really got going. While she liked and appreciated the apprentices, the commotion of summer and the demands of so many young people were sometimes too much for her. The more she fed everyone else, the less she fed herself.

After washing our hands in a bucket of water from the well, we served ourselves into our personal wooden bowls. As they ate, the apprentices talked with Papa, who rallied the helpers by inspiring them with the mysteries of the garden and sharing his books on soil and plant health. In Papa's telling, the soil held within it the secrets of the universe. One topic of discussion that summer was why plants grew so much better in soil recently turned over from the forest. Papa called it the X-factor, and everyone was always trying to solve the mystery. Even after he left, Kent sent Papa materials that helped to explain the phenomenon of what they eventually learned was the release of nitrogen stored in the forest floor.

Mama sat apart at the shadier end of the patio, sipping her soup, her navy-patterned bandanna pulled low over her forehead.

"Mama," I said, planting my naked bum next to her on the cool stone of the ledge. "Can we go pick berries?"

"Yup, sure, um-hum," she said in her checked-out voice, the profile of her face outlined by flickerings of light in the trees.

"You come," I begged, tugging her arm with my fingers. "The big patch."

"No, too busy," she said, setting down her unfinished bowl of soup.

In the evenings, if he had the energy, it was Papa who would make a batch of popcorn with butter and brewer's yeast and bring it over to the campground to hang out with the apprentices and increasing numbers of random visitors who came to see the Nearings and now our farm, too. The oil embargo had ended in March, but not before the country's energy innocence was lost, leaving many seeking a simpler lifestyle and finding in us an example. The visitors were young and free and adoring of Papa, especially the women. When they turned to him, they shone brighter. It wasn't a party in the traditional sense, but everyone was high from hard work, fasting, and the low-protein diet. They talked into the night about soil and compost mostly, but also of the effects of the energy crisis, Nixon and Watergate, and other more personal topics. Papa enjoyed the attention and gave it back in return, while Mama stayed home and kept to herself.

IN THE WARMTH of July Mama often sent Heidi and me out to pick berries, "for pie," she promised as a bribe to keep us from coming home belly-full and bucket-empty. It'd been difficult of late to buy the mason jar lids for putting away the magic stores of raspberry juice. The reason was said to be because people were nervous over the oil shortage and were growing and storing their own food in numbers unanticipated by the lid manufacturers. Happily for us kids, we made pies instead of canning.

Heidi and I walked barefoot and bare-bellied under the coolness of the fir trees, where the air smelled of sap and the ground was covered in brown and fallen needles, soft underfoot. The trees opened up to the scraggly berry bush area around the foundation from the early settlers, with the campground to the left, empty tents flapping in the breeze.

Raspberry bushes loved places inhabited by the people who lived before us. The old stones of the foundation were sunk into the ground, round and bleached from the sun. Nearby the shallow dry well was full of berry bushes, too, but harder to get in, so the berries weren't eaten by others as quickly. I made Heidi wait at the top as I climbed down the well. Cobwebs tied the spaces between the brambles, and the air was heavier from the heat of sun on the stones, berries red and overripe. They fell off into my hands so easily I had to eat them because they would be too mushy in the pail. My fingers quickly stained red.

"Wa ba-ba," Heidi said from above. Her eyes were blue pools of want, bare belly pushing out.

"Just testing them," I said. "Yum, yup, pretty good."

"Me!" she said.

I put some of the less ripe berries into the empty bucket. They made *plink-plink* sounds like those in our book *Blueberries for Sal*, and the thorns on the bushes left raised welts on my arms as I reached into the deeper clumps. Soon the berries made a layer in the bucket and didn't *plink-plink* anymore. When I climbed out of the well Heidi reached in for a handful and put them all in her mouth, leaving her with red lipstick lips like Skates. She took another handful.

"Stop eating all the berries," I said and held the bucket up so she couldn't reach in. "Let's go, you can pick your own."

Down in the larger space of the foundation the berries had been combed over by others. We scavenged what we could find, but the bucket wasn't getting any fuller for pie, and our arms and legs were covered with scratches. I knew where more raspberries might be. Old places. Secret places. The big patch past the graveyard with the many granite headstones above the blueberry field—but I was scared to go over without Mama. Sometimes I could hear the sounds of people who lived here before, just beneath the surface, like layers of time in the earth. Every so often they reached through and touched, leaving a trail of goose bumps across my skin.

A LOCAL ELDERLY lady named Lucy, who sometimes stopped at the farm stand, told Papa she was related to the people who lived on our land over a century ago. "They were the Colsons," she said. There were two daughters, Christina and Eliza, who was her great-grandmother, and both married Blakes, also Irish. She said most of them had farms, and the men worked at sea as Grand Bank fishermen and at other odd jobs. The children harvested blueberries and sold them door-to-door in Castine. There were no cars, and horses were too expensive to keep, so they often went around by boat. "Some walked all the way to Bangor for work," she remarked. Most of the Blakes were buried in the graveyard by the blueberry field, but she also said a Colson child was buried next to another headstone in a little graveyard on our property. She took Papa out to show him the spot near the road and just down from our driveway, overgrown, but still an opening in the forest around two small stones sinking into the earth.

"It was a hard life then," Lucy said, nodding over the stones.

In the quiet of winter, when I'd asked Mama about the people who came before us, she got books from the library about the Indians who first inhabited the land, the warrior Micmacs and peaceful agrarian Wabanakis. The Wabanaki creation myth told of a god named Koluskap who came down from the sky and turned stones into the Mihkomuwehsisok, little elves who dwelled among the rocks and made music with flutes. I was sure I'd seen them myself. Koluskap then shot arrows from his bow into the trunks of ash trees, and men and women stepped out, strong and graceful with light brown skin and shining black hair. Koluskap named them Wabanaki, People of the Dawn.

Another book told of Leif Ericson and a crew of Viking sailors who explored the Maine coast in their Viking ship with its dragon head and many oars, and of John Cabot, an Italian sailor employed by King Henry VII of England, who sailed to North America and explored the Maine coast six years after Columbus. Our cape was named for James Rosier, an explorer hired by Captain George Weymouth to write an account of his 1605 voyage. According to the report, they found a land of dense forests with pine trees two hundred feet tall and ten feet in diameter, "birch, ash, maple, spruce, cherry tree, yew, oak very great and good." The natives, he said, referred to the land as "Mawooshen."

In the mid-1700s, we learned, Massachusetts offered hundred-acre lots free to anyone who would move to the northern province. It was during this time that Cape Rosier and surrounding towns were settled by our predecessors, but the land was later abandoned after the Civil War, when many pioneers headed west to find new fortunes. Papa said the oldest tree he'd cut down on our property had eighty-three growth rings, indicating that at the turn of the century the area was fielded land created by the original settlers, but as people moved away, trees reclaimed the land once again. My favorite tales of this time were, of course, the Laura Ingalls Wilder books, especially *Little House in the Big Woods*, as I often felt I had more in common with Laura than with my contemporaries.

By the 1900s, Henry Ford's success at mass-producing the automobile brought a new type of settler, summer folk and out-of-staters, like us, who would become Maine's grudging bread and butter. With them came Robert McCloskey, who wrote and illustrated some of my favorite stories, *Blueberries for Sal*, *One Morning in Maine*, and *Time of Wonder*, at his summer home on Scott Island, just off the coast of Cape Rosier. These books, and others by E. B. White, Sarah Orne Jewett, and Elizabeth Coatsworth, captured Maine's remote beauty and brought more visitors, including Helen and Scott in the 1950s, who found that the rugged nature of the landscape and the long winters afforded the privacy they sought and provided the ideal setting in which to re-create the lifestyle of the original settlers.

But as much as we had in common with our earlier predecessors, the difference was that even in our remote corner of Maine, the modern world, in my parents' opinion, was still too close.

THE SOUND OF a plane tore the quiet blue of morning sky. Customers were chatting on the green swath of grass in front of the farm stand while Papa weighed and bagged their vegetables and Heidi and I sold potted flowers.

"That son of a gun!"

Papa's voice was like the plane, too loud for the morning air. He strode out with hands on hips looking up, the silver in his hair catching the sunlight like the glint of the plane as it passed. Our heads all tilted to follow his.

"That SOB is spraying," he said, waving his arms, save-our-ship style, in big crosses over his head. Papa marched out to the parking lot, and we could hear the sound of the jeep sputtering away as he went, as usual, to take it up with Herrick, who owned the blueberry fields. He'd once tried getting a group of people to stand in the field in protest, but the planes always returned. It was an ongoing fight that eventually saw some concessions, but Herrick, for the most part, kept spraying.

"Guthion," Papa spat when he returned, "is a fancy name for a nerve gas used to kill people in wars." People didn't know much about it at the time, but Bayer, of the aspirin, a Nazi-owned company during World War II, had registered azinphos-methyl, a neurotoxin derived from nerve gas, as an insecticide for fruit and berries in 1959. Guthion became popular for management of the wild blueberry fruit fly, as it could be sprayed on the large, rocky barrens by plane. This also meant it was easily carried to nearby areas on the breeze, but manufacturers and advocates claimed the levels were too small to do any harm to humans. Papa trusted his gut—if pesticides killed bugs and were derived from nerve gas, they couldn't be good for us.

The blueberry industry, as Papa saw it, had gone the way of big agriculture, stripping the nutrients from the soil and replacing them with chemicals. In the early 1900s, when True Cannery began canning blueberries in Hope, Maine, blueberry farmers developed the wild lowbush blueberry barrens for commercial harvest, fostering the plants with an age-old method learned from the Native Americans—burning. Every other spring, marsh hay was spread over the fields and set aflame. The seedless hay didn't spread weeds and burned low, so as not to damage the humus layer of the earth, but killing diseases and weeds and re-placing carbon in the soil. The plants recovered quickly and vig-orously after a burn and produced higher yields the following year. However, when machine burning later gained popularity, marsh hay was no longer needed, and as the berries received less nourishment without the hay, they began to attract more dis-eases. Calcium arsenate was initially used to kill the fruit fly, but was highly toxic to the farmers who spread it manually, so airplane-sprayed Guthion became the potion of choice. Not until 2006 would the EPA finally begin phasing out Guthion due to its adverse affects in humans—including respiratory problems, abnormal heart rate, anxiety, and coma; but a full ban won't take effect until 2012.

In those days, people were getting sick from pesticide drift but had little support for or acknowledgment of their complaints. A number of local miscarriages, including Mama's, were thought to have been induced by commercial blueberry spraying, but such theories were dismissed by doctors and the chemical indus-try alike.

"Sons of bitches," Papa swore about the sprayers, once out of earshot of the customers.

COME AUGUST, MILLIONS of dusky blueberries covered the field across from our driveway, and Heidi and I snuck over to the hollow above the gravel pit where no one could see us stealing them. We weren't allowed to for two reasons, the spray plane

and the seagull gun, which shot a loud report every few hours to
scare the seagulls.

"If Herrick sees anyone picking blueberries he'll shoot them
with the seagull gun," Papa said, to deter us from the spray-
covered blueberries, but we just couldn't resist the call of plentiful
snacking material across the road.

"The seagull gun won't kill us, will it?" I asked Papa, just in case.

"It might bust your eardrums," he said.

Eardrum-nervous, we walked elflike on our toes across the crinkly carpet of stems with folded leaves. We'd figured out the gun
didn't shoot bullets, just made the sound, and once you got used
to it, it wasn't so scary anymore, even though it made me jump
and Heidi cry.

"Shush!" I'd say before she cried out. "They'll catch us."

There were so many berries in the hollow, you could sit in one
place and eat handfuls without having to move. The best ones
were nearly as big as Helen's big-bush berries. We pulled them off
in handfuls and blew away the leaves before depositing the berries
in our mouths all at once, the juice dribbling from the corners of
our lips.

"Boom!" went the seagull gun, and we jumped. "Shush," I said
to Heidi. A car crawled by on the gravel road, raising puffs of
dust, and we hunkered low in case it was the dreaded Herrick.
From that position, I realized we could eat the berries right off
the bushes with our mouths, like the bear in *Blueberries for Sal*. It
was much easier that way, and more filling.

When we got home Mama took one look at us and said, "You've
been into the blueberries."

"Nunh-uh."

"Well, your faces are covered in blue. You better wash before
Papa sees."

"I have a tummy ache." The sick feeling would remain, I knew from previous experiences, until I pooped all the blueberries out like bear scat.

"You ate too many blueberries with spray on them," Mama said.

"Nunh-uh."

"Well, whatever you do, just don't tell your papa."

"DID YOU HEAR they accidentally dug up some graves above the gravel pit?" our neighbor Jean asked Mama when delivering the bread and sticky buns she baked to sell at the farm stand. "Yeah, just across from our driveway." Heidi and I slunk nearby like foxes around the chicken coop, our mouths watering at the thought of cinnamon and honey on our tongues, hoping a stray bun might find its way into our dirty little hands.

"The guys were digging gravel when they struck something buried in the earth up there," Jean said. "Turned out to be a coffin."

Mama made the appropriate facial expression in reply.

"There's that one big gravestone for the Blake family over there. When I went over to check it out, I noticed the husband and wife died the same day in 1894. That's kind of odd, I thought to myself. Then I looked at the dates for all the kids. November 23, November 29, November 30, all in 1863. Six of them died within three weeks of each other. That poor mother, I thought. So I asked in town if anyone knew what happened. You know what Louise Grindle said?"

Jean paused and pushed up her glasses, working her audience. Mama was busy arranging vegetables, part listening, but something about this story made her stop and look up.

"Diphtheria, she told me," Jean said. "It used to wipe out whole towns. Very contagious before people knew about those things.

Often brought back from sea. A terrible way to die—they get this thick membrane in their throats and can't breathe. They choke to death."

"Oh," Mama said, looking as if she felt a constriction in her own throat.

"Yeah, well, I was thinking to myself," Jean added in a casual tone, "what with those graves opened up, who knows if there might be old diphtheria germs floating around in the air. I'm taking Becca in to get her DPT shots. Diphtheria, pertussis, tetanus. I know you and Eliot don't want to get shots for your kids, but you might want to think twice about it."

"I'll mention it to him," Mama said.

"Well," Jean said, smiling a bit, "you can pretty well assume the Blakes were eating a good pioneer diet. Some of these diseases don't care how healthy you are."

"Hmmm," Mama said, not liking to be bossed into anything.

"Scram," Mama added, when she saw Heidi's and my fingers on the glass lid of the wood breadbox containing the cinnamon buns. "Hands off!"

MAMA AND PAPA didn't like the idea of inoculating their children with vaccinations that might contain harmful chemicals, but the local school, where I would be attending kindergarten, required it. After some debate, Mama took me in to the doctor's office to get the necessary shots. The first time we went, I got to push the button for the elevator, an entirely novel and magical contraption similar to a time machine I'd heard about. You went in one place and came out another. The button with the number 2 lit up, and the doors magically slid closed behind us. My stomach dipped as we time-traveled to arrive at a destination that would become my worst nightmare.

The second time we were also taken to the same small room with bright lights and paper-covered table. The same nurse as before came in, all large and white-jacketed. Her eyes were small and crinkly, reminding me of the pain she had inflicted on my behind during the previous visit. Knowing all too clearly what would happen next, I quickly stood up and opened the door.

"I'll be right back," I said.

"Lissie . . . ," Mama called; Heidi was on her lap, so she couldn't grab me. I ran down the hallway to the elevator and pushed the smooth button. The nurse hustled out the door and down the hall after me, calling, her white jacket pressing against the swaying of her bosom. Another nurse came along behind her, and the people in the waiting room looked my way. The magic doors slid open.

"Hey! Stop!" the nurse yelled as the doors slid closed. Saved by the time machine.

When we got home, Mama told Papa what happened.

"The nurses had to chase Lissie up and down the floors by the stairs to try and catch her when she came out of the elevator," Mama said. "Boy, were they huffing it. She must have gone up and down a couple times before they got her."

Papa's eyes went from hard to soft, and he began laughing gently.

"Not funny." I pouted from the couch.

"She screamed and kicked when they brought her in," Mama continued. "She was really pissed. They kept missing her butt with the needle because she wriggled away. The other nurse had to hold her by the hips. When the shot finally went in, she screamed like hell."

It made my bum hurt just thinking about it.

"The nurse told me we could stop there," Mama said. "She was still red and sweaty from chasing. 'Are you sure?' I asked. 'Absolutely!' the nurse said. 'You can do the rest next time.' "

"One smart little kiddo," Papa chuckled, sensitive himself about doctors as he tried to diagnose what would turn out to be a hyperactive thyroid.

"Well, at least we got the tetanus," Mama said. "Whatever everyone else thinks, that's the most important one, with kids going barefoot around rusty nails."

In my mind, the only good thing about the whole episode was Papa's and Mama's laughter together, something that I had been missing of late.

BY THE END of August, June's bottomless light began seeping away from us and the trees rustled around the farm, whispering about it. Heidi and I lay under the ash tree by the house, grass thick beneath our backs, and listened. The firs, spruce, and cedar kept quiet while the birches, maples, oaks, and ashes chattered amicably. In winter when their branches were bare and gray, they didn't have much to say because they were hibernating, like the animals, but in summer they were full of talk, full of themselves.

Gazing up at the rustling leaves, we suddenly felt as if our backs were glued to the ceiling and we were hanging above everything, looking down from the surface of the earth into space. The tree roots went up under us, and the branches went down below us. My stomach lurched, but then, just as suddenly, everything shifted, and I was lying on the grass under a tree again. The light made patterns through the leaves as they shimmered with the breeze and played across the walls of the farmhouse. Pretty soon my mind drifted with the movement, and I could hear what the trees were saying in my head, as if reading words from a book.

Change is coming, the big ash said, old and wise-sounding.

I lifted my arm over the top of my head and clasped my opposite ear with my fingers. As if on cue, the wind shivered the leaves of a distant oak and the acorns shattered the ground, their impact reverberating in my chest.

PAPA TOLD ME I was old enough for school when my arm could reach over my head to grab the opposite ear with my hand. Some back-to-the-landers homeschooled their children, for a variety of reasons, but Mama felt she had enough to manage as it was. So despite my initial protests, on a cool September morning she took me to meet the bus off the cape on the main road, the closest it would come to us at that time. The narrow door of the yellow beast cranked open, and the driver looked down at us with a scowl.

"Mornin'," he said.

I clung to Mama's hand and twisted my body behind her legs.

"Go ahead," Mama said.

"No." I wouldn't let go of her hand. "Mama, I want you to come with me," I pleaded into the back of her knees.

"I don't think I'm allowed," Mama said. She looked up at the bus driver.

"You can com'on up." He nodded.

So Mama led me up the steps, and we sat down in a seat a couple back from the front. The bus was not that bad with Mama on it. She looked pretty with her Nordic sweater and clean hair, smiling and happy next to me, her eyes big and skin glowing. When the other kids got on, Mama stuck up higher above the seats than anyone else, so she tried to hunker down to be little like me, and we giggled together. I cried when it was time for me to go into the school building and for Mama to ride back to the jeep on the bus, but that was easier than getting on the bus alone would have been.

At school was where I began to realize I was different from other kids. I was the only one whose mother came on the bus that day, for starters. At lunch everyone had white bread sandwiches with pale flat meats. If I was so lucky as to have a sandwich, my bread was dark and heavy with peanut butter and honey on it. No one else had half an avocado and a spoon to eat it, or a jar of yogurt with a dollop of jam. My treat was a mixture of sunflower seeds and raisins, rather than Hostess Twinkies or potato chips.

Another problem was that I didn't always remember to put on underwear, as no one cared about those things at home. The teacher said young ladies must wear underwear and pull up their tights in the bathroom, but the bathroom was yet another source of trouble. At first I would forget to flush and was reprimanded for that. Then, once I got the hang of it, I began to flush too much. It was a miracle to watch the water swirl down the hole and then fill up again. I flushed until the toilet wouldn't flush anymore and got in trouble for that, too.

The other kids played kickball, Red Rover, jacks, marbles, and jump rope and had exotic things like piñatas at birthday parties. At one such party, the piñata hung by a string from the center of a room that smelled of cookies and chocolate milk, its rainbow crinkly paper on the outside like colorful curly hair. Someone said it was a cow, but it looked more like Ma-Goat to me, with her horns and short legs. All the kids were boiling around underneath, chasing each other in circles, until we lined up and one by one were blindfolded and sent out in the room swinging a stick, trying to break open the cow/goat.

One of the boys hit the body square on, making the piñata swing haphazardly. He braced and struck again. There was a ripping sound as the paper gave out, and suddenly the butt of the cow fell off and confetti, pieces of candy, and small toys stormed to the floor.

Kids rushed in, pushing and scrambling to grab anything—stuffing pockets, filling shirts. There were swirled candy sticks, wrapped suckers, penny boxes, party horns. By the time I realized I had to grab my share, all that were left were the penny boxes. They were small clear plastic boxes the size of a hard candy with a penny inside and a lid with a raised magnifying orb so that you could look through and see the ridges on Abraham Lincoln's brow.

Arriving home, still crazy with the thrill of candy and toys falling from the sky, I proudly showed my penny box to Papa.

"Amazing," he said, shaking his head. "They give you kids money like it's a toy."

I kept my penny magnifying box for a long time in my collection of treasures, a token, as it was, of the incomprehensible world of money and politics to which school was introducing me.

As much as he didn't want to admit it, Papa was concerned that autumn about money as he made plans for his first European farm tour. Through the Small Farm Research Association and the money from Scott, he'd raised just enough to do research that winter in libraries and on farms as far away as England. Papa wanted to bring back Old World secrets of "biological agriculture," as organics was called in Europe, to convince those in power to pay attention to the emerging voices of organic farmers, the little guys. He was ready to get pushy about it.

"My mother was a pushy realist and my father a laid-back idealist," Papa liked to say. "Now my sister is the laid-back realist, and I'm the pushy idealist."

Papa hoped to see organics taken seriously by the agriculture industry rather than being dismissed as some hippie thing. "The scorn in which organic agriculture is held by the University of Maine and by the Extension Service is something which should be changed," he told a reporter for the local paper. "Their attitude probably isn't based on malice but on misinformation. The organic idea has been presented in a naïve sectarian way, and I can understand the reaction of the professionals but can't condone it because they are not fulfilling their hired role to be investigators instead of front men. They should be the first to say, 'Let's look into it.' Instead they are the first to pooh-pooh it."

Papa had a button pinned to one of his jackets that read, "The meek are getting ready," a tongue-in-cheek reference to the beatitude, "Blessed are the meek, for they shall inherit the earth." Papa was getting ready, but he was finding that action required a lot more power and money than the farm stand could provide. The outside world was far more concerned with financial returns than with Sir Albert Howard's law of return.

In Washington, Secretary of Agriculture Dr. Earl Butz had made sweeping changes in the 1973 Farm Bill that would significantly alter the course of agribusiness in the United States, but not for the better, in Papa's opinion. Butz's motto, "Get big, or get out," further encouraged agribusiness to buy up small farms and plant thousand-acre crops of government-subsidized, pesticide-sprayed corn. As some farmers saw it, Butz's policies gave the chemical industry carte blanche to control the nation's food supply and push all but the most determined small farmers out of business. While Butz's motivation was born of the scarcities of the Great Depression, his solution—cheap food for all— had its own set of consequences. High-fructose corn syrup and corn-fed beef, two by-products of cheap corn, were soon sold into every channel of the American diet, leading to the prevalence of fast food, which in turn contributed to what would become a nationwide health and obesity problem. Papa hoped to encourage a healthier alternative.

HURRICANES BLEW UP the coast from the tropics in fall. You could tell one was coming by the heavy-humid-warm feeling in the air. The gulls lined up on the rocks, waiting. Clouds slunk in from the sea. The radio squawked out staticky warnings.

"She's a comin'," the locals said on such days in Robert McCloskey's book *Time of Wonder*, written about his summer island just off the coast from us. "It's a gonna blow."

"Let's go!" Papa—the Departure Nazi, as we called him— hollered. The clouds hung just above the farm, full of the coming storm. Papa moved out the door with a force greater than his wiry body, a strength beyond muscle. His hair stood up with the energy of it. There were airplanes and faraway places in his eyes and a thrill in the smoothness of his shaved cheek. Papa would be doing research in Europe for two weeks, the longest he'd ever been gone from us. We followed him out the door, Mama trying to button her shirt after nursing, Heidi and me hustling behind. The farm was quiet, waiting to see what would happen. Papa swung his satchel into the back of the jeep and clapped his hands.

"All aboard."

"I love Papa so much, I don't want him to leave," I said to Mama as I followed her to the jeep, and knew she agreed by the way her face went soft and distant. When we dropped Papa off at the church in Penobscot to meet his ride to the airport, I remember kneeling in the back seat watching Papa out the window as Mama drove away down the hill. He stood beneath the white upward angles of the steeple, his figure getting smaller and smaller, and when he finally disappeared over the crest of the hill, I began to cry.

Papa was our air—our bodies becoming listless and slack in his absence. Soon I realized I was still breathing on my own, but it was an effort to take those first breaths. There was the feeling of something stuck in my throat, not a loneliness egg, but a hollow robin's egg, the kind you find in a bird's nest in summer after the other fledglings have hatched and flown away. The stuff inside simply vanished, leaving only the fine tiny blue shape of the shell in the matted palm of mud and straw.

On the way home Mama stopped at Bucks Harbor Market, the coming of the storm making everything restless. The Condon's Garage sign creaked back and forth on its metal hooks. Boats sighed against the docks in the harbor as people readied for the storm. Houses along the ocean braced themselves. Birds sought shelter. My bones ached.

"She's a comin'."

"It's a gonna blow."

Our nerves tingled with the charge of electricity in the air. You could feel the blood pulling in your veins to join the water gathering in the atmosphere. At the same time your brain said, "Hurry, rush, go deep into the forest, find safety under a rock." The stop sign shuddered in the wind at the turn onto the cape road. Halfway home, along the open stretch by Carolyn Robinson's drive, the rain hit us. It pounded horizontally against the jeep, driving in through the canvas flaps. The raindrops were furious on the windshield, wipers working at high speed, *twap-twack, twap-twack*, and dead branches cluttered the hood. When we entered the woods by Hiram Blake's, the forest shielded us, a bubble of peace, then out again into the open by Hoffman's Cove, where the wind was driving the ocean to madness, a roil of wind, rain, clouds, and waves washing up nearly onto the road.

The Vegetable Garden sign wavered dangerously at the end of the driveway as we turned in and drove up the back road to the house. You could feel the floorboards shifting under the high pressure when we stepped inside. Then, slam! The outside door blew open against the side of the house, knocking a clatter-crash of snowshoes from the outside wall.

Mama rushed to close the door, and we huddled in the kitchen as she tried to light the stove, hair wet to her face.

"Ma-ma, Pa-pa, Ma-ma, Pa-pa," Heidi repeated in a murmur to comfort herself, rocking beside me on the floor by the stove. Outside the wind tore the air like fabric and trees shuddered and cracked. The next day we would find trunks toppled, roots askew as if the backhoe had pulled them from the earth, exposing white piles of ancient shell middens, the only remaining evidence of the ancient peoples who had once lived off our land.

WHILE PAPA WAS in Europe, a female apprentice named Chip helped Mama with the many chores of readying the farm for winter. Chip was twenty-four, a couple years out of Springfield College, with short brown hair, thick glasses, and a compact athletic build so that from a distance she might be mistaken for a guy. Her mother had died at a young age, leaving her a comfortable sum, but she barely touched the money, preferring to live simply on the road and in the woods. After hiking the Appalachian Trail from Georgia to Maine, she finished the last segment of the trail at Katahdin and hitched to Brooksville to see Doc Brainard, whom, like Kent, she'd met when studying at Springfield. Doc brought Chip over to see our place, and while helping search for a runaway goat, Chip had the sudden inspiration to ask Papa if she could stay and work. "Sue could use some help while I'm in Europe," he replied, so just after Halloween, Chip returned with her stuff and moved into the log cabin in the campground.

Chip, it turned out, was a meat eater. She loved to hunt and often tanned the pelts of her prey—anything from squirrels and skunks to roadkill—on the cabin balcony. The Nearings were, of course, scandalized by her predatory ways, but our neighbor, Keith, also a hunter and carcass eater, connected with Chip over their shared passion for game. Mama was too busy to care about Chip's choice in diet; she was just glad for any help she could get, and Chip was a hard worker. If it was tough raising two children and running the farm for a couple, it was twice as hard for a woman alone. In Papa's absence, Mama gained new respect for all he did on a daily basis to keep life running smoothly. She wrote down the litany of tasks in her journal:

November 14, Thursday

Got two loads of seaweed before lunch at Hoffman's Beach. Lots more too. Took Liss between loads to catch bus.

November 17, Sunday

Looks, feels, smells like snow. Rained instead. Worked on wood stack and also immediate firewood. Took goats a load of rhubarb chard. Brought in entrance, welcome and park signs. Spaded up entrance flower bed.

November 19, Tuesday

Took Jeep's starting motor to Steve to check it. We need a new one, plus bushing. It made me realize that I don't take care of Jeep very well since I don't know enough about what to listen for: When something doesn't sound right, I just ignore it.

November 20, Weds

Moved frames into garden and placed over parsley and for lettuce. Transplanted lettuce—25 Boston and Webbs into frame #1. Covered back field kale frame with windows. Rototilled manure in the well and rose hip patch. Also cross-tilled back corn field. Anne took Tansey and young goats.

We'd been caring for a herd of Nubian goats over the past year as a mutual favor for the owner, but it was time to cut back on numbers and return them to their home, leaving us just one milker. They bleated and flapped their short tails as we herded them into the trailer where they looked out through the slats in the walls, the black bar of their pupils making a minus sign in the round unblinking marbles of their eyes.

Mama, though relieved to have one less responsibility, cried dearly to see her goat friends depart. After keeping herself together for a week on her own, she couldn't hold back any longer. Heidi and I cried, too, for the goats and because we couldn't bear to see Mama sobbing like that.

"Don't cry," we pleaded, pulling at her hands that covered her face as she knelt in the kitchen by the stove. "Please, don't cry." The top of her head leaning toward us was divided by the jagged part of her hair as she rocked her upper body over her knees.

"It's okay," she said finally. "It's okay." But we weren't convinced.

Mama was learning in Papa's absence both that she could hack it on her own, and that she preferred not to. Life without Papa made her sluggish and lethargic. As long as she was working, she was fine, but the minute she stopped, fatigue slipped in and all she wanted to do was sleep.

When Papa returned we nearly suffocated him, we so desperately wanted to fill ourselves up with him, but though happy to see us, he seemed preoccupied, his hands shaking and eyes popping with the excitement of all he had learned in England. The timeless techniques of the farmers he visited made more sense than anything he'd seen in America and laid the foundation for his later contributions to the organic movement. He was also skinnier than before and the lump like an enlarged Adam's apple in his throat was bigger. Not long after he returned, the heart palpitations began. He knew the doctor in Blue Hill wouldn't tell him anything new, so he went to see a specialist in Bangor.

"They want to put me under the knife," he said to Mama, shivering from the cold drive home in the jeep. "To remove the part of the thyroid that isn't functioning right." The only option to surgery was ingesting a radioactive iodine capsule to shrink the overactive gland, but Papa thought that sounded even worse than the illness.

"No!" Mama whispered. It was their greatest fear—expensive doctor bills accompanied by the loss of Papa's manpower while he recovered—but Papa was most disturbed by the fact that he'd gotten sick in the first place, considering all the effort he put into eating well. Somewhere along the way, he'd pushed too hard and his body rebelled. Instead of slowing down and resting, he pushed harder, did more.

According to the standard medical explanation for Graves' disease, which is what Papa had, the hypothalamus region of the brain senses a need for increased output and instructs the pituitary gland to release more thyroid-stimulating hormone, which in turn tells the thyroid to release more thyroid hormone. This stimulates the metabolism and the sympathetic nervous system, which speeds up body functions with adrenaline. Papa, as we know, found comfort in the adrenaline from hard labor, easing as it did his mind. While certain people are genetically inclined to Graves' disease, it takes a trigger to set it in motion. Perhaps that trigger was our low-protein diet, which, as we know, was lacking in B vitamins, the absence of which can cause the body to experience more stress on top of the natural stresses in our lifestyle. Papa went into his extra gear, and I imagine that each time he went there, the hypothalamus set its emergency plan into action. Eventually his body finally said, Enough. You've pushed too hard. I'll force you to rest, take care of yourself, change course.

As Papa usually did when someone or something tried to tell him what to do, he became furious. And because there was no one person responsible for the cause of his anger, it came out in various ways on whoever crossed his path, most often Mama. What about this? his actions seemed to be saying to Mama. Will you put up with this, too?

It was around then that Chip decided she should clear out. Keith invited her to live with him and Jean in the unfinished second floor of their house, and she accepted. The log cabin in the campground was cold, and besides, she thought things were getting a little too intense on the Coleman farm.

THE VOICE ON the Zenith battery-powered radio squawked flat and tinny on the ledge by the window. It talked about President Nixon's resignation that August, Muhammad Ali preparing for the Rumble in the Jungle that October, poet Anne Sexton's suicide, and Ed Sullivan's funeral in New York. When it talked about the weather, Papa, as usual, turned up the volume and moved close.

"Temperatures for Penobscot Bay and the surrounding area were in the high fifties today, and partly cloudy," the voice droned. "Temperatures will drop to the teens tonight."

"I'll be damned," Papa said. "Frost." He shot for the door and slammed out.

"Weather's changing," Mama had said earlier, looking up at the clouds and pressing a hand to her back. The air wrapped cool fingers around me when I jumped down from the patio and followed Papa through the garden. The two things that made the most trouble for us were animals, like voles, raccoons, and deer, that ate plants, and frost that could freeze them—not the hardy plants like kale and cabbage, but the tender tastier things like lettuce, tomatoes, and summer squash. In the morning after a frost, the plants were covered in white crystals that sparkled and glinted when the sun first caught them. Anything not protected by plastic, greenhouses, cloches, or cold frames might be dead. The leaves looked fine at first, but after a few hours of sunshine, they would turn translucent and soggy, then wilt. The fall before we'd lost a whole patch of late lettuce to a sudden frost when the covers weren't on the cold frames. "Damn it all to hell," Papa had said. We wouldn't have salad until the light returned in February and new little lettuce seedlings could germinate.

Now he had rolls of plastic that he spread on the garden like long blankets.

"I need more plastic," Papa yelled to Mama, heading for the jeep.

"I want to come," I begged.

"All right, hop in."

He tore out of the parking lot, past the campground, and down the road to Keith and Jean's driveway, long and close with trees, rutted in the middle, dark with foreboding. Keith had been slaughtering livestock for cash, and this made Mama less keen on my visiting young Becca, since you never knew what gruesome chores might be in progress. We bumped into the clearing and braked abruptly beside the barn-style house.

A large buck hung from a tree by its hind legs, the rack of horns dragging on the earth with the swaying of the rope. Its fur was dark burgundy, and burnished with blood along the center of the white belly, cut open to reveal a complication of innards. I couldn't look away. The deer was both majestic and robbed of its majesty as it hung there, eyes turned to black stones in the encroaching dusk.

"Looks like Keith got his deer," Papa said.

Keith emerged from the house, bearlike, an uneasiness beneath the contours of his strong jaw. There might have been a human hanging from the tree, the way he looked at Papa. Continuing to hunt and eat meat, despite the Nearings' disapproval, lent Keith the unapologetic guilt of an addict who didn't know how to quit.

"Frost coming," Papa said. "I need to get that extra roll of plastic I stored with you."

I stayed in the jeep, having no desire to enter the shed, which might contain the carcasses of butchered pigs or chickens.

"At least they know where the meat comes from," Papa would later concede. "Much better to eat animals you feed well yourself than buy the crap they raise under poor conditions in the commercial feedlots." If it hadn't been for the lack of refrigeration and the Nearing taboo against "carcass eating," perhaps Papa would have added more meat to our diet, but in the competition for the Nearings' favor between Papa and Keith, like competitive siblings, vegetarianism was the one thing Papa had on his side.

As it was, Papa couldn't hold too high a candle over Keith,

because he killed animals, too, the ones that got into the garden. When the dried blood sprinkled around the crops and the radio left on at night didn't scare the coons away from the sweet corn, you could hear Papa out taking shots with his old .22. He hated to do it, but had few options in the competition with wildlife for our food supply.

Papa and Keith came out of the shed on either end of a roll of plastic and loaded it in the jeep. We hightailed it back to protect our food source from frost, leaving the silhouette of the buck swaying from the tree, its blood seeping into the ground in a darker circle beneath it.

IN THE QUIET of winter, we found some of our old happiness. The pace of the farm slowed to the rhythms of hibernation as Mama sewed and mended and Papa rested and dreamed over seed catalogs and snow fell endlessly outside the windows. Oh, the beauty of those snowstorms! The flurries muted the landscape and united the details of the farm under one soft blanket, silhouetting the bare ash branches and accumulating on the boughs of fir and spruce trees, hanging them to the ground. Squirrels, chipmunks, jays, and chickadees retreated to the inner parts of the forest to wait out the storm, and we followed their example in the house, the dark lifted up by white outside the windows, our faces glowing from the charge of negative ions in the air.

"Snowstorms remind me of living in the mountains as a ski bum," Mama said.

"Yes," Papa agreed, an old light in his eyes to match Mama's. Determined to heal his thyroid on his own, he'd been taking B vitamins, kelp tablets, and concoctions fortified with seaweed to provide the much-needed iodine he seemed to be lacking.

Heidi and I snuggled on the padded benches with our blankets and warm milk and honey, kerosene lanterns humming, and listened to *The Spider's Web*, a radio program on WBGH that featured English-accented readings of children's books.

"It's a web like a spider's web, made of silk and light and shadow," the theme song began, as Heidi and I leaned close to the Zenith. "Spun by the moon in my room at night. It's a web made to catch a dream, hold it tight till I awaken, as if to tell me the dream is all right." We shivered with excitement at the familiar words.

A story called *Otto of the Silver Hand* particularly captured us. It was a complex tale about a boy who was raised in a monastery until age eleven, when he was retrieved by his father, who told him of his mother's death and family's dark past. "This tale that I am about to tell is of a little boy who lived and suffered in those dark Middle Ages," the story began. "Of how he saw both the good and the bad of men, and of how, by gentleness and love and not by strife and hatred, he came at last to stand above other men and to be looked up to by all." The world expanded around me as I wandered the far places of the tale, the snowy night outside transforming itself into the dark castles and towns of Germany in the Middle Ages.

The next day, temperatures dropped and sunshine sparked the whiteness into a field of diamonds that made the sky seem vastly bluer. Our snowshoes pushed through the drifts on the way to the outhouse, flakes clinging to our pants and falling in explosions from the trees. Soon the paths around the clearing became packed underfoot, our boots squeaking against the hardened snow. Heidi and I tunneled with our hands and kitchen bowls through the banks below the patio to carve a maze of passages like voles in the earth of the greenhouse. We'd lie for hours in the caves and retell stories from *The Spider's Web*, safe from the cold in our snowsuits, the walls glowing a pale ice blue with the light beyond, peace of the snowstorm preserved within.

The next day I put on the snowshoes the Tomten had given me and trekked the half-mile path down to meet the school bus, which now picked me up at the end of the Nearings' driveway. "Not many kids get to snowshoe to school," Papa said with enthusiasm.

On March 30, Mama and Papa made time to listen to the "non-lectures of ee cummings" on Maine Public Radio, cummings being one of Papa's favorite poets.

"Less than nothing's more than everything," cummings read, his Old World Harvard accent reminding Mama of her father.

Mama copied the line into her journal, one of her few entries that year.

"Beauty is more now than dying's when," she added, a line from another cummings poem, and sat for a while after the program ended, staring out the windows at the remnants of melting snow.

RELIABLY AS ALWAYS, spring and the white-throat returned. Another blanket, this one of mist, settled on the farm with the thickness of a cloud falling. It filled the spaces between tree branches, lying heavy in the hollows and blending all colors together into one pale shade of blue-green-gray. I watched out the window from the table while eating breakfast with Mama, as the mist wound between the rows of the garden and danced in muscular bodies with the plants.

We could hear the *thwack* of the ax and the tumble of logs falling apart as Papa chopped wood out by the shed. The mist and birdsong surrounded him with mystery. When Papa came in to make his breakfast muesli, his hands shook as he grated apple over the oats, cinnamon, and goat's milk. He was often in a state of low blood sugar from the hyperactivity, but food didn't soothe him, and he became easily upset about things Mama did—not cooking the oats right, forgetting to pick up something in town, harvesting the wrong lettuce from the greenhouse. The more Mama tried, the more she got it wrong and the more needy and insecure she felt in the wake of his rejection. Instead of fighting or even arguing, they went inside themselves and stayed apart. Papa to work, and Mama to the house. I could feel the elastic cords of their connection stretching further and further, becoming thinner and thinner with the strain.

Mama, Papa, and I sat in silence at the table by the window, eating our oats. Light from a lantern bit a semicircle of yellow into the blue-green vapor outside the window, but as the sun burned through from above the mist fell back like a curtain, exposing all that it had kept hidden.

Papa was teaching a part-time course at the College of the Atlantic for the spring semester, which meant driving the hour and fifteen minutes to Bar Harbor and back one day a week to share the joys of farming with a group of ecology students. The students were drawn to his youthful energy and contagious enthusiasm for plants. Mama was not so enthusiastic. The class was taking Papa even farther away from her and the farm than the trip to Europe had, and she worried about the beautiful young students. There was a female student in particular that he sometimes drove with to MOFGA meetings. While Papa enjoyed having a driving companion, Mama imagined he was more interested in the student than in her of late, but she was afraid to speak about it and make it become real.

*   *   *

HEIDI SLEPT ON her stomach with her head turned on one cheek, lips pouted, legs bent froglike beneath her bum. When I tickled her chin to wake her, her eyes were blank for a minute before the spark of her being returned from somewhere far away and lit her pupils with an iridescence of blue. Some mornings I'd wake to Heidi singing below me in the bunk. *Oooo auuuu iiieees* in her own kind of tune. Her secret language.

It started with Heidi trying to sing a song Mama sometimes sang:

> *Go tell Aunt Rhodie*
> *Go tell Aunt Rhodie*
> *The old gray goose is dead*
> *Drowned in a millpond*
> *Standing on her head*

But then I realized Heidi was talking to someone in her bird language. "Go tell Aunt Rhodie" had become "Tel-on-Ferdie." Mama called her an imaginary playmate, but that wasn't exactly correct—Telonferdie came and went on her own. She came from a place of wisdom about all things of the world. Sometimes I could see her and sometimes I couldn't.

As Heidi sang to Telonferdie, the birdsong shattered down on us like rain in the early morning, coming as if from everywhere, from the trees and the woods, even, it seemed, from beneath the earth. At night you heard the frogs instead, rising from the low wet places of the farm—the pond, the drinking water spring— places that turned misty when the air was warmer than the water. The frog voices were like music on the radio, echoey and squarky, calling you to them. If you walked by the pond it was as if someone turned up the volume dial, each *crick-crick* part of the whole, becoming so loud you couldn't hear anything else, then fading back into the night as you walked on.

I wished I could hold all these beautiful sounds safe in my belly, to keep them for my own the way Heidi used to put the things she loved into her mouth as a toddler. But when the sun rose, the sounds escaped me and spread out into the world.

"You cannot own these things," one of the apprentices told me when I tried to catch a bird once, "because they belong to God."

"What's God?" I asked.

GOD WAS SOMETHING I did not understand the way kids who went to church did. They said God was a man in the sky with white hair and a beard like Santa. This seemed strange to me. When I thought of God, I imagined only mist over the pond, a sliver of moon in a dark sky, scatterings of stars, birdsong.

The only person I knew who went to church every Sunday was Skates. She was "an Episcopalian," she told me, the sound of the word rolling nicely off the tongue. Skates said Heidi and I were heathens. Pagans. Atheists. Unbaptized.

"Wouldn't it be nice if you kids were Episcopalians too?" Skates said. When we visited her over Christmas, she took me to church to pray. "And forgive us our trespasses, as we forgive those who trespass against us," the voices hissed around me. Our collected souls rose to sing, then sat, then rose again. Skates was tone-deaf, though it didn't matter to me because so, it seemed, was I. While the singing in the church was beautiful, it could never match for me the sounds of Heidi and the birds in the morning.

"Even though we do not belong to any organized religion, we are very religious people," Mama had written in her journal a couple years earlier. "We believe in the individual who can be trusted, who is capable of loving, who can carry his own weight and who has a basic goodness."

But by the spring of 1975, Mama was no longer so sure. The principles of trust, love, hard work, and basic goodness that Mama and Papa had founded their lives on were changing as their relationship began to grow and change. Over the course of history, organized religions had developed to provide a compass for small tribes of outcasts like us. The Old Testament, it seems to me, was essentially a guide for the survival of a tribe of Jews as they left behind the civilized world of Egypt to make a new life in the Promised Land. In the Ten Commandments, Moses gave his people the moral laws needed to survive in the wilderness.

Our small community, too, had become a tribe of its own, one consisting of Helen and Scott, Keith and Jean, our family, Greg (a new neighbor), and the seasonal apprentices in the campground, all living on the Nearings' original hundred acres and following the customs and rituals of homesteading. As with any group of people united by certain customs, our tribe was fortified by the belief that its way of doing things was the best way to survive the myriad dangers of the world.

We didn't have a connection to God in the traditional sense, but rather a spiritual reverence for nature. We appreciated the power of the sun to germinate our crops, the rain to keep them growing, the beauty of a sunrise, the glory of the sea sparking with diamonds. Each found his or her own sources of wonder and mystery in the unfolding of the universe, without the guarantees and assurances that church provided. This life was the priority, and in the effort to survive we didn't worry about what would happen afterward.

The problem with our unorganized religion was that we had no constant, no Bible or church, no compass—aside from *Living the Good Life* and the now-expired five-year plan—to refer to in times of confusion. And *Living the Good Life* didn't provide guidance for more personal matters outside the Nearings' experience. Mama knew how to put away food, but what she needed was advice on the increasing distance in her marriage, and other more esoteric concerns.

Helen believed in the Theosophical tenet that all religions were explanations for the bigger mysteries of the universe and therefore each religion held a piece of the truth, although little discussed in the Good Life books. She espoused the Eastern idea of karma, similar to the Christian saying, "What ye sow, so shall you reap," and reincarnation, which holds that the spirit is undying and is transferred into a new body after the body's death.

Our neighbor Jean said she once saw Heidi running through the woods like a little sprite; when asked where she was going, her reply was a familiar, "Helen's." Helen likely treated Heidi as if she were an adult, the way she did most kids, respecting an older wisdom inside each child's body, and Heidi perhaps connected to a shared spiritual spark in Helen. Despite Helen's spiritual inclinations, the Nearing formula of four hours a day each for work, intellect, and society was missing the quadrant of the spirit.

Heidi, with her innocent joyfulness, was our primary representative.

CHAPTER EIGHT

Paradise

YOUNG ANIMALS WERE everywhere in the spring before Mama's leaving. Our remaining milk goat, Swanley, named after the goat in the book *Heidi*, had a kid, not a billy, luckily, that we called Turnip because she was white like her mother. She had soft noodle legs and liked to butt her head into my hand, the way she butted into Swanley's udder to nurse, so you could feel the bumps where her horns would be.

Mama and I were walking down the path to the Nearings' when we saw a fawn with its mother in the woods next to the path. They stopped to watch us over their shoulders, the small one with white freckles across its back and dark wet nose and eyes. Suddenly the mother flicked her ears as if to say, "Come on," her tail flashing white as they leaped away, cracking sticks through the woods.

"When you see a deer, that means something new is coming," Mama whispered. "We saw a baby so maybe it means we'll have a new baby, too."

"How do you know?" I asked.

"Oh, I don't know."

"Will you be able to take care of it?"

"Of course," Mama said. "That's what mamas do."

"Really?" I felt like asking. It seemed a challenge for Mama to take care of herself that spring. The business of readying the farm for summer overwhelmed her body, which longed to remain in hibernation mode. Checkout times had been more frequent, and fasting was often the culprit, as she resorted to juice diets for energy.

Then Papa found six baby mice when cleaning up the woodshed and brought them out to us in a wood box. I peered in to see a pile of small brown tear shapes with pointy noses and eyes sealed tight as peapods.

"Where's the mama mouse?" I asked.

"She must have gotten lost or hurt," Papa said. I held the box against my stomach so I could show Heidi. She looked in, then up at me, that sweet smile of hers flooding her eyes and twisting her mouth into a bow. We gave them goat's milk and water, but had to push their noses into the milk so they would drink. The first thing I did when I woke the next morning was look in to check on the mice in the box next to our bunk. Some were making cheep-squeak sounds, but two of them did not wake up. We tried to get the others to eat lettuce, oatmeal, and more goat's milk, but they just crawled to the far corner of the box. The next morning there were no more cheep-squeak noises. I sat next to the box for a while, swallowing at the lump in my throat, then took the dead mice to bury them with the others by the compost heap.

When I found a young bird that had knocked itself out against the front windows, I was afraid it would die like the mice if I helped it, so I left it next to the greenhouse. A little later I snuck out to find the bird still there in the leaves with its eyes closed, as if sitting on a nest. Worried about foxes, I picked it up and carried it inside, a warm shape in the palm of my hand. To my surprise, it began to perk up, and its eyes brightened. When I took it back outside, it flew out of my hand, flopping to the ground at first, then lifting up and alighting on a tree branch. After a while I saw it fly away with some other birds, and over dinner Papa said the fledgling was just stunned and would be just fine, thanks to me for helping it recover.

"Some will die, and some will survive in nature," he mused.

I may not have known much about wood-paneled station wagons, shag rugs, *The Rocky Horror Picture Show*, *Wheel of Fortune*, or other high points of 1970s culture, but I was learning to understand the laws of nature. The one thing you could count on was its predictable unpredictability.

"It's paradise here," I once overheard a woman say to her friend.

"The very nature of paradise," the friend replied, "is that it will be lost."

ON AN AFTERNOON not long after my sixth birthday, I walked up the soggy path from the bus, the last crusts of snow still hunkering in the dark hollows of the forest, to find the farmhouse empty. Papa was out in the garden spreading compost.

"Where's Mama?" I asked.

"She went to visit your grandparents," Papa said.

"Where's Heidi?"

"Heidi went too."

"Why did Heidi get to go?"

"Because Heidi is still little, and you are in school."

I kicked the log along the edge of the path until my shoes filled with damp sawdust. Heidi always got to do everything now that I was in school. My lips started to curl away from my teeth. The cry was there right beneath the surface, waiting for this to happen.

"Don't cry," Papa said.

I tried, but I couldn't stop. I sat down in the sawdust as the tears fell out the corners of my eyes, down my cheeks, and into my open mouth.

"Come on," Papa said, reaching for my hand. "Let's go in and get you something to eat."

"No." I pushed him away.

He lifted me up and I kicked against his knees, screaming. When he put me down in the house my legs became rubber and I lumped to the floor. I lay on my back and screamed louder. Crying made the anger go away and replaced it with sorrow. Sorrow was gentler.

"Why don't you lie down for a minute," Papa said, lifting me to my bunk. There was a calmness to him when he was certain about things. Something had been decided, and it was done. Pretty soon everything faded to dark.

Papa later told me he showed up that morning with a rental car and asked Mama to drive it down to Westport to stay with her family for a while. Something had slid shut inside him with the smooth clunk of the old wood latch on the farmhouse door. "I don't know why I did some of the things I did," he said. "Sometimes I didn't realize in my haste to solve a problem that my solution might hurt the other party."

"It's not working out," he'd said to Mama, hands shaking, heart beating too fast. The solution seemed simple—remove the emotional burdens so he could focus on work, his old escape. As if anything is ever that easy.

"Mammm-maaak." The sound came from my throat like a hiccup when I woke to a kerosene lantern in the darkness. Papa was reading at the table. Papa. I slipped out of my bunk and shuffled across the floor to climb onto his lap. He didn't say anything, but his arms wrapped around me as he rested his chin on the top of my head. I leaned back into the warmth of his chest, the way we used to sit when he seeded flats.

Mama was miserable and misunderstood at her parents' house, her mother, Prill, fearing the situation might give my grandfather another heart attack. Mama tried to figure out where things had gone wrong, thinking as far back as the winter Papa was building the addition, pushing too hard to finish before Heidi was born. With the hyperactivity he'd become a different person, and said he was no longer in love with her. Her only hope was that Papa's condition would improve, and things would return to normal.

AFTER SCHOOL LET out, the long summer days sighed lonesome and empty without Heidi. I longed, more than anything, for companionship. If Papa was my air, coming and going, Mama was more internal. I didn't know how to adjust to Mama's absence; the shape of her had been with me since before birth. She was a lung. The other lung could still breathe and keep me alive, but there was a hollow space on one side of my chest that made me "needy-needy," as Mama called it. Needy was not good, but I couldn't help it.

"Play with me, Papa," I begged, and he would try, but he was racing across the farm trying to finish the work of both parents. "Just a minute, Lissie, I'll be right there," he'd say. He always came for me as promised, but those minutes might turn to hours.

Then Frank arrived, his glow as big and warm as a bear eating honey, intent on the joy in front of him. The son of a southern lawyer, he'd gone to boarding school and recently graduated from Harvard. Inspired by the Nearings' maple sugaring book, he decided to stop and visit them while hitchhiking to Canada, and, hoping to find himself through the work of the body rather than the mind, he'd returned to apprentice with us.

The wooden screen door slammed behind as I leaped off the patio and into the green space beneath the ash tree. Where might Frank be? I listened to the sounds of the farm filling the bowl of the clearing—metal of garden tools clanking against buckets, birdsong, whispering of the trees. Across the back field I heard the scrape of a shovel and then saw a curved toss of earth fly up to a pile at the edge of a hole. I ran over and looked in at Frank's bare back, glistening as he dug. Giggling, I took a handful of dirt and sprinkled it down so it stuck to the sweat on his skin. He spun around, brown eyes alert behind horn-rimmed glasses, then shook his head at me in exasperation.

"Don't put the earth back in, okay—I'm working hard to get it out of here, can't you see?" His laughter started small at first but got bigger until it burst like thunder. The rumble filled the hole, making me laugh and filling the hole inside me, too.

Dowsing had worked for finding water before, when Helen divined the spot for our other well, so someone went out with a rod and walked in a grid across the field. When the rod dipped downward to purportedly indicate a vein of underground water, Frank started to dig. He had a regular old curved shovel with a smooth wooden handle. Each time I came to find him, he was deeper into the earth. Up to his knees, then his waist, then his bushy head. He dug and dug, but the water didn't seep up from under the earth the way it did when the backhoe dug the pond.

"Might as well stop digging," Frank grumbled at me. "There's no water here."

SOON MORE APPRENTICES began to arrive, eventually forming the biggest group we'd ever had. When running through the garden looking for Frank, I would find Julie, Naomi, and Michèle harvesting carrots in the nude. It was Michèle who started going naked in the gardens that summer, and everyone followed suit, competing with me for the best overall body tan, a fact that visitors found much more notable than the nudity of a child.

"*Bonjour, ça va,*" Michèle called out, teaching me French words. "*Comment allez-vous?*"

"Come on tally who?" I repeated, and she loved that, tinkling with laugher, her body slender with small breasts and hips and a long brown ponytail hanging like a rope down her back. Passionate about learning to farm and happily existing in the moment, Michèle was from a politically inclined family in Montreal, her father a union leader who knew of Scott Nearing. Having lost interest in her anthropology major, she attended a farm conference where Papa was speaking and, feeling inspired, asked if she could come work for him. "Write me a letter," he said, as usual, which she did. There being a mail strike in Canada, she didn't bother waiting around for a reply, so with tent and sleeping bag in her backpack, she took the bus to Bangor and hitched to Cape Rosier. A neighbor drove her the last ten miles to the farm. As she walked up to the house in darkness, she felt herself surrounded by the growing plants of the garden, the earthy smells of spring evening in the air.

I've come to the right place, she thought, and smiled. Papa brought her to the cabin to stay with Frank. "I was an impressionable baby goose when I first came to the farm," Michèle liked to say. "Frank was the first apprentice I met, so I imprinted on him."

When Kent, the gymnast, returned for his second summer, he was thrilled to find Michèle out at the well in the cool of morning, stark naked, dumping water over her head for a shower, and singing "*le soleil, le soleil*," her arms stretched above her head to the rising sun.

Everyone was in love with Michèle, but most of all Frank and another newcomer, Greg. Michèle meted out her joy slowly to those around her, but Frank wanted it all for himself, so she was careful with him, letting him have only enough to keep him wanting more. While Frank was warm and bearlike, Greg was a mystery Michèle wanted to solve, his silence like a pool reflecting you back to yourself. The summer before, he'd come to the cape in his International pickup while on a road trip around the country. He found an elderly woman trying to roll a rock out of a ditch alongside the road, and she, of course, turned out to be Helen. After he helped her with the rock, she invited Greg to join her for a dinner of beans and ketchup, and Scott asked him to stay.

Lean and muscular, Greg became Scott's helper, looking after him in his increasing dotage so Helen didn't have to worry he'd fall or get lost in the woods. Recently, when dumping a wheelbarrow load of unneeded gravel over the slope to the cove, Scott had tumbled heels-over-head after it. Scott eventually sold Greg the piece of land on the other side of our farm, where a Franconia student had built a cabin before he left to sail around the world and the land reverted back to the Nearings.

In the evenings, when I missed Mama most, I'd visit Michèle and Frank in the log cabin. You could get so much more out of human friends than animal friends, I was learning, but there were tricks to it. You had to give more to get more. The secret to Frank

was that he enjoyed telling stories. He knew how to use his mind
in structured ways, he told me, from growing up with an attorney father who expected him to be a lawyer, too, but he was still
searching to find his own way. As he worked in the garden, he liked
to let his thoughts flow freely and see where they ended up, his
mind drifting into what he called the never-ending story, a magical
tale he narrated to me about a little girl who went on adventures
to other planets. Though he never said she was me, I knew it was
so. She came across troubles and strange creatures that threatened
to take away her powers, but she always won out in the end. Every
time I found Frank, there was another adventure to be told. And
as the girl in the story was saved each time, so, too, was I.

"PANTS DANCE!" MICHÈLE called out with her French lilt, the
urgent code to announce the 10:00 a.m. opening of the stand.
At the warning, apprentices scrambled to find their clothes, shed
in the heat of the morning sun. Running for the Enchanted Asparagus Forest, they tugged and pulled into T-shirts and shorts,
and casually emerged to greet the string of summer folk walking
down the grassy lane from the parking lot. Kent always looked
cute enough with his muscular gymnast's chest and cutoff shorts
not to scare them away.

"At least they weren't friends of my parents this time," Papa
said over lunch with a laugh, referring to the last, less successful pants dance incident when Frank tried to hide his nakedness
behind the compost heaps to the horror of some visitors from
New Jersey.

"You should have just stood there buck naked, pretending you
were the normal one," Kent said, and Frank's trademark laughter
rolled over the patio.

The local gossip lately was about Mama leaving and the apprentices riding nude on a hay wagon through the sleepy—but not sleepy enough—town of Harborside. It was all a bit more excitement than the locals could appreciate. Papa had volunteered to help clear the hayfields around Harborside in exchange for free hay. Lacking a tractor, he and Scott usually cut hay the old-fashioned way, with a scythe, the ancient blade from Europe and Asia popularized in art as the tool the Grim Reaper used to harvest souls. Its long wooden shaft was slightly curved and as tall as a person, with two handles, one at the top and one in the middle. At the bottom was a pointed metal blade the length of a man's arm. Papa and Scott held the scythes like dance partners, swinging the shaft around their bodies as if it were a lady in a ball gown as they waltzed across the fields, each stroke of the blade cutting a swath of grass that fell under the feet. Once they got into a rhythm, they could make significant progress, stopping every so often to run the sharpening stone across the blade.

On the large Harborside fields, the scythe was no match for a mower pulled behind a tractor, but the owner of the fields needed help loading the hay and carting it to the barn. Papa and the apprentices hitched a wagon to the jeep and everyone rode over in the back, armed with pitchforks. They tossed the hay from the field onto wagons and unloaded it into the barn until, hot and sweaty and itchy, they headed home on top of a full wagon. Michèle, of course, had been chafing at working in her clothes, so she stripped down and let the breeze cool her skin as the wagon weaved through town.

"Well, I'll be a hot crossed bun, that's something you don' see every day," a local allowed.

"Hippies," others said, frowning.

Either way, it got people talking, which Papa wasn't very happy about, worried it would scare customers away from the farm stand. As it turned out, it may have scared some, but those were replaced by others who came in hopes of catching a glimpse of Michèle's glorious full-body tan.

I, TOO, LOVED to ride naked on the hay wagon like Michèle. It was a soft bed, if a bit itchy, smelling so sweetly of clover and timothy, you could almost imagine eating it like the goats. But Papa said I couldn't go over to the hay fields, I was too little to help, so I had to stay behind with the apprentice tending the farm stand. I sulked all day until they returned, then ran up to climb onto the wagon.

"We've got to unload the hay," Frank said. "Time to come down."

Everyone else climbed off, picking stems from their hair.

"No," I said.

Frank laughed his booming laugh, and it was hard to resist him, but I wanted to stay on the wagon.

"Come on down," Frank said.

"No," I said, throwing some hay on him.

"Hey," he said. "Hay is for horses."

I threw some more. It blew back in my face and got stuck in my mouth, so I spit it out. The spit fell on Frank below me.

"No spitting," he said.

His face was calm, but the glow was gone from his eyes.

I spit out another piece of hay on him and laughed.

"If you do that one more time," he said, very serious now, "I'll give you a spanking."

Frank was my friend, but I felt like a wild animal, trapped. So I spit on him again.

"Okay, that's it," Frank said. He climbed up and grabbed me under my armpits, lifted me screaming off the wagon, turned my naked body over, spanked me twice, then put me back down.

It was still a common punishment then. Papa had spanked me before, usually behind the woodshed, where he'd make me sit and consider the errors of my ways.

Frank later apologized to Papa for the spanking. He felt badly, but also thought things were a little too loose around the farm, quite different from the parental strictness he'd grown up with in the South. He'd simply reacted to the situation as he'd been raised. While I was mad at Frank for a long time after that, I also felt a reverence of sorts. He'd drawn a line, the boundary I so badly needed in Mama's absence, and I loved him for it.

After haying, the shorn fields of the cape sprouted a white blanket of Queen Anne's lace. "Queen Anne was sewing her lace when she pricked her finger and a drop of blood fell on it," Mama told me once when I was younger. "See." She showed me the small maroon dot of dried blood at the center of the lace doily flower.

"Drop of blood," I'd repeated.

That tiny drop of blood was so much more interesting than the lace.

ON A WARM day in June, six weeks after the day she left in the rental car, Mama walked down the grassy lane with Heidi and Papa, as if they were just coming back from the store. I looked up from selling potted flowers, and there she was. Mama. My first instinct was to run to her. She was more beautiful than ever, her hair flowing back from her face and skin glowing. She was nervous, too, but her beauty covered that. She looked around the farm, breathing it in. Something in me held back for a beat—the torn place was used to being torn, and I wondered if it was easier to keep it that way—but then I gave in.

"Mama," I shouted and ran across the grass to her. The sun was warm on my face as she bent down and opened her arms.

"Lissie," she said, and drew me into a bear hug, wet where our faces touched. "I've missed you so much."

Heidi was glad to see me, too. She looked so much bigger than I remembered her, the baby fat disappearing into her longer frame. I couldn't help but love her, though underneath I was angry, too. She got to go with Mama, and something would always feel unequal after that—she was favored. It didn't matter that she got to go because she was still nursing, and I had to stay because I was in school; it made me want to pinch the soft juicy places under her arms. The sibling rivalry that had smoldered between us ever since she got all the attention as a baby caught the tiniest bit of flame, the way coals ignite in the firebox.

Uncomfortable at her parents' home, the weight of their disapproval prodding the tuggings for her own home and family, Mama somehow managed to get Papa on the phone. "Please, I want to come home," she whispered into the line so Grandma couldn't overhear from the next room. Papa was silent on the other end, standing in the Nearings' new hand-laid stone garage, his ear resting on the black earpiece of the phone Helen had installed there with a pad and pen next to it to record calls. He'd been taking his cupfuls of vitamins religiously and his doctor was amazed to say the blood tests showed tremendous improvement. Unsure of his feelings for Mama, but missing Heidi dearly, Papa made plans to pick them up at the bus station in Bangor.

It must have been something of a happy reunion, family being an organism that when separated wants to pull back together. Mama and Papa's wedding anniversary was a few days later, marking the day they got married by the justice of the peace in Littleton, New Hampshire, nine years earlier on the way to Colorado. Nine years was a long time, when you thought about it.

As happy as Mama was to be home, summer was still summer, her quiet homestead overrun, the farm teeming with youthful naked bodies. Everywhere you looked, apprentices and visitors were climbing out of tents or rolling up sleeping bags from the ground. You had to be careful where you squatted in the woods to pee, as someone else might be squatting nearby—and there's nothing worse than having your bum unwittingly exposed in that vulnerable position. They bathed under buckets from the well, cooked in the kitchen, and ate lunch on our patio, coming and going from the house as they had in Mama's absence. They were like kids, too, each competing with the gardens for attention, their energies pushing Mama into a smaller and smaller space for herself.

Heidi and I fought more often—pinching, screaming, pulling hair. Mama covered her ears and ran from us, the sounds of our crying at odds with her capacity for calm. She felt, more than ever, other people's emotions as if inside herself. It doubled the confusion in her mind. She needed quiet to sift through the feelings and throw out the ones that weren't hers. So she did what she always did in times of overload: she checked out.

"I just need some space," she said to Heidi and me.

But there was no space. What we needed were boundaries, but we had done away with boundaries. Boundaries were uncool. And so we felt the loss of each other more deeply because we were all part of each other.

"I was not born to be forced." Mama copied these words from Thoreau into her journal, which had evolved from a daily log to a place for quotes from others, reminders to herself that she was not alone in her feelings, and in these musings she hoped to find the strength she sought. "I will breathe after my own fashion. . . . If a plant cannot live according to its nature, it dies; and so a man."

*   *   *

WHEN MAMA RETREATED into the addition's bedroom to rest, Heidi and I ran from the house, screen door slamming, to find engagement in the life of the farm and intrigues of summer.

"Let's go to the campground."

"Yeah, yeah."

Once our minds were set on going somewhere, we never walked, we always ran. Running was as free and light as flying, and the more you ran, the longer it took for the heavy feeling to catch you. Heidi padded behind me with fast little steps as I ran down the sawdust paths of the garden, along the lawn in front of the farm stand, up the grassy lane, across the packed gravel of the parking lot, and into the campground that sloped down from the driveway in the woods between our homestead and Keith and Jean's.

At the top of the slope sat the log cabin and cook shack, below which platforms were scattered across the fern-covered ground like floors without houses, topped with the canvas peaks of tents. A laundry line hung between two trees, flapping with drying towels and clothes that never came entirely clean. At the far side sat a granite boulder, the size of a VW Bug almost, smoothed and dropped by an ancient glacier. Hanging from a tree was a rope that you pulled back to the rock; you then hopped onto the knot and swung over the clearing, nearly into the trees.

Apprentices harvested what they needed from the garden to make their meals and got goat's milk from Mama, digging little holes next to their tents to keep the perishables cool. "My goat's milk keeps going sour and turning pink," Kent complained over breakfast. "That's one way to ruin granola!"

"Morning, Franklin," everyone chimed from the cook shack when they heard the sound of Frank blowing his nose from his hayfever, loud as a foghorn and regular as an alarm clock. Eventually Frank had enough teasing and moved his tent to the back field, where he could make his noises in peace. Trips to town were rare, but when the laundry situation got desperate, everyone piled into the back of a truck and drove the forty-five minutes to Ellsworth to use the Laundromat and indulge in mushroom and onion pizzas at the joint next door, or to Brooksville to dance to the Caribbean sounds of a steel band that sprang up on the steps of the post office that summer. After hearing the unique music in Trinidad, my friend Nigel's dad, Carl, had bought a Pete Seeger songbook, built some pans from steel drums, and taught himself and friends to play.

Much to my delight, a girl my age had arrived with her father, another bearded and long-haired apprentice named Michael. "I came to the cape with fifty dollars in my pocket and left with fifty dollars in my pocket," Michael would say at the end of his visit. He'd heard about the Nearings when working for the photographer Lotte Jacobi, who put together *The Good Life Album*, a photo book on Helen and Scott. Recently discharged from the army, Michael was looking for a place to stay with his daughter for the summer, so Greg offered him the cabin on the hill behind his house.

Heather joined me at the beaches where everyone swam after work, and naked and free, we spied for hours in the tide-pools and seaweeded rocks for starfish, sea urchins, and snails. We loved to collect the bleached discs of sand dollars and watch the gulls drop shells on the rocks to break open for dinner. The ancient-looking cormorants perched nearby with wings outstretched to dry in the sun, as S-necked egrets stalked fish in the shallows.

At night, we hung out at the campground, ignoring calls for bedtime and listening to Frank and Michael improvise tunes around the campfire, the starlight exploding across the navy sky.

Frank loved to play bluesy riffs and popular tunes of the time, folksongs and ballads. He and the others also improvised, with much amusement, lines to a song about the high—but often unreachable—values the Nearings were supposed to stand for, though didn't always meet themselves. There was Helen's weakness for ice cream, despite her belief that too much dairy and sugar were unhealthy, and the trips to warm places to escape the cold Maine winters, despite tough public personas.

Each stanza detailing the various Nearing commandments was followed with the refrain: "Likely it's not, with Helen and Scott."

It was rebellious humor of the best kind.

"Milk and honey, milk and honey," I'd always beg for my favorite song, referencing as it did Heidi's and my beloved bedtime snack.

"Michael row the boat ashore . . . ," Frank hummed in reply, a tune he liked to play for Michael. "Halleluuujahhh":

> Sister help to trim the sails,
> Hallelujah.
> River Jordan's deep and wide,
> Hallelujah.
> There's milk and honey on the other side,
> Hallelujah.

He explained it was a slave song sung by freed black men as they rowed from an island off the southern coast, and that the Jordan was a river in the desert, and Michael—wink, wink—the angel who took you across when you died.

"You get milk and honey when you die?" I wanted to know. By then Heidi was asleep on my lap, and Michael told Heather it was time to row home to our beds.

*   *   *

THAT JUNE, EVERYONE was talking about the Rockefeller Commission's report exposing the CIA for "unlawful and improper" activities, including the opening and reading of mail belonging to private citizens. Dot Crockett's possible involvement at the Harborside post office was certainly not disclosed, but Helen and Scott were indeed on the list of watched citizens.

Two days later, we appeared in another big article on homesteading, this time by the *New York Times*. "Self-sufficiency, the distant call of a small band of young enthusiasts in the early nineteen-seventies," the reporter Roy Reed began, "has become the battle cry of a full-scale back to the land movement. . . . Established politics and economics are beginning to feel the movement's pressure in several places, especially in New England."

"Mr. Coleman," Reed went on to report, "is a leader of an organized effort in Maine to promote a return to biological agriculture, as he calls it."

"There are just not enough resources in the world," the article quoted Papa as saying, voicing what was then a still novel concept. "Especially the oil and natural gas from which the chemical and nitrogen fertilizers are made, and the resources to transport the other chemical fertilizers, to continue farming the way [this country] is farming. And so it's necessary to think in terms of large-scale nonchemical farming."

The article was not the glowing first-blush portrait that the first *Wall Street Journal* pieces had been, but a harder look at a movement that was becoming an often contentious segment of the public consciousness. The reporter pointed to Census Bureau numbers showing population in nonurban areas growing faster than the cities since 1970, but said that while many were serious about the move to the country, "some portion of back-to-the-landers are leftovers from the escape culture of the sixties who were chiefly interested in smoking marijuana and sitting on the porch talking philosophy."

"Self sufficiency," the article also noted, "proves too difficult for many. Marital stresses, for example, are exaggerated in isolated areas around the country."

Certainly, our isolated tribe was not immune. The increased foot traffic and drama over Mama's departure and Papa's hyperactive behavior led Keith to cut a new path so people would no longer walk through his property on the way from the campground to the Nearings'. Chip, who had been working for both us and Keith, decided to work only for Keith and take a break from the tensions at our farm, but her choice also marked the beginning of the end of Keith and Jean's marriage.

MORE AND MORE, the farm was overrun with reporters interviewing Papa about advances in organic farming. When a reporter showed up, everyone did the "pants dance" and Papa talked a mile a minute, his excitement over his experiments with natural fertilizers doubled by the hyperactivity of his thyroid.

"This farm is like a large canvas, and I enjoy making paint splashes all over it," he told the *Ellsworth American* reporter, sharing his discovery that planting cabbages in soil with tilled-under oak leaves made the cabbages immune to maggots, and onions and asparagus seemed to grow twice as well in beds spread with calcium-rich clamshells.

"Healthy plants aren't troubled by insects," he explained to the *Country Journal* writer, laying the foundations of his plant-positive theory. "Insects are symptoms of ill health and disease. Substituting [natural repellents like] garlic spray for [the chemical pesticides of] DDT removes the symptoms. It doesn't create healthy plants. It's like removing the spots of chicken pox; you still end up with the disease."

"If you use aspirin for a headache," he elaborated for the *Maine Times*, "you mask the symptoms rather than find the reason, such as your hat is too tight or your glasses aren't right. If the bugs ate plants indiscriminately, the world would have been defoliated long ago. So when a bug is on a plant, it shows me that the plant is unfit."

After numerous tests with different soil amendments, Papa was ever more certain that the secret to healthy, happy plants lay in creating good soil.

"At first people thought we just sat around and blew pot," Papa told the *Country Journal* reporter. "But when they came out here they saw we work hard. New Englanders appreciate hard work."

"It's very exciting here," an apprentice named Marcie was quoted. "Last summer I worked in a bank. Next year I'm going to get a job in a greenhouse."

"We don't get too old with young people around," Papa added.

As much as Papa's public face had a genuine enthusiasm and true excitement over the magic of clamshells, he possessed an uneasy skepticism about the outside world that sometimes alienated him from a mainstream audience.

"New York City is an aberration," he was quoted in none other than the *New York Times*. "If we can do anything so places like that don't exist, we're doing the world a favor."

"LUNCH!" MAMA CALLED out the door every day at noon.

"Lunch!" Papa echoed. Summer was, as always, a match struck in the darkness burning furiously until spent, with farm lunch the centerpiece of our days.

Frank emerged bearlike from another unsuccessful well hole he'd been digging. Julie, Naomi, and a new girl with long blond hair un-folded from seminude prayerlike crouches for weeding the garden patches. Kent came up bare-chested from tending the farm stand, and Michael unstuck his ponytail from the sweat on his back and leaned his pick against the stump he was extracting in the back field. Michèle helped Mama bring out the usual fare of soup and salad, along with Helen's sourdough bread made with sprouted rye berries.

After lunch people practiced throwing the wooden curve of a boomerang in the back field with a visitor who was the previous year's national boomerang champion, and relaxed in the shade of the tree as Kent practiced walking on his hands, a sheen to his brow and jaw as he moved upside down across the yard, forever trying to beat his record of twenty steps.

"Come on, Eliot, catch him," someone called. Ever up for a chal-lenge, Papa sprang to his hands, skinny legs twisting out of his shorts like crooked tree branches, vying to match pace beside Kent's ramrod-straight gymnast's form, all to the cheering and laughter of the audience. Heidi sat on the lap of the apprentice whose golden hair hung in thick sheets on either side of her face. She could have been the mother to Heidi's fair hair and blue eyes. As Skates always said, Heidi looked like a Coleman, while with my dark hair and wide face, I took after Mama. Cheering erupted when Papa's wiry upside-down form began to gain on Kent's solid one, until Papa teetered sideways and snapped back to his feet with a good-natured laugh.

"Fourteen, fifteen, sixteen," Kent bragged aloud with each ad-ditional hand step.

"You gave him a run for his money," the new blond apprentice said to Papa. He smiled, the silver in his hair catching the light as he bent toward her to lift Heidi onto his shoulders. I watched from the patio where I sat with Mama, part of me wishing I had blond hair, too.

Seeking attention of my own, I went with my fingers out in front of me to tickle Frank. "Tickle you till you cry," I giggled. Then I ran screaming around the yard until he caught me and tickled me so hard the laughter made my stomach ache and tears leak from my eyes. Then he would try to tickle me when I was crying to make me laugh instead. Laughing and crying were opposite sides of the same coin that summer.

THERE WAS A cookout at Secret Cove, a pebbly beach accessed by an old wagon road that led across the uninhabited head of the cape. The curve of the starlit sky over the cove was edged with the swaying of fir and spruce, and the waves tap-tapped the pebbles against each other as apprentices relaxed after dinner, talking-laughing-singing in the warm evening. Having chased each other across the rocks and eaten too many berries, Heidi and I were tired and "winding down," as Mama called it.

"It's time to get you girls home to bed," Mama announced, bending to put some things into her pack, her hair falling around her face in long sweeps that caught the light from the kerosene lantern. There was the sound of paper bags being crinkled up and the smell of raspberries that had become dark pulp on the rocks.

"Leave them," Mama said. "The sea will wash them away."

Mama shouldered her backpack, and Heidi and I followed her without dispute, pebbles grating against each other under our bare feet.

"Where's Papa?" Mama muttered, turning on the jar-size red flashlight with the white padded knob on the top. She shone the light across the beach, its beam making monster shadows of the rocks and catching on bodies in various states of re-dressing after swimming, a bare back there, the side of a face, white butt cheeks.

My eyes narrowed on the beam of light leading the way.

Laughter came from out on the water, and the beam jumped to the sound, illuminating for an instant the pale color of flesh, arms and legs entwined.

"Oh!" Mama gasped, and the tunnel of light skittered out into the emptiness of sea and sky. Then the spotlight moved back like a magnet to the bare bodies.

"Oh," she said again. There was the glimmer of blond hair, pale skin.

"Come on," Mama said, snatching my hand. "Let's go."

There was a feeling in her grip of something broken, or lost. I knew she thought Papa was out there, though you couldn't see for sure. Mama swung Heidi onto her hip, and the flashlight zigzagged across the woods until she found the path. Dark columns of trunks took us in, the wind calm down low on the path but whistling high up in the branches like something trying to escape. Distant laughter echoed behind us as we hurried too quickly to ask questions, my breathing coming in gasps.

We all pretended to be asleep when Papa came home. His footsteps creaked across the floor into the addition.

"You took the flashlight," he said to Mama. "We nearly got lost in the woods."

"Well," Mama began, but that was all she said. Her uncertain fears had no words.

I lay in my bunk staring into the humid night air of the farmhouse. When I closed my eyes, the darkness was broken by a beam of light catching bare skin. A leg, an arm, a breast. The pieces fell apart and came together and fell apart again to the lapping of the waves.

CHEAP TO BUY and quick to set up or take down, tepees were especially popular with apprentices that summer. Chip lived in one at Keith and Jean's, Greg had one up at his place, and a handsome visitor named David set his up in the back field while studying and working with the Nearings. Tall and dark-haired, David came from Arizona, where he'd lived in this tepee the winter before. I liked to visit David in his home made from buff marine canvas stretched over the pointed triangle of twelve thin poles crossed at the top. Wooden slats across the front held the canvas together, and a flap opened for a door, with wooden pegs to secure it. The space inside was roomy, about the size of a bedroom, and David set up a ring of stones in the center for a fire that puffed out through the hole in the top where the tepee logs met. At night the canvas was lit up by the fire inside, glowing in the darkness of the back field like a paper lantern.

While kind, David never became as friendly with me as Frank and the others. Mama later admitted that she thought him magnetic and found herself wishing he would take an interest in her. If Papa was no longer in love with her, as she feared, she might as well get her needs met, too. Everyone else, it seemed, was doing it. Scott Nearing himself, in his younger days, had often strayed. Soon Keith next door with Chip. This apprentice with that one. It was the 1970s, after all. But though adulterers were not stoned in our tribe, a memory of the ancient moral code lingered deep in the bones. Mama, while she may have found David attractive, was not the type to stray, even though she suspected Papa of flirtations.

BY AUGUST, THESE distractions were lost in the frenzy of ripening vegetables. The farm stand was a hungry mouth to feed every day with an abundance of produce, and the three-hundred-some mason jars of vegetables and fruits had to be put away for our winter sustenance. We were consumed by picking. Beans, corn, raspberries, tomatoes. Picking the crawling yellow-black-striped beetles that appeared on unhappy potato leaves—much to Papa's disgruntlement—and putting them in a metal can. Most of all picking, in my case, on Heidi to show it was not fair that she had gotten to go with Mama when she left.

"No-no-no!" Heidi said when I put a creepy beetle on her hair.

"Stop picking on Heidi," Mama yelled as she carried a basket of tomatoes into the house. "Mama doesn't like fighting." When I followed Mama inside, I found her singing under her breath as she made farm lunch.

"Work your fingers to the bone, what do you get? Bony fingers—bloody fingers, more like it," she mumbled. "Work your fingers to the bone, what do you get? Bloody fingers."

"Why do you have bloody fingers?" I asked. Mama hunkered over the stove, sizzling onions in a pan as she talk-mumbled. She was so tired from the new baby, she said. Mumble. Mumble. The first three months were always the hardest.

"But you don't have a big belly," I interrupted, surprised.

"No," she said. "The baby is just a sprout. It hasn't gotten very big yet."

Something about the thought of a baby made me feel needy.

"Mama, uppie," I begged like Heidi did, hugging the back of her legs.

"No, Lissie, get off, please, I'm cooking." She pulled away from me. "You're a big girl, I can't lift you up anymore." I slunk back to the table and hung there for a minute, trying to act like I didn't care, then snuck out the back door and kicked over a bucket set under the edge of the roof to catch rainwater.

Back in the garden Heidi had dumped over the can of potato beetles. She stood watching as they crawled all over each other, sliding on shiny backs in the straw around the potatoes.

"No-no, Heidi," I said. "Bad!"

"No-no," she repeated. "Bad!"

I picked up the beetles in handfuls mixed with the straw mulch and put them in the bucket. They tried to crawl on my hands and cling to my fingers and made me feel like they were crawling all over my body. My thoughts felt like that, too, thinking about Mama.

"HEIDI!" MAMA CALLED.

"Lissie!"

L's and *i*'s and *e*'s echoed across the curve of the beach as my bare feet sank in the sand beneath the water, pants clenched up in fists against my legs. The surface of the bay was covered in an excitement of diamonds that sparkled and bounced in the swell. I was wading toward that place of light, but as I neared, it always moved farther away.

"Where's Heidi-di?" Mama's voice tripped across the beach.

I turned, dropping the grip on my pants, to look back at Mama. She stood in her green galoshes in the ragged band of seaweed that had washed up at high tide, a wood-handled three-tine pitchfork in her hands to harvest seaweed for mulching the gardens for winter. Mama worried because Heidi liked to go right into the ocean, as if she had a magnet on her for water. I pointed behind the rock island, where I could see Heidi bending over, looking for sand dollars, and Mama nodded her head and returned to work, her pregnant belly protruding as she slid the pitchfork into the seaweed and lifted a mop of it onto the old wheelbarrow.

Heidi came to me bearing a perfect round sand dollar. When I shook it to rattle the small bird-shaped bones inside, her eyes grew nearly as round as the sand dollar. "Let's go find snails," I said, the wet hem of my pants pasted to my legs. Nearings'

Cove—so called because it was directly below their property—fanned out in a clamshell shape around us, wide and gradual at the top where the seaweed lay, and deep and narrower down by the water. The sizable rock island slumbered in the middle of the beach at low tide, its surface full of crystal pools left behind in the crevices where you could find snails and starfish. A whole universe lived inside those tide pools, everything fresher and more beautiful when wet and magnified by water. We pulled up the snails and marveled at the way the coil of the shell was similar to the coil of fiddleheads in spring, or the coil of the lines that made up the fingerprints on our fingers. What kind of magic was this?

"Lissie," Mama called again. "Bus-sss!"

"Oh." I sighed. Time for school. It was not fair, nature was so much more fascinating than school. I scrambled down the rock, found my wet shoes, and ran up the beach to the bus waiting above on the road by the Nearings' driveway. I was always missing the bus, it seemed, and we'd gotten a note from the town, asking that *since* the bus had to come thirty minutes out of its way to get me, and *since* gas prices were so high, could I *try* to be there. *Especially* since they would be plowing in winter for the bus, unlike in previous years when the local plowman might "forget" our road simply because he didn't like hippies.

"You're soaking wet," Mama squawked when I passed, but there was nothing she could do as I left her world for the world of school.

SKATES SHOWED UP that fall of 1975 with Lyn and Lucky and the kids in a fancy rented motor home. It was the fall of heiress Patty Hearst's arrest for bank robbery and Charles Manson's acolyte Lynette "Squeaky" Fromme's attempted assassination of President Gerald Ford. Our wayward lifestyle seemed harmless by comparison.

"If Boots won't get modern conveniences, we'll bring them ourselves," Skates quipped, radiating pleased-ness with herself for having overcome the obstacles of our remote lifestyle by bringing what we lacked—generator, bathroom, kitchen sink, stove, and comfortable beds—all coupled with the ultimate in mobility and modern style. They established the motor home in the customer parking lot, generating much amusement and joking at Papa's expense by the apprentices in the campground.

"You sure you don't want to get one of those for yourself?" they teased. "Or how about one for us?"

Skates brought gifts to appease us, chilled brown bottles of Guinness beer for the apprentices and Papa, and for me and Heidi a stuffed beaver and a Fisher Price farm set with animals and a barn door that mooed. It was better than Christmas. "Plaaas-tic," Papa commented out of Skates's earshot, with a half-joking, half-derogatory nasal accent, but we didn't care, mooing the barn door endlessly until its batteries were stolen in a pinch for a flash-light and not immediately replaced.

Skates also brought Papa the infamous red Mustang convert-ible that fall, driven up by Lucky in tandem with the motor home. Skates had recently purchased herself a shiny new Pontiac and decided to donate the Mustang to the cause of her penniless son, as she generally did with her cast-off vehicles. It was a bright red 1963 convertible with leather seats, reminding Papa of a sweet little MG he had back in his school days.

"A car is the biggest expense of homesteading," Papa always said, referring to the constant repairs our old vehicles required, not to mention the pricey state registration we were always late to renew and the insurance that was generally beside the point. Our history with the automobile had certainly been an eclectic one, from the white VW truck Mama and Papa had in Franconia, with its built-in camper on the back, to the old army jeep of Skipper's.

The problem for me was that I'd always been particularly prone to car sickness, especially on those curvy hilly roads of the cape. Once Papa let me drive in his lap, hoping it would build my resistance, but instead I caused the jeep to go off the road into a ditch and dinged the fender. After years of such mishaps and the work of pulling out tree trunks and hauling trailers full of seaweed and other creative loads, as well as serving as our only form of transportation, Good Ole Jeepie was starting to fail us, so Skates had volunteered the Mustang. It wouldn't last the winter. On the winding road to Harborside, Papa hit a patch of ice going around a ninety-degree turn, and the car slid into the tree at the corner.

"Wrapped the car around a tree," he said to Mama, after walking the two miles home. Papa was unscathed, but the car sat there for a few days before he could get it towed into a garage in Bangor. When it turned out Skates hadn't kept up the insurance, Papa, lacking the money for repairs, quietly disappeared from the garage, leaving the mechanic an unexpected, and rather valuable, gift. Only the mark in the tree remained as a memento of the car's short life with us.

Sometime after that, Skates gave us the silver Pontiac station wagon that Papa dubbed the "Silver Bullet," back in the quiet days before its muffler fell off, never to be found again. He said it drove like a dream, but my sensitive stomach didn't agree. We had to roll all the windows down, summer and winter, to prevent vomiting. Once Heidi and I were on an errand with Mama that took us over the Waldo-Hancock, a long-span suspension bridge passing 135 feet above the Penobscot River narrows near Bucksport. Mama's hair flipped wildly in the front seat, windows wide open, wind rushing in, as Heidi and I, carseatless as always in the back, hung out the windows to see the river far below. Heidi had her little hand-knit brown Greek fisherman's sweater on backward, and her blond hair was blown into its customary nest over her tall forehead. She looked over at me with that little tight-lipped smile and began flapping her arms like she was flying. I joined her, and we flapped our wings on both sides. The ride was so smooth and the water so far below us, it really did feel like we were flying.

"Flying-di-dying," Heidi chimed.

"Flying-di-dying," we chorused. And we were.

Until it was replaced a couple years ago, I thought of Heidi every time I drove over that bridge, her hair nested and sweater on backward, arms flapping, eyes alight. Flying-di-dying still.

MY EYES OPENED to a child's cry in the night, air cool, fire banking in the stove. Outside I could hear the branch of the ash tree rubbing with a creak-shush on the edge of the roof, my skin prickling with goose bumps.

"I half to pee, I half to pee," Heidi cried from below me in the bunk. "I haaalff to peeee."

No rustlings came from Mama or Papa in the addition, so I slid down the bunk ladder and patted the lower bed with my hands until I found Heidi's taut shape and fingers reaching out to meet mine in the darkness.

"Come on."

We shuffled to the door and lifted the latch to a wall of sub-zero air. The moonlight lit the snowy clearing with a pale luminescence, like the wintry scenes in our book about the Tomten making his night rounds.

"Mama says no pee scars by the doorstep." The outhouse being too far to go in the dark, I pulled Heidi over the edge of the patio to the snow-covered yard, teeth clicking furiously, the cold burning our bare feet. Heidi squatted and pulled her leg-gings down, moonlight lighting the perfect rounded W of her bum hanging over bent legs, steam rising around her from the hot rush of pee.

"Ggg-got on my leg."

"Just pull up your pants, hurry."

"Got-a wipe."

"Use snow."

"No-no-c-cold."

Unwiped, we left the pee scar in the snow and dashed for the door. I pulled the edge of it open with my fingernails, pushed Heidi up the step from under her bum, and helped her back into bed.

"Snug me," she said into the dark. I clambered into her bunk, pulled the blankets over us, and Heidi stuck her ice-block feet between my calves until our combined body warmth began to thaw us out. There was the odor of pee, but underneath Heidi smelled like baby, clean as if she'd just been born and hadn't gone for weeks without a bath. You couldn't help but love that sun-warmed honey smell, the comfort of it filling my chest as I fell to sleep.

We learned to hold our poop at night because a trip to the outhouse was too scary in the dark. Our outhouse didn't have a toilet seat and lid like the Nearings' did, just a slit in the floor that we squatted over above the hole in the ground. In the dark you were afraid of what was down in that hole, and even more afraid you might fall in.

About once a year we moved the outhouse, which meant Papa or an apprentice dug a hole as deep as he was tall. Then they lifted the small A-frame and carried it to the new hole, covering the old one with the dirt of the new one. At first, Papa found spots that had nice views of the farm through the window, but after a while it was more about privacy and distance from the house. Sometimes you'd forget that it'd been moved and follow an old path to find a filled-in hole indented in the earth from the sinking of the decomposing organic matter, like an ancient grave. "Old poop paths," we called them.

"If the ground doesn't thaw soon, we'll be up shit creek," Papa said one morning that spring. The poop mountain was rising closer below the gap in the floorboards, and he had to push it down with a shovel.

"Pee-yew," Mama said as it began to thaw. "Be sure to use lots of peat moss." The soft tufts of moss were harvested from the swamp and dried for wiping our bums and dumping in the hole to absorb odor.

"Yikes!" Heidi and I agreed when using the outhouse.

One day Mama heard Heidi's crying coming from the woods. Running in the direction of the sound, she followed it along the path to the outhouse, where, to her shock, she found Heidi down in the hole, screaming like bloody hell, of course.

"Luckily it was so full I could just grab her out," Mama told us. "Otherwise it would have been a disaster!"

"Ha-ha, you fell in the outhouse," I teased Heidi for a while after that. "Hidi-didi, poopy breath."

"Yuck," Heidi admitted.

Later I'd take pity on her tears and hug her tight. Even falling in the outhouse couldn't erase that tender sweet smell.

HEIDI SANG-TALKED IN the bunk below me, having a conversation with herself about my tree-branch fort.

"Let's go," she whispered to my stirring. "We half to see if she's there."

I rubbed my eyes, stars popping and swirling behind the lids.

"Who?" I asked, protective. The fort was my place, made from a heap of spruce branches cut from the trunk of a tree and left in a pile a little way into the woods on the path to the drinking water spring. The curve of the branches formed a dome, and I'd noticed that the bristles were falling away to make a space to crawl inside. While I was still in school that spring, Heidi'd been hiding in my secret places. Disappearing and making Mama crazy.

"Telonferdie," Heidi said.

"She's coming?" I asked, goose bumps rising.

"Yes."

Covers shuffled and bare feet padded the wooden floor.

"Wait." I climbed backward down the bunk ladder, dirty toes clinging to the rungs as my hair parted like grass around my face. Heidi waited by the door of the cabin, skinny legs and arms sticking from the shirt and shorts she slept in, blue eyes deep as a well, hair a bird's nest atop her forehead. She turned on tippy-toes to reach the latch, and the heavy wooden door swung open. We exploded from the house into the morning. The air was warm and moist, full of light that vibrated where the treetops formed the crooked edge against the sky of a broken eggshell, trunks fading into darkness down by the earth.

"Race you!"

Our bare feet leaped across the grass of the yard and onto the smooth, cool indent of the path in the woods. The forest closed around us with the smells of cedar and spruce and the white of bunchberry dogwood flowers popping from the muted greens and browns. We hopscotched over the exposed roots and past the old log covered in wiry-green moss and an army of red-hatted British soldiers.

When we neared the fort, I reached out to hold Heidi's three-year-old hand, so much softer than my seven-year-old one. We slowed and ducked into the trees at the edge of the path around the fort. It was quiet down there below the cackle and chirp of birds above. We crawled into the cave of branches and waited.

"She's not here yet," she told me.

I had to trust her on this.

"She's coming," Heidi said.

After a while I could sense more than see an outline of something against the forest. The shape was constantly shifting, like tree leaves in a breeze. I could make it look however I wanted. "Yes, I see her!" I said to Heidi.

With a voice of rustling leaves, Telonferdie began to tell us an ongoing story that always picked up where it left off the last time. It was woven of the details of the day-to-day—the names of animals and plants and the little worries in our hearts—together with the greater knowledge of the world that flows through all our brains. Telonferdie became the key to this wisdom that would, in its way, save me.

When we'd tell Mama and Papa about the things we did with Telonferdie, they'd smile gently, but the more Mama and Papa began to fade in their vibrancy, distracted by their own troubles, the more clearly I could see Heidi's imaginary friend.

CHAPTER NINE

Bicentennial

AS THE DAYS warmed, Heidi and I often sat on the swing together under the ash tree by the house, gazing up at the crown of still-bare branches. I can see our two little figures hanging over the face of the curved green earth, the universe sighing above us, vast and unknown. The soil, forests, and waters held in them the promise of survival if we could learn their secrets, but pumping our legs together on the swing, Heidi and I hoped only to reach the sky. We were, all of us, caught up in the excitement of the apex, the high before the decline.

Soon the chartreuse buds would unfurl in the breeze like miniature flags as the sun relaxed across the farm, igniting the edges of new leaves. A kaleidoscope of young people would again fill the campground to work for us or help the Nearings finish their stone house, and the pregnant bellies swelling on many of the women—Mama, Jean, and Bobbie—would turn into babies. Soon July of 1976 would mark America's bicentennial, two hundred years of democracy, and shortly after, *Viking 1* would capture images of what looked like a face on the surface of Mars, sparking countless imaginations.

"The universe is ever expanding," said some. "Democracy begins to fail after two hundred years," said others.

"Rain coming," Heidi said from next to me on the swing.

"How do you know?" I asked.

She turned to me, hair falling across her forehead so it didn't seem as oblong as it used to. The skin of her hands was still soft as a baby's, but she was becoming a little girl, an impish sparkle in her pale blue eyes.

"Listen," she said. I felt the shift inside as my mind drifted into the flickering of light upon the leaves. All knowledge was in that moment; the trees were merely gossiping about it.

"See," Heidi said, nodding at me. "Rain."

The rain began the next day and continued for weeks. Leaks ate their way through roofs, moss grew on the vacant tent platforms, and our clothes never came dry. The mist collected in fine drops on the skeins of cobwebs, and the pond grew deep and dark as night. We began to forget what the combination of blue sky and sun looked like, growing morose and dull as mushrooms despite ourselves, our faces puffy and pale, eyes wary. A beam of sun falling through a brief patch of clear sky was godlike in its rare beauty, similar to finding the exotic lady's slipper flower in the forest, but the moments of brightness hurt the unaccustomed eye, making us squinty and sullenly ungrateful, as if seeing an old friend we were sure had forsaken us.

*   *   *

ANNE ARRIVED BEFORE the white-throated sparrow on a wet day in early April. Her tan Ford Fairlane, with a trunk big enough to sleep in, crunched over a crust of snow clinging stubbornly to the north side of the driveway, despite the rain. She was pregnant, due in winter. We did what we did with everyone: we took her in. Mama, due in May, immediately felt the connection pregnant women sometimes feel with each other. Anne had a short bounty of curly chestnut hair and equally brown and large eyes. She radiated the spiritual purity of a nun, coupled with a beautiful singing voice and skill at the guitar, leading someone to call her a brunette Maria from *The Sound of Music*.

Coming from a Catholic family of seven kids in western New York, Anne had sought her own path by majoring in French and spending a year in France before taking a job at the whole food supplier Erewhon in Boston, cooking for employees. She later decided to apprentice at Wildwind Farm—where Frank had also apprenticed—and there she found herself pregnant. Things didn't work out with the father, so, seeking a new home, she heard about us, and decided to visit in hopes of finding refuge.

"I was not a person with my feet solidly on the ground," she realized about herself. "My head was in the ether."

Anne found the cabin occupied by another new apprentice named Bruce. Despite his offer for her to move in, she insisted on putting up her tent on a mossy platform below. Papa started her on spring seeding, along with Michèle, the French Canadian nymph of the previous summer, who was living with Greg in his cabin, Greg having temporarily won out in the competition with Frank for Michèle's heart. It would be Frank, however, with whom Michèle would eventually settle and raise a family. Particularly taken by Anne's serene purity was Brett, who'd built the log cabin in the campground a couple years earlier and was now the chief carpenter for the woodwork in the Nearings' stone house. Papa had recently sold Brett a couple acres of our land, passing on the original Nearing discount of $33 an acre, and Brett planned to build a cabin of his own when he finished work at the Nearings'.

The gardens began to fill with naked bodies and new growth alike. A blond woman named Bess, beautiful and reserved, with fair Norwegian skin and eyes, arrived to stay with Bruce in the cabin, and a couple from Connecticut took up residence in the lean-to behind Greg. Two curly-haired guys named Larry and Barry arrived in a pickup, having driven across the country from California to work for the Nearings. Everyone thought they were gay because they slept in the back of the truck together, but they were just friends who'd connected over the Nearings' books back in San Luis Obispo.

Larry's interest in organic farming began while he was running a wholesale tree nursery, when he nearly passed out from exposure to Metasystox, a chemical spray that was used to control aphids at the time. He began to experiment with beneficial insects for pest control and got a degree in soil science from Cal Poly. Then, while starting a community garden in San Luis Obispo, he met Barry, who'd read *Living the Good Life*. Barry wrote the Nearings to ask if he could apprentice, and when Helen replied in the affirmative, Barry asked Larry to drive to Maine with him. Today Larry oversees, with his wife, Sandy, a cooperative of certified organic farms in Baja whose cherry tomatoes can be found at Whole Foods markets around the country.

"There's something happening here, what it is ain't exactly clear," blared Buffalo Springfield from the battery-powered transistor radio in the campground.

"For the times they are a-changin'," Bob Dylan's worldly-wise voice followed, as prescient as when he first sang those words more than ten years earlier.

"Hot damn," Papa said about the farm that year. "Things are taking off."

After the success of the farm stand the previous summer, Papa's dream for the farm seemed just within his grasp, but still a mountain with no top, still so much to be done, his thyroid driving him with supernatural energy. He was tired beneath it all, but it was a fatigue that nudged him onward. I sensed that familiar summertime distance in his attentions, as if he were constantly looking toward his goals and unable to focus on me standing in front of him. Or perhaps, like Mama, I needed more from him than he had to give at that time.

Mama's belly was taking off, too, filling the space of the kitchen as she tried to prepare lunch for the new crew until Anne, with her experience preparing meals at Erewhon, offered to cook lunch, much to Mama's and Papa's appreciation. We kids also liked having Anne around. Heidi called her Anner, short for Anner Eater Alligator, and the nickname stuck.

"Anner," Heidi would say, "sing me a song." Heidi would listen intently to the tune and then jump up and say, "Gotta go," and she'd be off to graze in the garden or run down the paths, leading Anner to call her "the little wanderer." There was something otherworldly about Heidi, one foot in this world and one in the next, Anner thought to herself, wondering as she did about the child forming in own her belly.

"When Heidi walks through the garden, it's as if she never touches a thing with her feet," Anner said to Mama.

BY THE FINAL weeks of first grade I'd become proficient in the skills of school—hula-hoops, jump rope, "onesie-twosies I love yousies," monkey bars, kickball, wearing underwear, and taking baths. I'd even earned the role of Mrs. Grindle's teacher's pet, entrusted with the coveted task of cleaning the chalkboard erasers by clapping them against the tarmac in the playground. But unlike other kids, I still had to walk the half mile down the path to meet the bus every morning.

"Lissie, keep your shoes on!" Mama called out the door after tying the laces double for me with a firm tug, but my shoes were already coming off as I ducked into the cover of the path. Going-to-school rules were getting in the way of barefoot training—I had to catch up to Heidi's school-free feet.

Spring walking-to-the-bus-alone mornings were the quiet of the day waiting for itself to happen. You could hear the morning's beginnings, little clinks and shushes like someone getting up early and fixing breakfast before anyone else is awake. I hung the heels of my sneakers from my fingers, swinging them just enough to keep balance with the pace of walking and not too much to send them flying. Telonferdie joined me, chattering about this and that, and the morning sun slanted through the trees in zigzags as the pale sky brightened to Heidi's-eye blue. The path sweated, hard and bony here, loose and cedary there, air warming, humid, and fat. Passing from the forest, I crossed under the scent of lilac trees by the Nearings' barn, past the sounds of Scott working behind the stone wall of the garden, and down to the bottom of the driveway, where I waited for the bus. Telonferdie drifted away when I unknotted my sneakers and put them on, my socks soaking up the muddiness to remain slightly damp all day.

On the days when Mama and Heidi walked me to the bus, I had to keep my shoes on and we sang Mama's favorite songs along the paths. "Tis the gift to be simple, tis the gift to be free," Mama belted out to the audience of the forest. "Tis the gift to come round where you ought to be." Or she sang Heidi's favorite, a round, with her nickname Ho in it: "Hey ho, nobody at home, no meat, no drink, no penny have I none, but still will I be merrrrry. Hey ho, nobody at home." They came with me less now that Mama was so pregnant. The last time Mama had to stop three times along the path to pee.

"Mama?" I asked. "Are you peeing *again*?"

She looked up at me squarely from her squatting position, eyes black in the shade of the tree.

"The baby is taking all the room, so there's no place for pee. You'll see. When you're pregnant someday, you'll have to pee a lot, too."

While waiting for the bus, I worried about what would happen if I had to pee a lot like Mama. It would be no good, though I enjoyed going to the school bathroom, with its clean tiles and running water. The problem was that I liked to use lots of toilet paper to make up for what we didn't have at home, my favorite trick being to roll the soft paper around my hand, pretending it was a bandage. I used the bandaged hand to wipe, dropped it in the water, then bandaged the other hand and did it again. When I flushed, the white wads swirled down toward the hole in the bottom. One time, however, the water slowed, the whirlpool disappeared and the bandages rose in the yellow water toward the top of the bowl. Afraid it would overflow, I ran back to class. After that Mrs. Grindle made an announcement. She said we had to CONSERVE. That meant not using too much toilet paper and not flushing too much. She was looking right at me when she said it.

ON MAY 14, a Friday, there was a party for a large group of students and teachers to celebrate the completion of the semester at College of the Atlantic, where Papa continued to teach his farming course. Papa asked Anner to help with the cooking, since Mama was more or less pinned to the padded benches by the weight of her belly. There'd been a full moon the night before, and she felt its pull, drawing the waters from her. The house was chattering with guests waiting for dinner when Mama motioned to Papa.

"I'm going into labor," she said. "I need space."

"Let's get you to the hospital," Papa replied. The plan was, as with Heidi, to go to Dr. Brownlow in Blue Hill for the birth.

"No," Mama said. She'd been in for a checkup that morning, and though she was having contractions, she hadn't mentioned them to Dr. Brownlow. He'd proclaimed her and the baby in great shape, giving her the confidence to carry out her secret plan. Over the past few weeks she'd been getting ready, sterilizing sheets in the oven, acquiring clamps and other items from a nurse friend.

"What do you mean?" Papa asked, hesitating to raise his voice around the guests, but Mama could see the fear in his eyes.

"Just get everyone out of here," she said, suddenly in charge. "We'll figure it out when you get back."

Papa ushered the group across the farm to continue the party at the campground. In attendance was Marshall Dodge, the Yale linguist known for his "Bert and I" monologues, a comedy act that utilized the Maine accent to great effect. He launched into one of his jokes as Anner played the guitar and the party drew Heidi and me into its embrace.

"Watch out for them socialists," Marshall said, in reference to the Nearings, telling a story about a fellow named Scott, who liked to preach socialism over the fence to his neighbor, Enoch:

"'So you mean to say,' Enoch asked the socialism advocate, 'that if you had two farms, you'd give me one of them?'" Marshall began in the classic Maine dialect that made his jokes so funny.

"'Yes,' said Scott. 'If I had two farms, I'd give you one a them.'

"'So if you had two hay rakes, say, would you give me one of them?'

"'Yes, if I had two hay rakes, I'd give you one of them.'

"'If you had two hogs, even,' Enoch asked slyly. 'Would you give me one of them?'

"'Darn you, Enoch,' said Scott. 'You know I got two hogs.'"

Everyone laughed hard and shouted for more. My favorite "Bert and I" joke came next, the one about the farmer who saw a moose on his farm and got out his rifle to shoot the moose in the leg, "just so as to wound him, you know," explained Marshall.

"Then he put up a big sign on his barn that said, 'See the moose, ten cents, fifteen cents for families.' Well, a family comes along and the man gives the farmer his fifteen cents. The farmer takes one look at the man, and one look at his family, and gives the man back the fifteen cents.

"'Keep your money, mister, I don't want it. It's worth a hell of a lot more for my moose to see your family, than it is for your family to see my moose.'" After I stopped giggling, I delivered a butchered retelling of the story to anyone who'd listen.

By the time Papa got everyone settled and returned to the farmhouse, Clara had been born. Mama was nursing in bed on the oven-sterilized sheets, a yellow orb of moon hanging in the darkening sky out the window.

"I got on all fours and slid her out, the way the goats do," Mama casually told an astonished Papa. "Then I reached back with one hand to catch the head." She hadn't felt any fear, she said. Something in her knew just what to do. The new baby had a blond fuzz of hair and a high forehead like Heidi.

"Another Coleman," Papa noted with admiration, once he regained his composure. And another girl, he mused, thinking of his theory of child gender—well, he was certainly more stressed at that moment.

When word of the birth reached Marshall Dodge back at the campground, Marshall quoted a line from another of his jokes. "I could take a sharp knife and a piece of knotty pine, and whittle me a better-looking baby than those two made." The laughter and party continued unhindered late into the night.

MAMA AND PAPA settled on the name Clara, also from the book *Heidi*, for Heidi's beautiful invalid friend who was healed by goat's milk and the fresh mountain air when visiting her in the Swiss Alps. And indeed, soon after Clara was born, the sun finally returned for good, its warmth drawing everything out of itself. Fiddleheads uncoiled into ferns. Seeds poked twin-tipped leaves from the earth. Mama's bleeding heart flowers dripped in pink formation over lacy fronds. Fields yellowed with dandelions.

In the evening twilight, Mama nursed her third child on the front patio as the earth released its damp smells of new life. Fireflies blinked come-hither signals across the clearing as a male woodcock performed his mating ritual, rising in a spiraling flight with a buzzing sound that increased in velocity as he rose, then exploding in a loud twittering that echoed across the clearing as he dived back to earth. It was the sound, Mama thought, of the ecstatic orgy of spring that she was both a part of and apart from, as a new mother. She felt such love for the small being in her arms that it momentarily replaced the missing passion in her marriage. Soon the days would warm and lengthen, and the garden would come back to life. Soon, she hoped, things would be right again.

THE GLASS BELL of night settled over the farm, turning the sky the midnight blue of church windows against the glow from the lighted house. Kerosene lanterns whooshed and sighed as Mama put Clara to sleep in the addition, and I read in the light as Heidi dangled her feet on the doorstep, looking out for Papa to return from the campground to tuck us in, the cool spring air breathing through the door.

"Bedtime," Mama called to us, but she was nursing Clara and couldn't do anything about it. The peepers increased in volume with the darkness. I knew the cricking came from the inflated sacs on the throats of the frogs, but it was hard to understand how the slimy shapes we caught at the pond with our bare hands could make such a piercing sound. Their concert filled the night with a noise so distinct it had a three-dimensional presence, solid with longing. The noise shapes came right up to Heidi's feet, praying to her like their goddess.

I looked up from my book to make sure she hadn't drifted from the doorstep, pulled sleepwalker-spirit-like into the night, across the dew-damp garden, but she just sat on the step, listening. I began to fade off, Papa coming and going in the distance, Heidi floating out over the night, becoming bigger and bigger like a balloon of light until she became the morning.

A CHORUS OF first-light birdsong shattered the morning sky with the same velocity as the peepers. Papa had returned last night but was already long gone out to the gardens, the endless list of all the things that needed to be done cycling in his head. No sooner had he recovered from his amazement at Clara's birth than Mama's baby blues set in, and his unsuccessful efforts at helping her left him afraid to try again. He began to confide instead in Bess as they worked together in the garden. It was simple talk about day-to-day details and the bigger questions of existence, but it filled for Papa an innocent need for connection and camaraderie. Mama began to imagine otherwise.

I knew Mama wished she could sleep all day, her body molded into the soft mattress tossed off by summer folk, the seldom-washed sheets, the old striped Pendleton blanket pushed down to her feet. The back addition was cooler and darker than the rest of the house, shaded as it was from the south-facing windows, luring her toward ever-elusive sleep. "Sleep deprivation is a form of torture," someone had told her recently.

I could hear the sounds of Clara's mewing cries as Mama pressed her breast to the tiny mouth. Then peace. Nursing was Mama's escape, her imprisonment and her freedom, when her mind could wander away from the more familiar and well-trodden paths of her darker worries. Papa's thyroid. Work your fingers to the bone. Bess and Papa eating breakfast together on the patio as they planned the workday. European farm tours she wouldn't go on. Broken seals on the mason jars that meant her canning efforts had been compromised. They all became someone else's troubles. But soon the milk would drain from her breast, Clara would satiate and squirm and beat her tiny fists in the air. Time to get up.

Mama slid from the bed, the sound of her bare feet padding on the cool of the wooden floor. From my bunk I could see Mama in the kitchen drinking water from a jar with a *glug-glug* sound as she looked out the front windows. She wore the same T-shirt she'd slept in, the same loose pants, her fine hair conformed to her head in yesterday's braid.

Mist was rising at the edges of the clearing, but the center of the garden glowed with sun from above. A child was walking toward the house on the path from the well, carrying something Mama couldn't make out. The child's fair hair caught the sun coming through the mist. Mama felt she was recognizing someone she hadn't seen in a long time—as if a face on a crowded street suddenly matched one stored in her memory.

"Heidi," she said to herself. Her middle daughter. Where had she been?

"Mama," I called from the bunk, tattling my morning knowledge of all secrets. "Heidi went down to the beach."

"The beach!" Mama exclaimed, opening the door and hustling Heidi in. "You must not go to the beach alone."

"Michèle took me," Heidi said, holding up a shell, then turned and skipped back out the door, and Mama's and Heidi's minds slipped out of mine to join the realities of the day.

PAM AND PAUL drove up from Goddard College in a red VW bug with brakes they had to stop to bleed every fifty miles. Mama greeted Paul, who had visited the previous fall, and he introduced her to Pam through the window of the car.

Another beautiful blonde, Mama thought to herself. She noticed that all of Pam's clothes were neatly folded in the back seat, as if she'd decided to come along at the last minute and quickly grabbed her belongings. Pam smiled at Mama, who was already slender and fit despite the tender baby on her back.

"What a great model of modern motherhood," Pam said to Paul as they parked in the lot. The two had met a few years earlier when Pam, having just graduated from high school in Wellesley, Massachusetts, was staying at a summer boardinghouse in Ogunquit. Taken by her fresh innocence, Paul, with his dream-filled

Italian eyes and dramatic way with words, soon won her heart. Paul was attending Hobart College, and Pam, William Smith, so come the fall of 1974 their relationship continued, though they found campus life lacking a variety of experience they both sought. When Paul read about our farm in the *Country Journal*, he wrote Papa, asking if he could come work.

"It's magical there," Paul told Pam upon his return. During his few months with us, he full-heartedly joined the ranks of middle-class, college-educated young people inspired to make farming a way of life. He convinced Pam to return with him to our farm the following summer.

Always good at encouraging the talents of apprentices, Papa noticed Paul's inclination for carpentry. "Listen, there's this big old swamp maple that's just begging for a tree house," Papa said, as Paul remembers it. "If you want to build something, knock yourself out, my kids would love to have a tree house, just don't put any nails into that tree."

Embracing the challenge, Paul and Pam set to work figuring out a Tinkertoy approach so as not to use nails. The branches of the tree made a natural palm for the floor joists, and one limb had a hollowed-out knothole, making it a logical place to sink a brace. Another branch went right through one wall and out the other, with canvas around it so it could move in the wind. In the afternoons, Heidi and I often took the little path past the pond and through the mossy woods to check on Paul's progress.

"When will it be ready for us to come up?" we called to Paul, our necks arched back to spot him perched precariously in the growing structure.

"Someday soon," he said. To our eager minds, that wasn't soon enough.

*   *   *

IN THE AFTERNOONS after work, there'd be people hanging out in the campground on the stumps around the fire pit, swinging on the rope, playing guitars and harmonicas, returning from swimming at the beaches, or picking raspberries in the foundation. There were always the smells of ferns and damp bark, wood smoke and baking bread.

"Have you heard about Barry and Larry and the fireflies?" Pam was saying to the group gathered outside the cook shack. "It's the funniest thing. They've never seen fireflies before, so they were chasing them around the campground last night, trying to catch them in their hands."

Larry and Barry, bushy haired in cutoff shorts, explained that they were from California, where fireflies did not live. "I thought we'd dropped acid by mistake," Larry said. "All these little lights blinking everywhere in the night."

"I forgot to tell you I put some tabs in your tea," Barry deadpanned.

"Or maybe some mushrooms?" someone suggested with a wink.

There weren't many drugs to be had in our neck of the 1970s, as far as I can tell—though Larry did once find a patch of marijuana someone was tending in the woods. Larry and Barry were, instead, edible-mushroom-hunting fanatics. Searching wooded groves and dells for the pods of pale leathery domes pushing though the forest floor, they found the rain had made for an especially good season. Most exciting were the golden chanterelles, which tasted like chicken when sautéed with garlic, Larry said. I knew not to eat the red toadstools with white dots—they were as poisonous as they were beautiful. Instead I preferred the puffballs, which in summer were round and white and edible, but by fall dried into a leathery sack that I liked to stomp on to release a cloud of dark spores. Sometimes we found artist conks, shelflike growths attached to tree trunks that had a smooth underside onto which we'd carve pictures, or we'd make prints from large-topped meadow mushrooms by laying the grooved underside on a piece of paper to capture its concentric lines of spores.

As we threaded the edible findings onto string to dry from the ceiling of the log cabin for later use we'd marvel that mycorrhizal fungi, the fancy name for mushrooms, were connected underground by a vast network of roots called mycelium, and the enzymes produced by this network were similar to those in the compost heap, breaking down the organic debris on the forest floor into food for the trees.

"If the soil is the earth's stomach, fungi supply its digestive enzymes," Michael Pollan, a modern-day colleague of Papa's, explains in his book *The Omnivore's Dilemma*. "They stand on the threshold between the living and the dead, breaking the dead down into food for the living." It was a concept that, to the child I was then, made perfect sense—the law of return.

MICHÈLE OFTEN CAME by to join us at the campground, as did Nancy, who was now staying in the cabin behind Greg's with her boyfriend, another Greg. One such afternoon in early June, when everyone was hanging around the cook shack before dinner, a new apprentice named Sandy rode up the dirt road on her ten-speed bike, nearly a month after she was scheduled to arrive.

"We were hoping you'd show up sooner rather than later," Papa said when she introduced herself, forgetting in his usual urgency about the farm that she'd just biked across the country from San Francisco. By nature sensitive and shy, Sandy was most comfortable swimming, running, or biking long distances; in the flush of those activities she could be fully herself, without the weight of other people's opinions. She had no idea of the effect of her long blond hair, strong body, and shy smile.

"Have you seen the new girl?" Larry asked Barry that afternoon after returning from work at the Nearings'. "Wow!"

Sandy originally sought to apprentice on a Mennonite farm, but my old friend Frank, who'd been her roommate in San Francisco and dated one of her close friends, told her about us. Frank wasn't having much luck as an encyclopedia salesman, but he was a great salesman for our way of life. "You don't want to go to a Mennonite farm where you have to wear a dress all day," he teased her. "You hate dresses. The Coleman farm is cool. You'll learn a lot."

Sandy wrote to Papa, and he told her to come in May. She didn't own a car, so she set out in April to bike the nearly three thousand miles alone, armed only with her favorite cutoff painter overalls, one pair of shoes, and a rubberized sleeping bag stuffed in her panniers. She met people along the way who gave her rides and took her in, but she mostly slept out in the open in her rubber sleeping bag, zipping it up against what seemed like the constant rain that spring. Even with the waterproof coating, water would leak in around the zipper and collect in the bottom as she curled her body around the puddle and tried to keep sleeping.

The life of the farm immediately took Sandy in. She sat around the campfire that first evening listening to Larry and Paul on guitar, Barry playing harmonica, Anner singing, and basked in the simple comforts of good vibes and laughter.

"Thank you, dear Franklin," she whispered up to the stars.

The working days were another story. Perhaps because of her athletic vigor, Sandy was assigned the grunt work with the boys, digging out stumps and hauling water for irrigation, while Bess did the less labor-intensive tasks of seeding and thinning, and Anner helped run the farm stand and cook lunch. Sandy soon bonded with Pam when they found they both loved to bake bread.

"Why don't you two bake for the farm stand?" Papa suggested, when he overheard them talking about bread one day at lunch. Our neighbor Jean was no longer baking the whole-grain bread and coveted cinnamon buns of the previous summer. So Sandy and Pam took on the task, rising before the sun to fetch water from the well; grinding wheat groats with the hand grinder; mixing flour, water, and sourdough starter in wooden bowls in the campground cook shack; then letting it rise and baking it in the gas canister oven, all before everyone else woke up.

Larry loved waking to the aromas coming from the cookhouse. He was drawn not just to the bread, but even more to the chef. From the moment he'd laid eyes on Sandy, he felt an immediate urge to protect and care for her. Hers was such an appealing combination of beauty and shyness, he had to restrain his desire to shield her from the slightest harm. However, the tough whole-grain bread that practically had to be cut with a saw was somewhat less lovable.

"It's not exactly flying off the shelves," Pam said, laughing.

THAT JUNE, PAPA and some apprentices piled into VW buses and pickups and headed to UMass-Amherst for the Toward Tomorrow Fair, a gathering to promote sustainable living. Scott Nearing was delivering the keynote address at ninety-three years of age, and a large crowd gathered in the speakers' hall, young people with cutoffs, healthy beards, and long hair, some sitting on the floor, others fanning themselves in the heat. Helen and Scott sat at a table onstage, Helen knitting as she often did at conferences, unable to let idle time be wasted, her fingers flying toward the completion of a scarf or mitten.

When Scott was introduced, Helen gave him a hefty push up toward the podium, shrugging off, as she did, the burden of the younger wife tending to an aging husband. Scott, his mind sharp even if his social skills were beginning to slacken, shuffled up to the podium, smiled, and said a few words of introduction before delivering his lifelong battle cry.

"Pay as you go!"

The audience cheered enthusiastically at the well-known Nearing belief in eschewing debt, even though Scott then turned and sat back down next to Helen. His job, he must have felt, was done.

One of the young hippies nodding in agreement in the audience was a tall, skinny, and bespectacled twenty-six-year-old redhead named Rob, founder of a new organic seed company. A few years earlier, George Oshawa's book on macrobiotics, the Asian-inspired diet of whole and raw seasonal foods, had been responsible for Rob's conversion from a bookish guitar-playing UMass math major to the manager of Amherst's first health food co-op. Eventually he'd dropped out of college and found himself working on a farm near Keene, New Hampshire, at a commune, of sorts, that provided lodging in the drafty attic of the old farmhouse. Lying in his sleeping bag in that attic, Rob began to dream about seeds, and those dreams turned to action. Where could you find the unique varieties of squash a Japanese buyer had requested, for instance?

He wrote to international seed breeders and farmers, asking for heirloom varieties. Soon he opened a business checking account, moved back to his parents' home in Massachusetts, and placed an ad in *Organic Gardening*, advertising heirloom and vintage organic seeds selected for a short growing season. He backed all of his products with an L.L.Bean–style 100 percent satisfaction money-back guarantee, and named his company for the legendary Johnny Appleseed, who wandered America in the 1800s, planting apple trees from seed. Before he knew it, Rob had forty inquiries in his mailbox.

As his business grew, Rob took friends up on an offer to locate his fledgling company on their farm in Maine. As a result of the energy crisis, there was a demand for seed tailored to the small home garden. Backyard gardeners wanted sustenance crops— corn, potatoes, beans—that tolerated the short New England growing season and provided ample sustenance. "Based upon our projected seed needs for the 1976 season," Rob advertised in the MOFGA newsletter, "we cannot possibly raise all of our own seed here at Peacemeal Farm. We have a need for growers." He was eventually able to purchase land in nearby Albion, where Johnny's Selected Seeds grew and prospered over the years to become one of the foremost organic seed companies in the country.

When Papa and Rob crossed paths in 1976, both scrawny and roughly dressed in soil-worn clothes, they didn't know each would contribute to the success of the other, but they did recognize in each other a similar passion and drive. They were the younger and hipper breed of organic visionaries who would soon replace the older and somewhat kookier J. I. Rodale evangelism.

ALSO IN ATTENDANCE at the fair were Winnie and John, former filmmakers at Rodale Press's media group in Pennsylvania, who had started their own venture, Bullfrog Films. The young couple had obtained permission from the Nearings to shoot a documentary on the good life. John, thin and bearded with an English accent, and Winnie, with a new baby in her arms, approached Helen and Scott after the talk. Helen took one look at them and said, "Pretty irresponsible to bring another little one into this world, isn't it?" Taken aback, but not deterred by what was known as the brusqueness of the Nearings, Winnie and John made plans with Helen to come to Maine that August with a cameraman and capture this newly in-vogue homesteader lifestyle.

Back on the cape, the Nearings' stone home was close to completion, thanks to the help of many free hands and Brett's fine woodworking skills. True to Helen's vision, the new house looked as if it had always belonged on the spot overlooking the cove.

"A building should appear to grow easily from its site," Helen would quote from Frank Lloyd Wright's *On Architecture* in her picture book *Our Home Made of Stone*, "and be shaped to harmonize with its surroundings if nature is manifest there, and if not, try to make it as quiet, substantial and organic as she would have been were the opportunity hers."

LANTERNS LIT A circle of people at the center of Hoffman's Cove as the ocean shushed on the shore. All the apprentices were there, and other people I didn't know. Heidi and I'd gorged ourselves on strawberry-rhubarb crisp, and our blood raced with the sweet-tartness of it. Mama said it was the shortest night of the year, so we were allowed to stay up after dark for the party, a special treat, but her face was somber in the firelight as she sat on a rock nursing Clara, while Papa sat with Bess and the others.

"Almost time to go home," Mama called, shy of parties, we knew, and glad for an excuse to leave.

"No, no," Heidi and I screamed. We ran from Mama in all directions. We were full of the light of the endless June days, fields swaying with the purple-blue temples of lupine. The light, too, was full of itself, sun rising before we woke and setting after we went to bed. It bubbled up from some endless underground spring, tumbling over itself to be free. Even after the orange of sunset faded from the horizon, the light burst through the darkness in the blink-blink-blink of fireflies and the flash of phosphorescence in the black water of the ocean, mirroring the sparks of stars above. The moon was like a hole in the fabric of night, allowing the constant light to show through from behind.

Everyone sang and laughed and talked all at once, swimming and splashing naked in the ocean. We chased fireflies with Larry and Barry, catching them in our cupped hands, and stirred the sea with our toes to watch the phosphorescence follow their path in the water. Heidi was another light in the night, a lively firefly, bouncing here and there, sitting on laps, singing in her little voice to herself, putting pebbles in her nose. And then she ran out into the ocean after Michèle, tripped on a rock, and fell underwater.

"Whoa!" Michèle said, grabbing her and pulling her soaking wet body to shore.

"Time to go home!" Mama called again.

A guitar strummed. Another joined in. People were blowing on the mouths of empty beer bottles to make hollow foghorn sounds. Someone was booming a drum, and a tambourine jingled. Bruce's harmonica jangled in reply.

"Hey, Mr. Tambourine Man," Anner's voice joined. "Play a song for me . . ." The rest of the sounds adjusted to follow the tune of her voice until soon the song turned into another. "I am just a poor boy, though my story's seldom told . . ."

The light of June was like the loudest crashing music at the end of that song. "Lie-la-lie, boom, lie-la-lie-la-lie-lie-lie, boom, lie-la-lie, boom." After this the light would still fill long days for the rest of summer, but it would get slower like honey. By July the fireflies would mate and extinguish, and the phosphorescence drift out to sea.

"Lissie, Heidi," Mama called. "Time to go home."

"Nooo, we don't want to go!"

We ran across the road to hide behind the rose-hip bushes.

"Watch out for the poison ivy," I called, but Heidi kept running into the darkness. I heard Mama calling, so I ran after her.

"Run, run," I said. "Hide."

A couple days later, we couldn't stop itching.

"You got into the poison ivy," Mama scolded. "Serves you right for hiding."

"STOPPIT," I SAID, my tongue worrying a loose tooth, as Heidi trickled water from her bucket onto my sand castle in the sandbox by the woodshed.

"Stop, you're ruining our home." We often played make-believe for hours until something—hunger, fatigue, or irritation—jolted us out of the imaginary and back to reality.

We'd been to the July 4th parade in Harborside earlier that day with some apprentices to watch the bicentennial festivities, but the games and costumes had left us tired and overstimulated.

Heidi tipped the bucket toward the castle again.

"If you do that you'll die," I said in a singsong voice. I don't know exactly when or why I started saying that to her, but I said it often that year, as her three-year-old precociousness began to get the better of me. It was the only threat severe enough to get her attention.

That day Heidi looked at me with those pale blue eyes. Something in her was always a bit of the prankster, as if she could afford to take life less seriously. She tipped her bucket forward, and the sand castle gave way beneath the flood.

"Oh, now look," I said. "Our home is ruined!"

I hit the remaining lump of castle with my shovel, flicking wet sand in her face. She rubbed it off while backing away, then ran across the yard and out toward the gardens.

THE PATH TO Paul's tree-house-in-progress led past the pond, a mystery of darkness after rain, hiccupping with frogs calling you to them. The frogs laid clusters of gelatinous sacs, each with a black dot in the center, attached to grass and twigs along the edges. The eggs hatched into hundreds of squirming pollywogs that became miniature frogs by the time the dimples of water-bug feet dented the water. Heidi and I often stopped to try and catch them when heading along the path to check on the tree house.

"Here we come, wittle froggies," Heidi chirped as our bare feet sank into the cushions of sphagnum moss. The frogs lay half submerged at the line where water met earth, their knobby skin an iridescence of greens, yellows, and browns, rounded eyes unblinking. We stood on a shallow ledge where you could see through to the sandy bottom, the warm water up to the middle of my calves and to Heidi's thighs.

"Catch me a frog," Heidi begged. If we were too sudden, they sprang into the water and breaststroked out of reach. It annoyed me when I couldn't catch one, cupping my hands on emptiness as the frog shot away. I wanted to feel the thump-thump as it jumped inside my closed palm like a beating heart.

"Stupid frogs!" I kicked the water, splashing Heidi. Some days she annoyed me, too, the reasons building a house in my heart. There was always the underlying grudge that she got to go with Mama last spring. And Heidi was the one Papa carried on his shoulders—I was too big, he said. She had such a funny way about her, the apprentices loved her best, but she drove Mama crazy, always into trouble.

"I catch one," Heidi said, wading farther in.

"You're too little to go deeper," I said. "You can't even swim."

Sandy had been teaching us how to swim down at the coves, but only I could stay afloat, though the cold water of the ocean made practicing less than appealing. Heidi kept moving forward, so I splashed her. She turned and splashed me. I splashed her again and she stepped back into the water, fell, and slipped under. The water was the color of pale tea near the sandy edge, so I could see her open eyes register the shock. She came up and immediately began to wail, sucking in air between the sputter of exhales.

"You got me wet!" she gasped.

"You have to listen," I said, then turned and leaped across the softness of moss to the tree-house path, bumping past Pam as I ran.

CHAPTER TEN

Loss

"Heidi. Hi-di. Heidi Ho. Ho-di."

Again and again Mama called, breaking into the train of my story about the mountain people. "And the little people were hiding behind a rock because they didn't want to get hurt. The big people were coming and the little people were scared. 'The big people are coming, the big people are coming,' they called, 'Run and hide in the cave.'"

The loft was stuffy and hot, the floorboards printing their grain on my leg. I shifted position and wiggled my tongue in the hole left by my lost tooth.

"Lissie," Mama called. My muscles clenched in place. Big people. Hide. "Lissie!" Again. She peeked up from below.

"Oh, there you are," Mama said. "Skates is here. Where's Heidi?"

"I don't know."

"Come say hello to Skates."

My body unbent from the crouch and shuffled backward down the ladder. It was a little cooler below, but no breeze, air thick as molasses. The swing hung unmoving from the ash tree. I listened for words from the leaves. Nothing. Then I heard Mama's scream.

JUST THAT MORNING the gardens were bustling as usual with apprentices and customers and vegetables needing to be picked. It was a humid-hot day, a Saturday near the end of July. Baby Clara was strapped to Mama's back in Heidi's old sling, sleeping mouth-open as Mama cooked lunch, skin glowing and tan from summer. Skates was coming to visit, and Mama needed time to clean the house, to hide from her mother-in-law the chaos her life had become: Bess and Papa having breakfast together that morning, mud tracked in from the gardens, piles of laundry to be washed by hand, Heidi and I running around the small kitchen pulling each other's hair and screaming.

"One more scream, and you're out," Mama yelled, her mind tumbling over itself.

"Pull my hair, and you'll die," I said to Heidi.

She pulled my braid. I screamed.

"Out." Mama pointed to the screen door, sweat shining on her forehead from the heat of the wood cookstove. Around the stone patio of the farmhouse, the daylilies panted their orange tongues in the heat. Rain had fallen the night before, and the air was heavy, as if waiting to rain again.

"I'm going to the woodshed," I said, marching away across the yard and climbing up the woodshed ladder to my perch in the loft.

Heidi followed me, reaching up the ladder that she was afraid to climb alone. "Uppie."

"No," I said, but after a while she came back again with a little red boat in her hands.

"Come an' play with me," she begged.

"No," I said. "I'm busy."

WHEN THE WORKDAY ended—at noon on Saturdays—some apprentices hiked down to Redman's Cove, accessed from a path across the road from the campground. They swam and relaxed on the beach, and Sandy started on one of her marathon swims. By the time everyone headed back up the path, Sandy was just the arc of an arm far out in the sequined water. Pam and Paul were sitting in the cool of the gravel pit by the road when someone came running over from the campground.

"Heidi's fallen in the pond!"

SOMETIME AFTER MAMA'S scream, I remember the silhouette of a woman coming over the rise from the garden. A few minutes later? An hour?

"There you are," she said. Was it Bess? Nancy? Michèle? She bent down to put her hands on my shoulders. Her eyes were not right, too bright.

"Come with me," she said. "Let's go into the farmhouse." She took my hand and pulled me up the patio and through the screen door. It slammed behind us. The house was hotter than outside, the cookstove still burning low.

"Come sit here and let's read a book," she said.

"Where's Mama?"

"She's down at the pond."

"Where's Papa?"

"He's down there, too."

"Where's Heidi?"

"Down at the pond."

She began to read one of the books. It was a kid's book, Heidi's now, but I didn't care, I could never get free of books. When their pages opened they pulled me in, even if I'd heard the story a hundred times. The apprentice's voice sounded funny. I looked up to find she was crying as she read, tears rolling down her cheeks. One splattered on the page, and she stopped reading. Sniffled.

"I want to go," I said.

"No, you have to stay here," she said.

"I want to go check on Heidi."

"No, that's not a good idea. You should stay here."

"I'll go down to the pond by the long way, so by the time I get there she will be okay," I said.

"No," she said. But after a while, it seems I was alone.

I slipped out of the farmhouse and onto the path to the spring. It was cooler in the woods, but the indent of the path was sweaty. Down a little ways was a turnoff to the tree house, and then another turn toward the pond. I walked slowly. "By the time I get there, everything will be okay," I repeated to myself. The light came into the woods from the clearing of the pond. I peeked around a bush, the moss spongy beneath my bare feet.

The pale shape of Heidi's body lay on the ground by the edge of the water, a circle of people around her. "What are you doing?" I cried. They all looked up at me. Someone grabbed my hand and pulled me away through the gardens to the farm stand. Other apprentices were standing around, talking in hushed voices.

"She threw up water," someone said. "That's a good sign."

Mumbles. Sighs. The sun bright on the gardens. Lettuces wilting in the farm stand. Then I was stumbling along a path in the woods with Mama to call the ambulance from Jean and Keith's phone. Mama wailed Heidi's name into the forest, and my toes clenched from the sound as I scrambled to keep up. Then I was behind the woodshed with Papa in the dusk of late afternoon. He was holding a blanketed shape in his arms as the afternoon sun burned the tops of the pointed trees around the clearing. Rocking back and forth, crying in a way I'd never seen before.

"But Papa," I said, "but Papa, you've got to uncover her face. She can't breathe."

"Lissie," he said. "Heidi is dead."

The lines of Papa's face were blurred with tears, the curve of his steel hair gone flat. He rocked her in that tight embrace. His body didn't understand such pain, the arch of his back was fetal. Up though the path in the woods came the sound of Mama wailing Heidi's name. But Heidi had to be okay, she had to wake up, I didn't mean it when I said she would die. She had to be okay so I could help her up the ladder next time. But around the farm the light began to fade, and the daylilies closed up into fleshy clothespins that looked like the fingers of praying hands.

"You're not taking her," is what Paul remembers Papa saying to the EMTs, responding with fury when the ambulance finally arrived and they tried to put her on board. He wasn't going to let an undertaker touch her, pump her full of chemicals. That's when the ambulance driver radioed the police. And that's when Papa slipped Bruce and Paul a piece of yellow-lined legal paper with handwritten instructions on where and how to dig a grave in the woods.

"Whatever happens," the note said in Papa's distinct scrawl, "just keep digging."

Pam, Paul, Barry, and Larry were all there with shovels in the graveyard where the Colson child had been buried a century before. It seemed to Paul to take an eternity to dig that grave. Sandy still hadn't returned from her swim, and Larry wondered if he should look for her. The grave site was bookended between the road, the parking lot, and the path to the stand. They heard the sounds of wailing, sawing, and hammering—Papa building the small pine coffin. Then, through the opening to the road, they saw the cruisers go by, one, two, three, four police cruisers and maybe four state troopers.

"It's a siege," Paul said, counting the cars.

"Keep digging," Bruce said, down in the earth.

DARKNESS FELL ON our little house in the woods with a final sigh, until the pale flashing lights destroyed it. I'd never seen a light like it before, filling our clearing with ghostly fury. Popping and flashing reds, whites, and blues, making the trees into black skeletons in the paleness out the window as engines and radio static ripped the silence of the forest and vibrated on my skin.

"Stand back, stand back," a voice crackled, and fast hands pulled me across the room to the back addition.

"What, Mama, what?"

"Shush, quiet, Lissie." Her hand on my mouth. Clara was lying next to me in Mama and Papa's bed, soft and mewing, tiny fingers clenching and unclenching. Mama pulled at us, pulling us to her, the trembling of her jaw against my arm.

Across the room, the small shape on the padded benches, still wrapped in the blanket.

"Get the fuck off my property!" Papa's voice was loud at the door.

"Please come out of the house," said a man's voice. Mama was whimpering into my hair.

"Papa!" I pushed free and stumbled up the step to the main part of the house. Don't let them hurt Papa. That strange pale light flooded through the open door, snapping red and blue around the distinct shape of Papa in the space of the doorframe. He summoned all his vitality to stand taut and bowlegged like a cowboy, his head thrown back, shoulders wide. Someone later claimed he braced in his arms the old shotgun for scaring coons, but I don't remember the shape of that.

"Leave her alone. Leave us alone and get the hell out of here." His voice had no trace of hesitation. Outside, the dark shapes of men stood near a thick car topped with those eerie flashing lights.

"Papa," I moaned, my stomach filling with heat.

"Get her back," Papa said without moving from the door.

Mama pulled me to the addition, fingernails cutting into my wrist. Let me go, let me go, but she held me on the bed.

"No, Mama," I cried.

"Listen, Lissie, listen, the police are trying to take Heidi," she said over me. "They want to take her away. We can't let them. She has to be buried here. On our land."

WHEN PAPA'S ANGER subsided and the pain returned, he agreed to go down with the deputy and use Keith and Jean's phone to call the commissioner.

"This fellow here wants to bury her on the farm," Jean remembered the deputy sheriff telling the DA. "Doesn't he need to take her to a funeral home? Doesn't he at least need to take her to a regular cemetery? Doesn't she need to be embalmed? Aren't there laws about this? I don't know. I've never had one like this before."

As it turned out, the district attorney was Jewish, and Jews don't embalm the dead, preferring to bury the body within twenty-four hours, so the DA said fine, as long as there was a historic grave site like the one we had at the farm. All Papa needed was a permit.

It was nearly midnight by the time we put her to rest. A few of the apprentices acted as pallbearers, carrying the little coffin into the woods and lowering her down into the hole they had dug. Everybody was standing in a circle, holding candles and lanterns. It was beautiful and eerie at the same time. There were words spoken, tears, maybe a guitar. Anner sang "Simple Gifts."

"After what was a horrendous day," Paul would say later, "the likes of which no one had seen before, there was a richness and a victory, certainly, that Heidi could rest at last in the earth of the farm."

Around the cape, the sea swelled and retreated with the ancient comings and goings of the tide, small waves shushing on the pebbles and erasing the footprints of birds and humans alike from the sandy coves.

LARRY FOUND LITTLE peace in the rituals of the ceremony. A voice in the back of his head kept repeating Sandy's name, the velocity increasing until it became a scream. "Sandy!" After the burial, he and Barry searched along the roads and paths with lanterns and called out into the night, but to no avail. Where the hell was she?

Sandy liked to swim out to the islands almost, the steady pace of arms and legs moving in unison to soothe the anxieties collected in her mind over the course of the day. She swam away the strain of hard work, the fatigue of waking early to bake bread, the social tension of living so closely with a group of people. The cold water felt especially delicious in the humidity, the pulse of adrenaline warming her as she settled into the rhythm. Who knew where the time went when you were in that place? An hour later, maybe two, she stopped to get her bearings and realized she had come clear around the head of the cape from Redman's to Ames Cove.

By the time she returned to Redman's and stepped ashore, the sun was sinking behind the peaked edge of spruce and fir surrounding the cove, the rocks purple in the fading light. Sunset was still a couple hours away, but the light had disappeared from the deeper places of the forest.

Sandy remembered the path leaving from the top of the cove, but it wasn't where she'd thought it should be, so she located her overalls and shoes and set out bushwhacking for it. When she hadn't found her way after an hour, the darkness began deepening around the moss and trunks of the forest floor. She knew the head of the cape was surrounded by sea on all sides, meaning she couldn't get too lost, so she kept forging on, the branches scraping her skin and her overalls chafing with salt. Soon she could see the silver sickle of the waning moon rising above the trees, and that served as her compass as she climbed up and down the rocky undulations of the forest.

When she began to tire, she decided to lie on the pine needles beneath a tree to rest. She shivered and hugged herself with her arms, having no protection from the surprising coolness of the night, as mosquitoes complained and trees creaked. Unable to sleep, Sandy continued to pick her way through the woods and eventually found herself on one of the old trails. She felt the way home with her feet, finally limping into the campground just before dawn, hair tangled with twigs and skin scraped by branches. Limp with relief, she crawled into her familiar rubber sleeping bag next to Larry, who woke with a lurch and furiously hugged her to him. Warming her hands with his own, blowing on them, he began to cry, his reddening eyes exposed without glasses.

"What is it?" Sandy asked.

"I'm glad you're safe," he said, but the words sounded hollow compared to the magnitude of his emotion. This was the woman, he knew in that moment, with whom he wanted spend the rest of his life. When he told her what had happened, Sandy felt it like a fist in her stomach—she had just the other day been trying to teach Heidi how to swim.

COME DAYBREAK WE heard that at 3:00 a.m., around the time Sandy was hoping for sleep under a tree, Jean, two weeks overdue, finally went into labor. A new child, a boy named Dagan, was born to our neighbors at 9:00 a.m. the day after we lost our own.

We drifted around the farm like shadows. We didn't talk or feel, or, in Mama's case, eat. Mama's parents came up to help, camping in the blueberry field, but there was nothing they could do. Mama hardly spoke to them. I watched the light fade through the windows at the end of the day, pale sunbeams full of dust. Come night the farmhouse was quiet save for the whooshing of kerosene lanterns and Clara's hunger cries. Helen and Scott held a memorial service in the long room at their old house, and everyone sat on the padded benches in numb silence while Helen played Mozart's *Requiem* on her phonograph. Skates, silenced with shock, retreated to Carolyn Robinson's.

BY MONDAY PAPA couldn't stand it anymore, his mind commanding his body to turn back to the only thing he could trust—work.

"I'm opening the stand," he said. Mama wanted to yell at him, shake him, punch him. Instead she cried in the woods along the paths.

"Heidiii!" Mama called. "Oh Heidiii!"

It seemed to her that the whole of the forest was permeated with Heidi's spirit. She felt something move in the bushes and spun around, expecting to see Heidi come running out. When Anner tried to console Mama, Mama ended up consoling her, still thinking in her shock that somehow everything was going to be all right.

"Heidi was just there behind that bush, scurrying away," she told Anner. "I feel her everywhere. In the leaves and the grass and the breeze. She's all around us."

Sandy felt Heidi's spirit, too. When she rose in the darkness to fetch water at the well for baking bread, Heidi's energy seemed to pulse in the darkness. As she dipped the bucket into the water with the well pulley, the spirit shape ballooned bigger and bigger around her until she couldn't breathe. Fearing the intensity of those morning excursions, she began to wake Larry and make him come with her.

I sat in the woodshed loft in the golden light of afternoons repeating Heidi's names to myself in a litany, a song to call her back to me.

"Hieds, Ho, Hi, Heidi-didi, Heidi-Ho, Hodie."

I sang and sang, but she never came to the foot of that ladder again.

AROUND THE CAMPFIRE in the evenings, Anner sat in silence now, hesitant to raise her voice or guitar in song.

"Remember that crow? It was wise somehow," someone said into the darkness.

"It was an omen," another agreed, the myth of ravens and crows as messengers, harbingers of death, coming to mind. The crow had showed up that spring before Heidi died, the hush of its black wings cutting the sky. It landed on the patio and cawed down at the gardens, guttural and insistent. "Caw-akkkk."

"Nevermore," an apprentice said in an ominous voice, evoking Edgar Allan Poe's famous raven. We'd gathered around in a circle where the bird had hopped to the grassy space beneath the ash tree. It was larger than most crows; perhaps it was in fact a raven. It nodded its head, strutted on ringed feet, and made a gurgling noise in its throat, its obsidian head jutting forward and back from its body and ocher beak like a dark cave when it cawed. It was different from the many other crows that ate from the compost heaps and struck dark silhouettes in the trees around the house. There was a wise knowing in the dark marbles of its eyes.

Larry had noticed a feather hanging out of alignment from the ebony curve of one wing and wondered if it had been hurt and was slightly lame. He leaned forward and tried to pull the stray feather free, but the crow hopped just out of his reach as he scrambled after.

"Stop," Anner had said. "Don't mess with it." It flapped onto the patio, then dropped off the rock edge, catching air under its wings, and flew up onto a branch of the ash tree.

"You know why they call it a murder of crows?" someone asked. "Because a group of them will gang up on a solitary crow and kill it. Maybe they tried to do that to this one."

Heidi took a particular liking to that crow, following it around and talking to it in her own bird voice. It would gurgle-purr back at her. Perhaps she could understand it the way she understood the trees and Telonferdie. It came by every day for a month or so, dropping in at lunch to eat scraps and establishing itself as a member of our eclectic community. Jean also reported seeing it next door at her house. Someone finally looked up the old rhyme and recited it at lunch:

> *One crow for sorrow, two for mirth,*
> *Three for a wedding, four for a birth,*
> *Five for silver, six for gold,*
> *Seven for a secret not to be told.*
> *Eight for heaven, nine for hell,*
> *And ten for the devil's own self.*

Heidi was especially upset when we didn't see our feathered friend for a number of days and realized the crow was not coming back. To ease her distress, we blamed its departure on the fact that someone had finally pulled out that stray wing feather and scared it away.

Lacking neat scientific summaries on the news at night and a minister at church every Sunday to provide comforting religious sermons, our little community was left to determine our own rationale for the things that happened. So it wasn't surprising that after Heidi drowned, people thought of the crow and felt something tingle up their spines.

One crow for sorrow . . .

As everyone shivered around the fire, a Theosophical Society friend of Helen's who was said to be clairvoyant—a medium—emerged from the log cabin. Robyn was a grumpy older woman who often complained about the living conditions and ate a lot of garlic, its sweaty smell permeating her skin. She was on a sprouted wheat cleansing diet that made her act a little strange, in Sandy's opinion. As she approached the fire, sparks shattered from a collapsing log and brought forth exclamations from the group. Robyn raised her bare arms for silence.

"I've communicated with Heidi," she announced. "She said she's fine, and she doesn't want to come back."

Anner and the others stared at her in stony silence, eyes glinting in the firelight. Just who was this woman to make such a claim?

"I wouldn't want to come back either," someone muttered after Robyn returned to the log cabin. "Not if I saw that woman calling me from the ever-after."

Soon after, Papa, in his sorrow, began to fill up the pond, shovelful by shovelful, returning it to the forest. Its waters bled back into the earth, leaving a dark wound beneath new moss, and eventually, the beginnings of alders.

CHAPTER ELEVEN

Atonement

WHEN THE INEXPLICABLE happens, everyone wants to find a culprit. Where was the mother? The father? "It's because they were heathens, because they didn't abide—they had it coming, living like that," some said. The attending sheriff has since passed on, and the files from that year burned in a fire, so I don't know for sure what the law thought, but as if we didn't have enough pain, my parents were blamed for the accident by the moral world at large—especially Papa, he being the man in charge. Sometimes the crucified are redeemed, sometimes they aren't. For our family, redemption would come through sorrow.

By August the fields were covered with the swaying blanket of Queen Anne's lace, but all I could see were those thousands of drops of bloodred at the center. On the Hebrew Day of Atonement, a goat was sent off to perish in the wilderness, carrying the sins of the people on its back. A scapegoat, and the thread tied around the goat's neck was red for sin and guilt, red like Heidi's boat.

We went about life, needing still to make a living at the farm stand during the summer months. Mama and Papa created the facade of normalcy for others, working together by necessity but avoiding each other and the urgings of their emotions, as if by ignoring the pain in their hearts, it would magically disappear.

Into the stunned warmth of that month came Winnie and John, of Bullfrog Films, with their young child, a handsome cameraman named Robert, and a 16mm camera. They stayed in a cabin at nearby Hiram Blake Camp, slipping into a week in the life of Forest Farm as the Nearings transitioned from the old farmhouse to their nearly completed stone house on the cove. At first Helen and Scott, perhaps in shock like the rest of the community, all but ignored the camera, feigning indifference to the project. But soon enough Robert was able to work his easygoing charms on Helen and win her interest by gently poking fun at her. She began to emerge in the mornings with rouge on her cheeks and engage in something of a flirtation with the camera.

Scott, too, saw an opportunity to expound on his favorite topics, from the importance of building up the soil to his distaste for bankers and big business, even remarking upon what he saw as the wayward career of his adopted son John, who had abandoned his once stalwart Communist beliefs to work for Henry Luce at *Time*. And Scott never missed an opportunity to denigrate banking, the chosen profession of his other son Robert. Uncomfortable in the realm of emotion, Scott far preferred the intellectual critique of the sociopolitical.

One scene in the documentary took place during Helen's music night, with Sandy and Larry and other apprentices gathered in the Nearings' living room. It was only a week or two after Heidi's death, and a collective mourning was palpable. Helen explained that she had selected "music of protest" by a young Vietnamese girl for that evening's score in response to Scott's opposition to the "dribbly" music of the previous weeks, played in memoriam for Heidi.

"Can't we listen to something of social significance?" Scott had requested.

I hover here in shock at Scott's words, but also with empathy. We were all prone to that self-serious and emotionally distant tone set by the Nearings, the intellectual realm being so much safer than the emotional. Those tidy little stages of grieving—from denial to anger, bargaining, depression, and acceptance—were unavailable to hearts clutched in the grip of the intellect. There were no gardeners of grief in our community.

FALL AIR HOLDS the smell of wood smoke more than any other time of the year. For me it will always be the scent of lost things. As I walked the path to the bus, the ashy disintegration of maple and pine mingled with a wistfulness for the barefoot freedoms of summer and life as it had been before.

Everyone in second grade knew about Heidi. They stopped whispering when I came near and looked at me with blank eyes. It made me different, so I didn't want to talk about it. My friend Jennifer and I were playing hula-hoops in the playground when I fell on the tarmac and cut my hip. Everyone ran away, screaming at the sight of blood. The third- and fourth-grade teacher, Mrs. Clifford, came and took me to the nurse's room to swab and bandage the wound. She had to unbutton and pull down my favorite pink pants to get to the cut, which made me uncomfortable. When I cried at the sting of alcohol, Mrs. Clifford looked at me with eyes made large behind her rimmed glasses.

"You have a lot to hurt about," she said. I thought she meant the cut was very bad.

"It must be quite hard."

"No," I said, crying more.

She stood back, the tears in her eyes disappearing behind the glare of her glasses.

"Can I go now?" I didn't want any more people's sadness. I buttoned my favorite pants, now stained with blood, and wiped my eyes with my knuckles.

On the way home on the bus my friend Paul let me choose from his marble collection. There was one that reminded me of the blue of Heidi's eyes, with swirls of light and dark blues that went deep into its center, and he let me have it even though it was his favorite. I held the cool orb tightly in my palm so as not to lose it.

In the mornings I sat with Jennifer on the bus, and she counted the freckles on my arms. We both had long hair, but hers was summer blond, with streaks of almost white next to her pale unfreckled skin. She said that even though I had freckles and brown hair, I was pretty, too.

"We're the prettiest girls in our class," she said. "Be sure to save me a seat because I don't want to have to sit with anyone else."

We walked around the edge of the playground holding hands as she talked of plans to make us popular. I didn't understand why it mattered so much, but I practiced hula-hoops in the courtyard with her and did jump-rope tricks. When everyone lined up and held hands to play Red Rover in the big field beyond the swing sets, I would run as fast as I could toward Jennifer in the line of kids, knowing she would let her hand break free so I could go back to my team and get cheered. I did the same for her. When we were together, it didn't matter what the other kids said. That she lived in a trailer. That I was a hippie with a dead sister.

The second-grade teacher, Mr. McGuffie, was new and a bit of a radical. He organized our chairs in a big circle, rather than traditional rows. I sat between Jennifer on my left and, on the right, Nigel, the grandson of Dick and Mary, our friends who had hosted the sauna parties of earlier years. With the two of them I could forget about my troubles and feel like a normal kid—until Mr. McGuffie had to separate the three of us for whispering and giggling.

"Your wrists are so skinny, I can circle them with my thumb and forefinger," Jennifer said one day in the playground, but when she tried to clamp her finger and thumb around my wrist, I twisted out of her grip.

"Don't touch my wrists!"

"Why?"

"I don't like it."

"Why not?"

"I just don't."

There was a blank space in my memory. Hands reaching for mine. Don't. Don't touch. Don't touch this feeling. It hurts.

PAPA LEFT ON his second European farm tour that fall as planned, struggling to keep his thyroid—and life—in check. Secretary of Agriculture Butz had resigned in October after outing himself as a bigot by quipping, "The only thing the coloreds are looking for in life are tight pussy, loose shoes, and a warm place to shit." Despite Butz's departure in disgrace, the USDA remained attached to the well-entrenched purse strings of the chemical and commercial agriculture industries.

Through grants and savings, Papa had raised enough money that summer to take a group of adults to a conference on biological agriculture in Paris, followed by a ten-day tour of organic farms. The itinerary included France, Germany, and Holland. Papa wanted to share with others the secrets of these European farmers, whose soil had been worked for centuries to produce some of the happiest and healthiest plants he'd ever seen. In these small farms and their ancient soil, he saw hope for the future, if only he could translate their methods for the American mind. It was a passion that grew with the loss of his daughter, as if through his dedication to this work, her short life would be redeemed.

Our apprentice Paul traveled ahead to work the grape harvest with a vintner in France, then met up with the group in Paris. It was there that Papa finally opened up to Paul about Heidi one night at a bar. He'd been holding it all in, trying to keep moving forward, not letting himself feel a thing. That night with Paul, far away in another country, Papa broke down and cried for the first time since July.

"He was completely devastated," Paul told Pam later; the loss of Heidi was coupled with the loss of the dream that happiness could be achieved through purposeful effort alone. Life, in the end, had demanded its pound of flesh. Papa's most tender feelings of joy, he realized, had been the moments when he left off farmwork and sat on the grass to let me and Heidi climb onto his back like two little monkeys, giggling and tumbling to be near him, or as he carried the solid weight of baby Clara's sleeping body from the jeep at night and settled her into bed. They were memories he could taste only in short sips, before retreating again behind the reserve learned from his father. There he was safe, more or less, as he returned from Europe to the demands of the farm. But the pain continued to wreak havoc on his thyroid, until the doctors told him surgery or radiation treatment were the only options.

THE LOW SUN of late fall streamed through the windows at an awkward angle, illuminating the residue on the glass and magnifying the dust that covered every surface. Mama and Papa joined each other for meals, but ate in silence. There was a screaming in my heart as I sat with them on the old tree-stump chairs, the wood worn to a smooth patina beneath me.

Mama looked across the table and knew in the angle of his jaw and distance in his eyes that Papa was lost to her. If she could have talked with him about that day in July, things might have been different. If she could have aired how her suspicions about his friendship with Bess had come out as anger at us kids, how her innocent dismissal of us had turned deadly, he might have felt compassion for her. He could have told her that nothing ever happened with Bess, or with any of the others. Perhaps they might have helped each other and gone on together. But Mama did not tell Papa the last thing she'd said to Heidi that day. She did not tell anyone.

Some lives are made of the hope that something not quite right might turn out right in the end. When did that kind of hoping begin for Mama? When was that first sign of dismissal from Papa, the first hint of her happy homestead slipping away? It must have been long before the spring Papa rented the car and sent her down to her parents. Perhaps she knew the moment she served him the mashed potatoes at Franconia College that they could never fully meet each other's expectations. Looking back now, it seems possible that Mama's passive nature needed Papa to reject her in the end. The only way to grow, her heart insisted, was to suffer.

When the meal was done, Papa rose from the table, rinsed his bowl, and headed out the door to the shortening day. Silence remained in the farmhouse, but the screaming in my heart would not hush.

THE NEARINGS DIDN'T know how to solve the troubles next door, and preferring to steer clear of the vagaries of emotion, they let us be. Their own children, and many surrogates, were always falling short of their hopes, it seemed. Angered at what he saw as the capitalist rebellion of his adopted son John—the editor at *Time* who had a big house in the suburbs—Scott had been returning John's letters unopened via his other son Robert. Then on December 1, John, still estranged from his father, died of a heart attack at age sixty-four, while on a speaking tour in Chicago. It's hard to know how the news affected Scott, as he never spoke of such things, but certainly it must have hit hard on the heels of Heidi's death.

Then, as always, it seemed, life renewed itself. A baby girl was born to Anner in December. Gabrielle, feminine in French for Gabriel, an angel of god. Gaboo, we called her.

BY JANUARY, THE snow came to cover the farm and our hearts with its cool blanket. Sometime after that, Mama, Clara, and I were eating breakfast by the front windows when Papa and a strange woman walked up the front path, the distinct outline of their figures set off from the backdrop of white. The woman wore a fitted coat and tan scarf and moved with a deliberate aloofness, as if she only just happened to be in the neighborhood.

When Papa introduced us to Gerry, her smile emphasized how much fuller her mouth and lips were than Mama's, and though her eyes were almost the same color, they were a more reliable brown, with no flecks of lighter colors in them. Her skin was olive in tone, and she had a defined nose like Mama's, but with more emphasis on the nostrils. Straight brown hair fell from a cowlick on her forehead and down over her shoulders. She wasn't prettier than Mama, but she seemed to me more assured of her presence in the world.

Papa and Gerry met at a MOFGA conference where Papa was speaking about the most recent European farm tour. "Would you like to buy a cow?" Gerry asked him when they were introduced, a slight smile in her brown eyes. She'd come to the conference with her husband, Zeke, and some friends from their homestead in Wytopitlock, a small settlement in the remote reaches of Maine's Hancock County. Having grown up an only child on a quiet middle-class cul-de-sac in the Shadyside neighborhood of Pittsburgh, Pennsylvania, Gerry found another world while attending Temple University. Dressed in the hippie wardrobe of the time, she met Zeke, who with his long hair, Hells Angels beard, and jacked-up motorcycle represented the rebellion her young heart sought. After college, they'd moved to an abandoned shack in Maine to start a homestead, but the thrill was fading with the realities of their relative poverty.

"Actually, yes, I am looking for a cow," Papa said. Our goats were gone by then, and our neighbor Keith seemed to be benefiting from his new cow, and his new relationship with Chip. As Gerry and Papa conversed, he was drawn to her self-assured manner. Unlike Mama, Gerry didn't seem to need anyone or anything. Papa never did buy Gerry's cow, but when Mama looked out the window that morning she knew, in the way you know, that Gerry was there to stay.

*   *   *

SHORTLY THEREAFTER, ON a morning in February when I was again at school, Papa brought home another rental car. "It's over," he said to Mama, wanting only for her to stand on her own feet and find her own way. He barely had the strength to take care of himself, and her need for him felt like a weight around his throat. Rather than undergo surgery, he'd decided to try what would be one of two radioactive iodine treatments. The pill was supposed to take several weeks after ingestion to shrink the swollen gland, but so far it wasn't providing the easy fix the doctors had hoped for. Instead of his thyroid, it felt as if the radioactive iodine was removing his heart, leaving only anger at the world as he turned and walked away from Mama and out of the farmhouse.

"Fuck you!" Mama screamed after him, but she packed up herself and Clara and drove away from the farm along the narrow, icy roads. When she reached the stop sign where the cape road met the main road, she stopped, then turned around and headed back to the farm.

"I'm not going," she said, standing in the door of the farmhouse, begging, ironically, like Heidi, to be let back in.

"This has got to end somewhere," Papa yelled, his calm assurance unhinged at last.

"Just go," he shouted, no longer caring about the pain it caused them both. "Go!"

The strength of Mama's resolve withered in the light of Papa's anger. She turned and went back to the car and drove with Clara, both of them crying much of the seven hours along icy winter roads, and the final lonely stretch of 88, to Westport Point.

Her parents were at a loss to see her return yet again, so she sought refuge at a nearby abbey. It seems incredible to me that this could be for real, but the nuns took her in, even with baby Clara, and she found solace in the hymns and quiet pace of life there. A school friend of Mama's who lived outside of Boston helped her apply for welfare. She couldn't believe the government would send her a check, just like that, but she rented a place in Cambridge with the money, where she and Clara stayed until she was accepted to Naropa, a Buddhist school she'd heard about in Boulder, Colorado. Then she paid for the tuition and bought a VW bug, driving out to Boulder with Clara to start summer classes in June.

"Can a woman's tender care cease towards the child she bear?" was the quote Mama copied into her journal that spring above a photo of Clara and me, fighting, as she was, the numbing plunge into depression.

BACK AT THE farm, the white-throated sparrow returned, heralding the still constant reliability of the seasons. "There's a special providence in the fall of the sparrow," Hamlet famously said, referencing the line in the Bible from Jesus. "Do not be afraid of those who kill the body but cannot kill the soul. Rather, be afraid of the One who can destroy both soul and body in hell. Are not two sparrows sold for a penny? Yet not one of them will fall to the ground apart from the will of your Father."

The death of even the smallest sparrow was thought by Christians to be part of God's plan, but that was a comfort unknown to all of us at the time. Helen might have counseled us on what she saw as the comforts of reincarnation. "Death, we felt," Helen would later write, "was a transition, not a termination. It was an exit-entrance between two areas of life." Scott agreed, adding, "Death is a change; a good deal like the change from day to night—always thus far followed by another day. Never the same twice, but a procession of days."

Helen held to the Buddhist and Hindu belief that the spirit survives death to be reborn in another body. That is, when a body has done its work in this world, the spirit makes a choice to move on to another. Why some stay longer in some bodies than others is open to speculation, but this concept eases the pain for the living. When I think of death as an opening and closing of doors, a flash of light, an end and a new beginning, it becomes easier to find peace with it and its part in this story. Perhaps Heidi, through some wisdom known only to her, had decided to take a new form.

I don't remember returning from school to find Mama gone that second spring. I don't recall anything about that spring, in fact. The next thing I remember is my first flight in an airplane that June—the excitement of going to see Mama in Colorado coupled with the agony of getting airsick and throwing up in the pocket of the man sitting next to me.

MAMA's VW BEETLE moved under the constant sun like a green ladybug. Across the plains of yellowing grass we flew, the abundance of open space sliding away behind us as we drove from Colorado to Maine. I carried my Colorado memories close to my heart, like the coins in the magnifying box from the piñata, treasures I could examine through the larger-than-life lens of memory. There were the crisp beauty of the mountains and hugeness of the Colorado sky, the dry warmth of the sun that erased shadows at high noon, the friends I'd made, the adventures inner tubing down Boulder Creek, hiking in the Flatirons, going to my first movies, *Jesus Christ Superstar* and *Star Wars*. My happiness made Mama's struggles all the more evident, and so she had decided it was time to go home.

Mama drove into the rising sun as Clara and I hung our heads out the open windows. The wind tightened the skin on our faces, ripping our hair and making it difficult to open and close our eyelids. We spilled our food and fought like baby groundhogs, rolling on top of each other in the back seat, the wind muting our

screams. Bounded only by the walls of the car, we climbed back
and forth from the front seat to the back, catching the legs of our
shorts on the round ball of the stick shift.

"Get in your seat," Mama shouted whenever her attention returned to the present.

"Mama," Clara begged. "Mama, lap." Mama tried it one time,
her arms holding the steering wheel around Clara's shoulders, but
Clara squirmed so much, Mama didn't let her after that. Still,
Clara kept asking.

"Maaaamaa, laaaaaap," Clara said for the hundredth time. I
pinched her arm. She screamed. I pinched again. She screamed
louder. "Stop it," Mama said. "Stop it, stop it, stop it." Her voice
was wavery and loosy-goosy, as we called it. She said, "Stop it, or
I'll lose my grip."

Don't lose your grip, Mama, I whispered out the window. Hold
on, hold on, or we will crash.

When it got dark we camped in Mama's tent, tossing and turning, arms and legs and heads all mixed up together. "Please let me
sleep," Mama said, "please just let me sleep."

There was the end-of-summer glow in the air as we drove, the
days too perfect to last forever—warm and lazy with a touch of
cool air underneath, so it didn't feel as humid as July. The car
sickness began as we left the open stretches behind, the wide
sky shrinking to fill the space of roads becoming hilly and curvy.
When I threw up out the open window, the wind whipped it away
as Mama kept driving. I breathed in the smell of late-cut hay and
the cool dampness of pine and moss through the open windows,
and knew we were getting close to home.

"We're almost there," Mama said. "Hang on a little longer."

We crossed the Flying-di-Dying bridge, and Mama started to
cry. Clara joined her, and they wailed as I watched Heidi in the front

seat, flapping her arms out the windows. Flying-flying-di-dying. She was wearing her little brown Greek fisherman sweater on backward, and the nest of her hair caught the light. I knew better than to say anything to Mama, even though I thought she should move her backpack from the seat so Heidi could have more room. At the far side of the bridge Heidi waved at me and flew away.

"H-O-M-E," I spelled out when we passed under the H.O.M.E. sign of the artist colony by Bucksport. Mama pulled the car to the side of the road to brush her hair and put on a clean dress. We ran the cricks out of our legs and jumped for joy.

"Come on," Mama called to us. "Let's go see Papa."

"Yay!" we said as we tumbled into the car. "Pa-pa, Pa-pa, Pa-pa," we chanted. "Gonna see Pa-pa."

Mama's smile had lost its dryness in the rearview mirror and become a living thing on her face again. My stomach didn't even feel carsick because I was so excited to be home. Papa would be glad to have us all back together as a family again, like the old days, before Heidi died, when he used to give us double piggybacks. Now we could do them with Clara.

"Papa will give us piggybacks," I said. "Yay!"

We drove past Hoffman's Cove and the wide-open view across the sea to Pond Island, where it looked like you could walk across the water into the blue spaces around the islands, the sun warm and yellow coming through the windows. Dust kicked up on the dirt road, and I hung excitedly between the front seats, almost in Mama's lap. She didn't tell me to settle, just smiled back at me. Clara sang, "La-la-la-la-la-lap. Lap." I no longer felt the need to pinch her.

When we emerged into the open space of the blueberry field across from our driveway, Mama pulled the car to the side of the road just past the place where the trees opened up to Heidi's grave. She looked back toward that opening, and her face shifted, became dry again.

Don't lose your grip, Mama.

"I'm going to see Heidi's grave," she said. "Stay here in the car."

Mama walked down the road behind us, disappearing into the trees as Clara and I fell into a waiting space. We heard voices through the open windows of the car and watched as two people came up to the Vegetable Garden sign to change the placards. Gerry held a TOMATOES sign that Mama had once carved and painted and varnished. She looked over at our car but did not see us inside, did not recognize the car. Clara started to moan for Mama and began picking at the door handle.

"Wait," I said. I could feel a shape like a cloud, twisting over me, over the car, over the farm, blocking out the sun. I turned to see Mama coming back from Heidi's grave, walking step-by-step the way she did after meditating at Marpa House. Gerry looked over from the sign to see Mama. Their eyes met and recognition passed across Gerry's face. Her olive skin burned dark.

Mama got in and closed the door. She took a deep breath that seemed to suck all the air out of the car, and when her breath released, we were surrounded by her sadness.

FALL CAME, APPLES ripening and shriveling in the Holbrook sanctuary, no longer to be smuggled home by Mama and Papa. Most days I walked across the garden and past our orchard to the campground to visit Papa in the log cabin where he was staying with Gerry, while Mama lived in the house with Clara and me. To say it was not an ideal situation was an understatement, but no one knew what else to do. Papa had been offered a job at a farm in Massachusetts, but couldn't start until after he and

Gerry returned from the third European farm tour in November. And Mama had nowhere else to go, she said. Papa, remorseful for sending her away before, decided to let her be, and we cradled the hope that somehow life would return to normal.

If Papa wasn't at the cabin, Gerry would tell me stories about her life in Wytopitlock with her husband, Zeke. "One time Zeke was driving on his motorcycle behind a logging truck when one of the logs slid off the pile toward him," she said. "He watched as the log shot forward like a cannonball, likely to knock him and the motorcycle over and leave him for dead."

She paused, with a slight smile for effect.

"But the end of the log landed upright in front of him like a tree, pausing there for a second as he hit the brakes, then bounced over his head and off the road!"

She said he kept driving for a few minutes as if nothing had happened, then had to pull over to the side of the road because he was shaking too much. She talked so fondly of Zeke, telling me things like this, but not the reasons why she was now here. Looking back, I see it must have been hard for Gerry on the cape, our small community frowning on her for trying to take Mama's place.

Gerry had a lot to learn, so I began teaching her, giving her spankings when she did something wrong. "What did I do?" she asked, as if it was a funny game. I had to come up with something new. It could be anything, but it had to be something she did that was different from Mama. Woke too late. Not the breakfast I wanted. Smiled too much. Didn't overreact to my tantrum. Sometimes I came up from behind and spanked her for no reason. My hand made a solid smack that bounced back, ready for the next one.

"Spank. Spank," I said in a serious tone, but she just smiled. Something about that smile made the spank bounce off her and back to me.

*   *   *

I SAT BETWEEN Papa and Gerry in the front seat of the Silver Bullet. Gerry didn't know to let me sit by the window so the fresh air would settle my stomach, and if it didn't, I could lean out and throw up over the side. She also didn't know not to let me drink red grape juice in the car. For some reason Gerry wore a white coat with white gloves. I'd have to remember to spank her for both things when I felt better. White clothes were stupid because they get dirty, and she shouldn't put me in the middle.

Papa was in his driving bubble, somewhere far away in his mind, but his eyes were watching the curves of the road as he went over hills too fast, a grape juice bottle in the V of his legs. It was his favorite juice because it was one of the few bottled drinks with no added sugar. The hills made my head heavy. A soft thing like a baby rabbit crawled up from my stomach and waited in my throat. No, baby rabbit. It got bigger, swelling with grape juice.

"Papa," I said, meekly.

"Uh-oh," Papa said. "Roll down the windows."

Papa and Gerry turned shoulders and their arms moved fast, elbow over hand, working the widow cranks. Cold air smacked in from either side, scattering my hair. I turned to my right where the window was supposed to be, but instead there was Gerry. The vomit landed right on her.

"I'm pulling over," Papa grunted.

The car slowed to a stop, but the red oatmeal continued to gush onto Gerry's white coat. Gerry escaped the car, peeling off gloves, unbuttoning buttons. Then she bent and looked in at Papa with the hint of a smile, the ball of her coat folded around the gloves, all traces of red buried inside.

"That was the most of it," she said.

I was the only one with any vomit left on me, wet on my cheeks.

"Here," Gerry said, wiping my face and handing me a mason bottle of water, not grape juice, this time. "This will wash it all down."

BY NOVEMBER, MOST of the leaves were gone and the garden beds olive with seaweed, nights cooling. Mama was entering her "hibernation mode," which meant lots of naps and checked-out time. Papa and Gerry were packing for the European farm tour, and Gerry asked me to take care of Pussy Tats while they were gone.

"Pussy Tats is my all-time favorite cat," Gerry said. "Take good care of him." Sleek black with a perfect white star of fur at his throat, he was quite handsome, especially compared to Helen's hairball striped coon cats, but Pussy Tats was not my all-time favorite cat. In fact, I didn't much like cats at all. I didn't like the way he purred and kneaded his claws into my lap when he wanted attention or sat in the sun in the farmhouse and licked his fur until it shone. In general cats seemed needy, like when Mama said, "You're being needy," if I hung all over her. But I did try to take good care of Pussy Tats.

When Pussy Tats had not come to the house for a couple of days, I looked everywhere for the black shape of him with his short stub of tail. We found him lying in the woodshed, cold and stiff in an area under the workbench where he liked to sleep. You could tell he was no longer alive just by the way his fur was not shiny from licking but dull and dirty. It had been cold enough that there was no smell.

I think it was Chip who helped me bury the body by the spring, digging a hole in the nearly frozen peat moss. Pussy Tats lay in the position I had found him as we covered his body with the stiff earth.

"Was it my fault?" I asked Chip. Keith and Jean were still in the process of splitting up, but Chip would eventually take Jean's place as Keith's wife.

"No, no, he must have been sick," she said, but it didn't sound very convincing. I was sure it was my fault, because I didn't really like cats, because I didn't like him to purr and knead his claws in my lap. Just like I was becoming sure that Heidi was my fault.

There was something else I didn't want to remember. When Heidi drowned, my heart grew a hidden thought. *Maybe now I'll get the attention I need*, it whispered. *Maybe now our family will be happy again.* But it didn't work out like that at all.

Chip made a small cross out of two pieces of cedar wood and stuck it in the ground over the grave.

"There," she said.

"We worried about you," Paul told me much later. "That you would feel guilty, that you would feel responsible. And you were too young to speak to about it. No one really had the ability to check in with you or get at what really happened. So there was this very sketchy sense of whether or not you were there with Heidi. Seven is little, too little to deal with that, but it doesn't change the fact that Heidi tipped into that water and drowned."

The next time I followed Mama down to the spring to get water, she said, "What is that?"

"Pussy Tats's grave," I said. "We made a cross for him."

"What? You buried that cat by the spring?" Her anger was refreshing in its strength. "This is not a graveyard!"

"Chip helped me," I said.

"It will pollute the water," she said. "Ask Chip to dig him up."

Mama slipped out of the water yoke and walked over to the cross. She looked at the grave for a minute and then pulled the cross out of the ground and flung it into the forest. She stared into the woods for a few minutes, beady-eyed, before coming back for the yoke.

"I can't bear to get water from this spring now," she spit.

I didn't remember Gerry telling me about Pussy Tats's food sensitivities, but when she got back, she said of course she had. Perhaps she told Mama, but Mama didn't care.

"Sorry," I said. "I didn't mean to kill him."

Gerry asked to see where he was buried, and I took her down to the spring, but the ground was covered in snow by then and I couldn't find the grave.

"There was a cross," I said. I didn't say Mama had torn it out.

Gerry was smileless about Pussy Tats for a long time. After that, I didn't give her any more spankings.

MAMA NO LONGER brushed and braided my hair for school or made me new dresses, even though my clothes were all old and too small. Once when Mrs. Clifford called me up to the blackboard, I had on a jumper dress from last year with straps up the back that buttoned on my chest. When I reached up to write, I heard the kids sniggering behind me. The skirt part must have risen up to show my underwear—at least I think I was wearing underwear. I quickly finished writing and went back to my chair. No one met my eyes. They were laughing so hard Mrs. Clifford made everyone put their heads down. I loved to put my head down and watch the condensation of my breath on the Formica desktop—there I was safe.

When the bus pulled up to Jennifer's trailer in the big field on Varnumville Road, she stood tall and proud, blond hair twitching in the breeze, as if she were just hanging out there, as if she couldn't possibly live in a trailer. She got on the bus and looked right through me, heading back to sit with a new friend. They were the popular girls now.

During recess, I tried to grab Jennifer's hand and make her walk with me around the edge of the playground, but she ran ahead like it was a game and she was running from me. I caught up with her and stood in front so she couldn't run.

"Count my freckles," I said, holding out my arms.

She didn't take my arms and start counting; she just looked at me, her eyes flat and hair flipping like a cape around her shoulders.

"Hey, you have a freckle right there," I said, lifting my pointer finger and pressing a vagrant freckle on her nose. She ducked away from my finger and made a pointer finger at my face. Her eyes got narrow.

"Well, you have a freckle right there," she said. "And there, and there, and there, and there." Her finger came forward onto my nose again and again, the sharp edge of her fingernail pecking like a bird.

"Oww," I said, but I didn't move until she ran away.

I WAS RUNNING up the path from the Nearings' after the bus dropped me off, always running to the beat of some increased urgency in my heart, when my toe snagged a root and I fell forward onto the damp earth and pine needles, arm crunching beneath my chest. A tiny protest shot through the bones near my wrist. Broken, I was sure. I ran again toward the brightness at the end of the path where it opened out into the back field, trunks of trees flashing past, dark-light, in the fading light. "Mama," I called, though I knew she couldn't hear me yet. "I broke my arm."

A boy in my class broke his leg, and I'd watched with interest to see that everyone gave him a lot of attention. One or the other of his parents drove him to school, the teachers helped him to the bathroom, and all of us kids wrote on the white plaster of his cast, drawing bright pictures with markers. I imagined Mama would hold me sobbing in her arms. Drive me to school and pick me up. Forgo work to tend to my needs. But the protest in my arm was already fading, blood pumping to soothe the ache, so I held my arm out to smack it against a tree. The pain sprang back into my wrist from the impact. Broken, I was sure.

Across the field of stiff shorn cornhusks that poked through my sneakers, past the woodshed, the ash tree with its dangling swing, up the stones of the patio, the granite slab of doorstep. The wooden latch fell away, and the house opened its emptiness to me.

"Mama?" Back out the door. Scanning with ears and eyes across the clearing. Mama? I slipped off my shoes and ran through the autumn remains of the garden, dampening sawdust clinging to my feet, its coolness creeping up my legs. The tears began to come, not from any pain in my wrist, the impact already forgotten by the resilience of my young muscles, but from the hollow pain in my throat, the egg rising up.

"Mama," I called. "I broke my arm."

Dew washed the sawdust from my feet as I ran by the farm stand full of storage, up the grassy lane, past the orchard of shriveling apples, and out to the parking lot. Mama's VW Bug was gone. The Silver Bullet gone, too. Only the sunken shape of Good Ole Jeepie remained, rusted and beaten down from years of work. The campground spread out on the other side of the parking lot, cook shack and tent platforms empty, rope swing hanging still and straight. I already knew the log cabin would be empty, but I went anyway, up the driftwood steps of the porch, repeating the words to the empty room. "Papa, I broke my arm."

Then I did something that seemed strange even as I watched myself doing it. I ran up and down the packed stones of the back driveway, running to keep myself running so when someone returned it would seem like I had just come up from the bus, just broken my arm. I ran until the lump in my throat blocked the air from my lungs. My legs weakened, muscles slackening as dusk closed around me, but I kept walking up and down the drive, willing the tears to roll down my face for effect, but they were gone, dried up, and by the time Mama returned from her errands the welcome pain in my arm was gone, too.

I see now that beneath it all was a feeling I didn't want to admit to myself. It felt like relief. Relief because for so long I was working to prevent just this from happening, the falling and falling apart, but when it actually happens, you realize that once spilled, your life never goes back in the same way. It isn't supposed to. It's only then that you know you are alive, and that despite the uncertainties, you will survive.

BOOKS ARE WHAT save us. The best place for reading was the space where the feet were supposed to go under Papa's built-in desk in the log cabin. I read in the story of *The Snow Queen* about a goblin who made a mirror that had the power to shrink everything beautiful and magnify everything evil. The goblin carried the mirror up to heaven to turn it on the angels, but it slipped from his hands and fell to earth, where it shattered into a million pieces. A little boy and girl named Kay and Gerda lived across the eaves from each other, and once, when he was sitting by the windows, the little boy felt something stick into his heart and eye. It turned out to be bits of that magic mirror, which made his eyes unable to see beauty and his heart into a lump of ice.

I was that boy. I even looked like a boy after Gerry cut my

hair short so it wouldn't appear messy and unkempt. The stories lived in a safer place. The solution was to find books that lasted a long time. I'd already made it through *The Hobbit* and was working on *The Fellowship of the Ring*, and there were two more books in the trilogy. They would last me at least to winter. My favorite tales told of the hero's journey—of the hero who was called, often guided by an aged mentor like Gandalf, to another world where he or she must find the sword of knowledge to fight the dragons blocking the way to the ultimate discovery, in the darkest hour, of some secret to save the land.

"It's too dark under there," Gerry said. "You'll ruin your eyes." She gave me a little flashlight so I could trace the sentences with the beam of light, like Luke Skywalker's light saber. I would have stayed under the desk forever, but the beam soon become paler and less yellow, like the sun on a wintery day. When it started to flicker and waver, you knew the end was near, and we were always out of fresh batteries.

That's when I realized I could live in the world of the book in my head. Papa always told me I could be anything I wanted, and through my imagination I knew it was true. I could be Frodo. Even better, I could be Strider or Arwen, Galadriel or Gandalf, and raise my staff to make bad things slink away into their caves. As in the Narnia books, I could go to my own private country as I walked the paths in the woods, passing through the wardrobe into a world where there was something to believe in again. I could do this while going back and forth between the log cabin and the farmhouse, while lying in bed, on the bus, in the outhouse. At any time I could escape through the door of my imagination. The words "once upon a time" hold the comfort that the world is a rational place. If we can weave the threads of the story into a pattern that makes sense of things, we can believe it so.

It was then that Telonferdie came back. I was on the path to the Nearings' when I heard her voice whispering in the trees.

"It's me, Telonferdie," she said.

"You're still alive?" I asked, astonished. "Even without Heidi?"

"Of course," she said. "I never die."

CHAPTER TWELVE

Mercy

GERRY LEFT FOR home near the end of November. Papa told us she'd gone to visit her family for the holidays, which she had, but the truth was, she couldn't take the tension at the farm.

"If you go to Topsfield I might join you there," she told Papa. The Coolidge Center in Topsfield, Massachusetts, had offered him a job running an experimental organic farm and a big house with electricity, running water, and an office and phone. His thyroid was showing signs of shrinking enough to bring its symptoms into check, but he would have to take pills for the rest of his life to do the work the healthy organ had once done. Though it would get worse before it got better, there was hope that he could reclaim control over his body and relief in the thought that he might be able to focus on just the intricacies of organic farming, leaving his illness and the work of homesteading behind in Maine.

A light snow dusted the winding roads as Papa drove away from the farm in the Silver Bullet with his few immediate belongings and a staticky tune on the radio. Much, much later he would look back and say those years on Greenwood Farm, despite the heartbreak, were when he felt the pulse of life beat the strongest. It hurt him to leave, but it was time for him and Mama to part ways, there was no mistaking it. He knew she had to find her own strength; he could never give that kind of thing to her, no matter how he tried. Though his later successes would be built on the humility learned from these early struggles, it didn't seem likely on the day he left. Deep down he felt only the pain of his marriage coming to an end.

As he turned from the cape onto the paved road heading south, the snow on the pavement fluffed up into the engine and stalled it out.

"Son of a gun," he muttered, fingers burning with cold as he fiddled under the hood by the side of the road. The memories came to him then, faint but determined, of rising at dawn to cut branches from the trees for emergency firewood, fixing the rototiller by kerosene lantern on a spring evening, Mama's singing along the wooded paths as she carried water from the spring, patching the flat tire on the trailer to get manure to the gardens, building the addition in the cold of December before Heidi was born, and the warm little bodies of his children sitting in his lap as he seeded the flats for spring. Through clenched teeth, he said the words to himself, then, under his breath, his old mantra, though the words held little comfort.

"Just how many sons of a gun are lucky enough to be doing what I'm doing right now?"

Only later would he realize that he could still trust in his findings—gleaned by trial and error—that anything really is possible if you set your mind to it, that attention to detail is the best teacher, and that if you're not getting anywhere, it's time to change course. Though his health and family had been broken in the process, he'd found his purpose in life—to share the ancient key discovered anew in the garden: if we feed the earth, it will feed us.

I see that is the secret, too, to living. Though the earth demands its sacrifices, spring will always return.

AS IF THERE hadn't been enough sacrifices of late, when Papa called Gerry to say he'd reached Topsfield, she told him her father had just died of a heart attack. She'd gone out for a jog on New Year's Day and returned to find him on the floor at the bottom of the basement stairs, surrounded by broken flower pots and EMTs. She and her mother could do no more than stand aside as the supine form of father and husband was wheeled out the front door.

At the sound of Papa's voice, Gerry felt an inexplicable urge to get pregnant—to meet death with new life. Papa's voice dangled the cord of a rescue rope, and she reached out to grab it. After her father's funeral, she packed up her bag and boarded a bus—with her widowed mother's blessing—bound for Massachusetts.

MAMA WROTE TO former apprentices Pam and Paul asking for help. They arrived in a red Datsun pickup with their new little baby, Mariah. The gardens no longer teemed with naked bodies, and music rarely drifted from the campground at night. There were only Pam and Paul in the log cabin, and the occasional visitor who hadn't heard the party was over. In Papa's absence the air became thinner, like the first time he left for Europe. It left us fatigued, as if climbing at high altitude.

I thought of Papa chopping wood out by the woodshed on the day he left, clouds of his breath rising in the cold air, or pushing the rototiller into the dark of evening to get the gardens ready for summer, and I knew we were lost without him. It was by the force of his will alone that we had lasted as long as we did. His was the strength the pioneers had possessed, but the world had become an easier place since then, and people didn't need to work so hard to survive, so they didn't. It was insanity to do so.

WHEN I WENT down the path to catch the school bus in the mornings, I waited on the Nearings' former lunch patio for my new friend John to come out and join me. John's family had moved up from the city to rent the Nearings' old house and try homesteading. As we walked to the bus together, John said I was weird, so he would teach me how to be normal. These are the things he taught me:

Boys are better than girls.

Gilligan's Island is better than *The Brady Bunch*.

Oreos are better than Chips Ahoy.

Cowboys are better than Indians.

Mom and Dad are better than Mama and Papa.

Fall birthdays are better than spring birthdays.

John had a dark blond bowl cut and two square front teeth with a gap between them. While we waited on stumps at the end of the Nearings' driveway, now his driveway, John taught me how to lie. He told me the plotlines of the previous night's TV shows so I could say I'd watched them, and what it felt like to zip your penis in your fly so I could pretend to be a boy. Once I got started, it was hard to stop. The stories you could tell by lying were much more interesting.

The bus driver yelled, "No runnin'!" as John and I scrambled to beat each other up the steps and down the aisle to get the smaller of the two back seats. Along the way to school, my friend Paul came back and sat with us. John said Paul was his friend now, and that I could play with them only if I pretended to be a boy. It was much preferable to play with John at his house than stay at home, so I decided to be a boy so I could watch TV and eat junk food. Given the choice of my two gender role models at that time, Mama and Papa, being a boy seemed the better choice. Mama couldn't win. Nothing worked out for her. She was always saying how hard it was to be a mother. Nursing all the time, cooking and cleaning. Work-your-fingers-to-the-bone.

"I try so hard, and no one appreciates it," she'd say. "It's shit."

"I don't want to be a girl," I said to John's mother.

"Oh, but being a girl is so much fun, you get to grow up to be beautiful and have babies," she said.

"No," I said. Those things were not much of a selling point, given Mama's situation. Papa, on the other hand, had always been excited about something. It wasn't necessarily the things I wanted him to be excited about, like reading *The Lord of the Rings* to me or playing the games I wanted, but at least he was full of enthusiasm for the world around him. He glowed with the energy of being in charge of his life, even if life had other ideas.

In his absence, I decided I would be in charge, too, I would be a boy. I read a book that explained that the way to get something was to pray for it every day. You simply had to repeat the wish hundreds of times. If you did this, it would come true.

"I wish I was a boy," I whispered to try it out, amazed at how simple it was. I sat on the swing under the ash tree by the farmhouse and pumped my legs back and forth as I repeated my prayer. I wish I was a boy. I wish I was a boy. I wish I was a boy. Sometimes I worried that becoming a boy might be irreversible, so I stopped wishing. Deep down I knew, as Papa said, that anything was possible.

SPRING RETURNED, THOUGH we no longer found much joy in the white-throat's arrival.

However, one morning, as I lay in my bunk, the good feeling returned. It hadn't come in a while, and I was afraid I would scare it away because you can't feel the good feeling and be aware of it at the same time. I was thinking about the way light creates the shapes of things, when suddenly I felt it, like a smooth stone in my mouth. My body dissolved its boundaries and became part of all things. Just as suddenly the feeling was gone, and I was me again, lying in my bunk as the ache of reality returned. Mama was always angry, Clara crying, Heidi dead, and Papa gone. Today was my ninth birthday, but not really. My birthday was October 10 now, because John said fall birthdays were better than spring birthdays.

The floorboards creaked as Mama drifted into the kitchen. From above in the bunk she looked soft in the light, her face still open from sleep, not closed up like during the day.

"Mama."

"Ummmm?"

"Do you ever get the good feeling when you first wake up in the mornings?"

"The good feeling?"

"Yeah, like a smooth stone in your mouth?"

"I'm not sure I know what you mean."

"Like warm light surrounding your body."

"That sounds nice."

"Do you get that?"

"Not recently."

"Why do I get it? Where does it come from?"

"I'm not sure."

I lay back down and tried to make the feeling come back.

"Happy birthday," Mama said. She was lighting the stove. Smoke puffed up, and the oaky smell filled my nose.

"It's not my birthday," I said. "My birthday is in October."

"If anyone knows what day your birthday is, it would be me," Mama said, her voice sounding like the old Mama. "I gave birth to you right here in this cabin nine years ago."

"Really?" I said, interested before remembering to deny it. "But not in April, in October."

"Nope. It was April. The roads were muddy, and the midwife almost couldn't get through. You slid right out. The umbilical cord was around your neck, but you were sucking your thumb. The midwife cut the cord and said you were a girl. Then Papa put you on my boob, and you started to nurse."

"Really?" I said again. A story like that was almost too good to deny. "But I'm not a girl."

"Whatever you say," Mama said.

WHEN JOHN AND I got off the bus on spring afternoons, the sun shone through the leaves of the birch trees below his house to fill our favorite glade with yellow light. Something about the light made me want to run to the rock where you could see the ocean.

"Where are you going?" John called.

I kept on up the path, so he came after me. When we got to the top, we climbed onto the rock and sat, out of breath, looking over the trees to the sea.

"Paul said we should kiss," John said into the silence.

"No way," I said, but part of me thought this sounded good.

"Let's pull our hats down over our mouths," John said, and we did. We reached out into the space between us and giggled. He pushed his hat face against my hat face, paused for second, and then scrambled off the rock and up the path toward his house. The birch leaves tittered all around.

"Wait," I called, hat still over my face.

Soon after that John told me he was leaving for good.

"The people we rented to in September left the end of May," Helen wrote about John's family in a letter to some friends. "The winter was too much for them, and they weren't up to the work or the place. They thought homesteading would be a lark, but they did little more than ride their car around and watch TV."

Sometime after, there was a gathering to determine who should buy the Nearings' old house. Our former apprentice, Michael, father of my young friend Heather, came up and gave a speech in favor of Stan, another onetime apprentice who would resurrect that old farm to liveliness, despite Helen's complaints that he was too fun-loving.

Papa returned in May with Skates and Gerry to celebrate Clara's second birthday and pick up Pumpkin the cow and other items in his new truck. Skates was not one to be easily upset, but she was certainly unsettled after the tragic events of her last visit. And then, when helping Papa chop wood, Skates swung the ax back and slashed Pumpkin's soft nose. The cow was fine, but Skates would never return to Greenwood Farm.

I SUPPOSE THAT final summer of 1978 was as warm and lovely as all the summers. It was the summer the world's first test-tube baby was born, and Pope Paul VI died. The long days stretched into warm nights, the flash of fireflies and phosphorescence in June fading into the humid days of July and the honey warmth of August, when everything ripened and fell from the vines. But something was shifting in the world, reflected in the changes all around me. The spirit was gone, moved on—back to the cities. Only the hardy and slow remained.

The farmhouse was dusty and cluttery, but safe, because all of our remaining numbers were accounted for. Clara was napping, and Mama was standing on her head on a folded towel. Her elbows rested on the floor and her hands were clasped behind her neck, hair splayed out in broken wings, as her body rose straight upward in T-shirt and jeans to bare toes pointing at the ceiling. When I tried to do a headstand beside her, it made my head want to split open.

"You must really need your space to stay like that so long," I said.

Her eyes were upside down, watching, steady and mutinous. She wouldn't speak to me when she was in a headstand. A headstand was her time.

"Mama," I said, "I'm hungry."

Nothing, so I tried a different tactic.

"Mama, are you hungry?" I asked, hoping to get Mama to eat so she would have energy for me and not be "low blood sugar."

"Try some, try some, you will like it, you will see," I begged like Sam in the book *Green Eggs and Ham*, but her silence always said, "You let me be."

When she righted herself, Mama reminded me that headstands were good for her hormones, her aching back, her stressed shoulders, all her aches and stresses, really, the house, the garden, us kids. Paul was helping her, she said, but Pam was mostly taking care of baby Mariah, and the farm was too much work for her and

Paul. She stopped her monologue to ask me to wash my bowl, and when I didn't reply, she said we needed to work on "communication."

"Maybe I'm having my time now," I said.

"That doesn't matter," she said. "I'm the parent here."

As much as I wanted to say, No, she was not the parent, I knew there were laws of love, and the first is this: we owe our lives to our parents because they gave us life. Whenever I looked at the photo albums that documented our earlier years, I saw the mother she had been, standing next to me by the goat pen, wheeling me and Heidi in the wheelbarrow, and the pictures I loved best, of Mama and Papa taking turns pulling me across the black ice of the blueberry field in a little bushel basket. So I washed my bowl.

Mama was suffering the death of a child and the loss of her husband and marriage, but none of that made sense to the child I was then. She was simply no longer the mother I desperately needed.

"I'm having trouble coping," she told Paul. "I'm just not sure I can hack it."

Her eyes looked big and whirly a lot of the time, like they weren't seeing what was in front of her, and a vein often pulsed visibly just under the skin of her forehead. There was a lack of focus to her movements, as if she didn't know what she was going to do next. One time she walked out of the cabin and stood in the yard, wailing into the space of the clearing.

"Mama, what's wrong?" I called out the door to her.

"I'm just getting my emotions out," she said when she finally came in. She didn't seem to think it was odd to scream like that. Sometimes we went down to visit Stan, who was camped in his silver camper behind the Nearings' old house, the Gray House, everyone called it now, and he'd get Mama stoned. Mama and Stan had a good rapport, though she teased him that he was trying to get in her pants. "You're so tightly wound," he said, "a little toke will help you let go." Getting high gave her the nervous giggles, and fat jokes would make her laugh until she cried. Stan had a party at the Gray House with regular brownies for the kids and hash brownies for the adults, but by the time we arrived, there were only adult brownies left. I ate a good number of those adult brownies, and Mama did, too, as we didn't know there were supposed to be two kinds. I was wearing a baseball cap, and soon felt like pulling it low down over my head so the brim made a beak.

"I'm Donald Duck," I repeated in a nasal voice, making use of the bits of pop culture gleaned from John. I ran in circles around Mama, hat over my eyes, flapping my elbows and waddling like I was too fat to walk. Mama laughed until her cheeks were wet with tears.

"LOOK AT ME, I'm Mama," I said, turning my lips down to make a frown face as I walked around the addition in Mama's boots. They were tall, up to the middle of my thighs, green rubber browned by dried dirt, with two small flaps through which dirty laces were tied in an old knot that never got untied.

"Me try," Clara said.

"Ha," I snorted. "You're too little. The boots won't fit on your short legs."

"Whoaa," I said, pretending to almost fall out the back door. It was warm out, but the cooler air of evening lay in wait.

"Me, me," Clara said.

She'd been playing with my Sunshine Kids on the floor, which I didn't care about because even though they were supposed to be natural dolls, we didn't have things like the empty toilet paper rolls to make their furniture.

"No, you play with the dolls," I said.

"Me wanna Mama," Clara said, hugging onto my booted leg.

"Oh, I'm just soooo tired," I said for added Mama effect. "I really can't fo-cus on you right now." The boots clunk-clunked on the wooden floor as I walked slowly away from the door, head drooping, Clara leeching onto my leg. Mama was clinking in the kitchen, not listening to us.

"Well, okay, you can try," I said at last. She wasn't used to me letting her do things. Usually all she got was, Can't come, can't have, don't follow, don't take.

WHEN ANNER AND young Gaboo showed up, stopping by on the way to visit Brett next door, Clara was on the ground behind the house, Mama crouching over her. Anner instinctually lifted Clara onto her lap and pressed her shirt into her chin to stop the bleeding.

"It's a good cut," she said. Mama shifted back and forth on her feet, back and forth.

"She cut it on the bucket," I said. I looked at the rusty bucket. There was a little bit of blood on the sharp tab with the hole that held the handle. "She fell out the door in Mama's boots." My fault, of course.

"Has she had her tetanus?" Anner asked Mama.

"Oh . . . yes . . . no . . . yes . . . I think so," Mama said.

"She probably needs stitches," Anner said.

"Oh dear," Mama said. "Oh dear, oh dear."

"It's okay," Anner said. Her eyes went back and forth from Clara to Mama, wondering which one needed the most help.

Anner and Mama put Clara to rest in the bunk and talked over her in low voices.

"You should really get her a tetanus shot just in case. That bucket was rusty . . . just to be safe."

"Oh. Oh," Mama said.

"It's all right."

"I don't think I can do this."

"Do you need help taking her in?"

"No, I mean, I can't do this."

"Oh, Sue, it will be fine."

"No, I can't bear it. It's too much."

CLARA SAT ON my old tree-trunk high chair across the table from me watching Mama with round blue eyes that had dark circles under them. At two years old, she had hair that was still only a pale blond fuzz, making her forehead seem especially high and her eyes extraordinarily blue and bowl-size. They followed Mama's movements from wood box to stove, from stove to counter, from counter to table with our oatmeal.

"Wait for it to cool," Mama said, setting the wooden bowls in front of us, "or it will give you bad breath." Clara began to eat, but her eyes stayed on Mama, even as I made slurping sounds with my oatmeal.

"No slurping, please," Mama said. "It makes me crazy."

By then, the times Mama had left took up almost all the fingers on one hand. That first spring with Heidi in the rental car, the next time with Clara when she ended up in Colorado, then last week when she left Clara and me with Anner while delivering a sailboat down the coast with Stan for some much-needed cash. Only my index and pinkie remained. When she left it didn't hurt at first anymore, like when your hand brushes the hot stove and it takes a few minutes for the spot to sting.

Since Mama returned from the sailing trip, Clara cried about everything. After breakfast, she didn't want to sit at the table, she didn't want to get dressed, she just clung to Mama's legs in the kitchen. Mama told her she was trying to clean up, she needed space. She put Clara on the couch and Clara sat there screaming, her hands reaching out. I went over and showed her my Gandalf staff, but Clara grabbed it and threw it on the floor, so I pinched her. She cried louder and ran to Mama, but Mama put her hands over her ears, her eyes were whirling in her face and her mouth was twisted like in the painting *The Scream*. She pulled her leg free from Clara's grasp, slid the latch on the door, and jumped down the step and ran across the yard. Clara stumbled to the open door, her body shaking as she stepped back and forth at the edge like she had to pee. Standing in the middle of the room with my Gandalf staff, I pounded the staff on the floor and squeezed my eyes tight to whisper a spell.

"Mama Come Back."

Clara dropped to her belly and slid out to the stone doorstep, her face red and crying looking back at me, snot clumped around her nose, eyes not seeing me. She backed off the porch, then started to run after Mama, the sound of crying wailing across the farm. From the door, I saw her trip and fall on her belly, making a louder *wah* from the impact. I couldn't see Mama anywhere, so I went to help Clara. It was cool and breezy outside, the sun turning everything the deep golden yellow of late summer. Clara lay facedown on the ground, kicking her feet behind her.

When I pulled her up, her face was covered with dirt mixed with snot. She was wearing a hand-me-down light blue sweatshirt that said BERMUDA, but we called it her MUD shirt because it was so dirty the only letters you could read were the ones in the middle.

I pointed at her chest.

"M-U-D, mud," I spelled. She looked down so her scarred chin lay on her neck, and some snot from her face drooled onto her shirt.

"Mud," she said, sniffling. "Mama. Mud."

"No, just mud," I said.

After a while she took my hand, and we went inside.

When Mama finally came back, she reheated the leftover oatmeal for lunch and sat, hands holding her head, hair greasy and face blurry, as we ate. The oatmeal was not too hot this time, so we wouldn't get bad breath, and was perfect for slurping.

"Slurp," I said.

"Slurp." Clara imitated me.

Mama got up and went into the back room. We could hear the sounds of her lying down on the bed and pulling up the covers as we slurped.

A BRIGHT FLICKERING and sighing consumed the darkness. I was standing in the doorway of the bedroom addition as flames raced across a spill of kerosene on the floor and walls.

"Get back, get back!" Mama shouted at me from where she stood before the fire. "Get back." But there was nowhere to go that you couldn't see and hear the spark and hum of the flames as they ate into the floor, the rug, the walls.

A minute or so earlier, I'd been sitting at the table reading as the last glow of orange sank over the tips of the firs above Heidi's grave. The whirring of the kerosene lantern filled the cabin, its special domed wick glowing with a blue flame. Lighting the lanterns at night always reminded me of Papa, and there was a big space of him missing. The other lantern in the addition was the older kind with the wick and bare flame that you didn't want to knock over because the kerosene would spill out. Papa said not to pour water onto a kerosene fire, it would mix with the kerosene and burn even more. Mama had been in the back room doing yoga, Clara asleep on the bed. There had been the noises of Mama getting up, moving around, and then something knocking over.

"Oh shit," Mama had said. "Oh shit!" I didn't turn around. Everything was always, "Oh shit."

Now she was screaming, "Water, I need water!"

I stared at the flames as Mama ran outside the back door.

"Mama, Mama," Clara sobbed from the bed. "Don't go."

The walls were streaming with flame, reaching up to the ceiling, when Mama returned with a bucket in her hands, water splashing over the edges.

"No, Mama," I said. "Papa said not to put water on it."

"Fuck him!" she said, pouring the bucket on the fire. It slowed the flames on the floor at first, but not the ones climbing the walls. She came back with another bucket and splashed it on the walls, but the water just slid to the floor and the flames kept climbing.

"Mama, no, no more water," I cried. "Papa said no water." I wanted to grab her and pull her away, run from this place, never return. But Mama kept pouring the water on the fire, splashing it on the walls. Finally she grabbed a soaking rug and used it to smother the flames on the floor and wall. And then, as suddenly as it had started, it was over. The walls and floor were wet and smoking, but there were no more tongues of red.

Mama stood in the middle of the burned space, her body shaking, the skin of her face and hands smudged black as her eyes.

"I've got to get out of here," she said to the smoldering walls.

* * *

SHIVA SHOWED UP on a silent and gray morning as I sat at the table playing with a cornhusk maiden someone had showed me how to make.

"You are the most beautiful maiden in all the world, you must be very lonely," I said.

"The beautiful are never lonely," she said.

"Everyone is lonely."

"Not lonely."

"Lonely."

"Someone's coming."

I looked out the front windows and the corncob doll was right. Over the rise of the hill by the orchard came three shapes. They walked down past the farm stand and up the path. The tall one had shoulder-length hair and tan skin and was smiling down at Mama. Clara clung to Mama's hand, stumbling along as Mama looked up at the man with a smile. It was rare to see her smile like that, but I didn't like it.

Shiva turned out to be the head gardener from a Hindu retreat in Connecticut that Mama called the Snatch-a-Banana ashram. He had a heft to his body and a look around the eyes as if he'd been crying, but he hadn't. Mama had met Shiva through our old apprentice Michael, who said Shiva had been a brilliant gardener at the ashram and could help us with our garden. Mama still cried a lot in big wet bouts that left her nose red and swollen, but now Shiva would come up behind her in the kitchen, turn her to him, and kiss her. She leaned into him, but something in her was also pulling away.

"Kiss, kiss. Kiss, kiss," I said, from across the room. Being in the room around two kissing people made me feel out of place in my own home. It was like the long-ago time I saw the naked couple out in the water of Secret Cove, the bare, entwined bodies caught in the beam of the flashlight.

When they weren't kissing, Mama and Shiva spent hours on the floor in headstands and meditation.

"Mama," Clara and I would plead. "We're hungry."

"In a minute," she'd say. The minutes stretched on and on.

WHEN SHIVA WAS out working in the garden, I would try to make Mama laugh, like at Stan's, but she would say she had to meditate, which meant sitting cross-legged on her hard round cushion, a *zafu*, she called it, with a mat called a *zabuton* under her feet. I imagine her sitting there on the cushion, trying to make peace in her heart, but her mind fought her every step of the way. As wonderful a tool as meditation can be, if you don't have the right instruction, the right teachers, it simply becomes a means for the mind to attack itself. I know that madness is inside us all, but we each decide whether to make it comfortable, to give it a chair to sit in. Her meditation cushion became that chair.

As she sat on her *zafu*, her mind kept coming back to that day in July, circling it like a criminal returning to the scene of the crime. It had rained the night before and the air was humid, as if waiting to rain again, but it was too hot for rain. The heat rose up at sunrise in visible waves, filling the bowl of the farm. The rain made the pond dark and deeper, but it was so hot the rain was forgotten. The cicadas fitz-fizzed. The birds were silent.

Skates was coming that day. Papa and Bess ate breakfast together. She knew her marriage was over, had been for a while now, though she kept holding on. There was so much she needed to hide from herself, and now from Skates. We kids were restless. The house needed cleaning, lunch needed cooking, Clara wanted nursing. The little fires went off in her mind, a scream, a need, someone's disaster, something important forgotten, she'd run out of butter, no, you can never run out of butter, Eliot will be mad if there is no butter. And then her mind scrambled, trying to figure out how to get some butter as the pot of oatmeal frothed over onto the stove. She swung to catch it, hit her funny bone, swore as the oatmeal became a volcano, but no matter, there was no butter anyway. Someone was screaming now, she ran toward the sound, the girls fighting over a toy. Heidi took it, Lissie wants it back. "Work it out!" she yelled. Her face became a mask of her mother. She was her mother, she was herself, and she was the person her daughters would become.

"Out!" Mama screamed at us on that humid July morning, pointing at the door, the sweat shining on her forehead from the heat of the wood cookstove.

"You kids get outside. Now!"

Years later, Mama's shrink would tell her it started when she was a child. A need not met by her parents that made it hard for her to meet others' needs, most of all her own. Her therapist would also say that when she lost a child, she lost a part of herself, and was afraid to love again for fear of further losses. But aren't those just reasons not to love?

What Mama never talked about with anyone is when Heidi returned to the house that day, after I wouldn't let her up the woodshed ladder to play with me. Mama, too, sent her away again, but Heidi kept coming back. She begged to come inside the house, perhaps sensing Mama's confusion and wanting to be near to make sure she was okay.

"Let me in," Heidi pleaded, standing on the stone step outside the latched screen door, the distinct outline of her hand silhouetted against the mesh. "I want to come in."

"No, I'm trying to clean," Mama replied.

"I wanna play," Heidi begged.

What Mama did next is something any parent might have done in a hurried moment and then forgotten about when it had no consequences.

"Well, then, go float some boats," Mama said, tossing the red wooden tugboat, the one that didn't float right, out the door to Heidi.

I HOVER NOW with compassion near Mama as she breathed in and out on the *zafu*, trying to erase her words and their results. Her secret only grew more terrible there in the darkness where she kept it hidden. After she left the farm, she would wander from Arizona to North Carolina to California, finally settling in San Francisco, where she lived in a sequence of one-room apartments. She often dreamed of the birds, she would tell me, the white-throat, the swallows and scarlet tanagers soaring over the farm, and comforted herself by imagining that Heidi flew with them now. But it would not be until recently, when she realized I was afraid I was the one responsible for Heidi's death, that she shared her words from that humid July day with me. Exposed to light, they are simply what they are—innocent words with terrible consequences—but in claiming them she took responsibility for the guilt we've all carried, and with that action it has at last begun to fade.

FALL PAINTED THE leaves with its cool fingers as daddy long-legs gathered under logs in the chilly evenings, entwining their gangly legs to keep warm. There was again the smell of wood smoke, of loss, as I walked through the woods on the path to the bus. New England's seasons are so exact, you can feel a chill

in the air on the first day of fall, as if Mother Nature had a cal-
endar in her pocket. Ask me how a world ends, and I'll say it's
like the end of summer. The cold seems to arrive with a bang,
not a whimper, but looking back, you realize cool tendrils had
begun slipping into the warmth long before, you just didn't want
to notice.

"Oh dear, oh dear," Mama was always saying, about the vegetables not getting harvested and canned or me not having shoes
that fitted and forgetting my lunch for school. "Oh shit."

As the 1979 energy crisis waned in the following year, so too
would the accompanying desire to live more simply. By the 1980s
oil glut, jobs and opportunities would become so plentiful in
the cities that few could resist the pull to return. Many families,
like us, would succumb to divorce or separation, and as Helen
had long ago predicted, those who stayed put were generally the
homesteaders without children. Soon the back-to-the-land movement would be a distant memory to all but the most stalwart.
In the mid-1980s, I would even neglect to mention to teachers
and friends that I'd ever been part of something so odd. It wasn't
until the 1990s that organic gardening rose from the derision of
hippie stigma to find its place in a changing world. Papa's ideas
from the 1970s were suddenly being touted by those very same
people who'd said he was full of shit. And slowly a more balanced
off-the-grid-with-Internet lifestyle has developed. But for Mama
there were only memories of what she'd lost.

THE ONE THING Mama could bring herself to do—between the
never-ending, face-reddening headstands and prone-seated meditation, the marijuana for her nerves, the long mornings in bed
with Shiva—was read a particular story to me, tears welling up in
her eyes and rolling down her cheeks at certain parts. She'd first

heard the Selkie story at a Gordon Bok concert, the song "Peter Kagan and the Wind" being about a man who found a seal that turned into a woman, became his wife, and later turned back into a seal to save him from freezing when his boat was lost at sea.

Our book version of the Selkie story was slightly different. A man found a wounded Canadian goose, instead of a seal, and nursed it back to life. After the bird was healed and he set it free, a beautiful woman with dark hair and eyes came to his home and offered to be his wife. When she bore him a child, he thought he could find no greater happiness, but they didn't have much money, so she wove special cloth for him to sell. A merchant wanted a large quantity of the cloth, and the man begged his wife to weave it for him. She said the weaving took all of her strength, but he continued to plead, so she agreed, though she asked that he not look in on her when she was working. She spent many days and nights in the room, and the man grew impatient and decided to check on her. He saw not his wife, but a large bird at the loom, plucking the last of the feathers from her bloody chest to weave into the fabric. She screamed when she saw him, and suddenly they were surrounded by a flock of geese. The geese lifted the mother in a storm of beating wings, leaving the daughter behind with her father as the birds disappeared into the sky.

I knew Mama felt about this book the way I felt about some of my books—that it explained her feelings better than she could herself. I could tell by the downward turn of her mouth that she wanted to say, "See, he pushed her too far, and she had to leave her child behind."

WE'D BEEN HAVING trouble with porcupines in the orchard. When they ate the bark off the trunks, the apple trees would die. There was one porcupine bigger than the others, his body the size of an anthill, with a small head and surprisingly wise eyes nearly obscured by quills sweeping back over his body. Though they looked like hair gone white at the ends, I knew from Normie-dog that the quills were nothing so friendly. If Clara and I surprised that big porcupine in the back field, he turned his back to us and the quills rose up like a lady's fan, quivering as if about to eject across the distance at us.

"Run, Clara, run," I cried. "Or they'll shoot into you." We'd tear screaming back to the house, grass catching between our bare toes, and Shiva came out to try and catch him, but slow as that old porcupine was, he always managed to escape Shiva's wrath.

Heading to the path for the bus in the morning, I saw Shiva over in the orchard, checking on the damage to the apple trees. Those dwarf varieties of russets, Northern Spy, and Spy Golds planted the year I was born were finally coming into maturity; Papa would be heartbroken if they died now. He'd always tended them carefully—fertilizing, pruning off dead and volunteer branches, and mending the fence to protect them from deer and porcupines.

Every spring that I could remember, the trees burst with pale five-petaled blossoms that intoxicated the air, and every summer small fruits grew from the center of the bloom until, in recent years, the branches became heavy with apples that we harvested and made into applesauce or stored in the root cellar. They weren't always as big as the contraband at the Holbrook sanctuary, but they weren't half bad, as Papa liked to say. Orchards, stone walls, and foundations, Papa also told me, are the only things that remain after a farm is abandoned. Long after the gardens grow up with trees, the barns cave in, and farmhouses turn to rubble, the apple trees might still be producing fruit.

At school Jennifer pretended to be nice to me again, taking my hand, but instead of counting freckles she folded back my fingers with her small, strong ones.

"Mercy?" she asked. I locked eyes with her, refusing to give in. She bent my fingers backward until my palm became the curve of a bridge, the muscles and tendons stretching past their space of comfort. The pain ran up my fingers, wrist, arm. I felt it in my jaw. When I could bear no more, I finally said it. "Mercy." And it stopped, just like that.

When you have suffered enough, that is all you need to say. Mercy.

On the way home from the bus, as I walked across the back field to the house, I could see Shiva still out in the orchard, his hair slung back from the sheen of his forehead, the glinting steel of a machete in his hands.

The next morning there was the bloody head of that old porcupine on a stake in front of the house, its rounded nose drying beneath the prunes of closed eyes. Shiva had chopped it off with his machete and carried it in bloody hands back to the house to show Mama, a cat bringing home his prize. He put it on the stake, he explained, as a warning for the other porcupines.

IN THE LIGHT of early mornings, it seemed I might see or hear the secret to it all. A map of meaning. As my eyes opened, the light from the windows made broken shapes on the yellowed pine walls around my bunk. Brightness and shadow danced in the space of those shapes from the movement of the trees near the house. My mind drifted and caught on the patterns as they vibrated and hummed. They brightened to fade the shadow and darkened to fade the light. I watched for answers. I knew this would last only a few minutes, but in that eternity my mind could wander within a truth not spoken in words, a connectedness to all things. Dead and alive did not exist. All was just a coming and a going. What remained was mercy. The broken shapes of light fitted together into one. At-one-ment. Atonement. My eyes were closed, but the light remained.

I can feel, as if it were my own, Heidi's longing. Water, with its infinite permutations, called to her. The cushions of sphagnum moss welcomed her bare feet as she approached the edge of the pond with her little red boat, the dark water reaching higher than usual up the slippery banks from the rain. Did the boat drift beyond her reach? The water was a welcome cool on her skin at first, but her feet couldn't find the ledge. Her hands reached out for the boat, fingers grasping, closing only on emptiness. Pale blue eyes slipped below the surface. She breathed the water in. The lack of oxygen, someone once told me, feels like falling asleep.

In the Narnia books, the lion Aslan said there was a law older than time: if a willing victim, a scapegoat, offers his life in a traitor's place, the stone table will crack, and death itself will be denied. Heidi was our scapegoat, and with her death she was set free.

I OPENED MY eyes in my bunk to the feeling of a hollow space in the quiet of the farmhouse, like the empty stomach under my belly button. Lump the shape of an egg in my throat. Chill of October morning in the air.

Earlier there'd been whispering. Clara crying. Footsteps across the wooden floor. My sleep self was waiting for Mama to say, "Wake up, Lissie, it's time to go." The words didn't come. I should have called out, "Wait, wait for me," but sleep held me under. The wooden door latch slid across the smooth spot, closing with a solid sound, then only the scuffling of mice in the insulation and flies bumping the windows.

My body seemed too heavy, muscles hardening as if made of

clay. There was the sound of voices outside. "Mama?" My head hit the ceiling boards as I sat up and slid down the bunk ladder and out the screen door, slamming it behind. The garden spread from the house down to the well in a tired patchwork dissected by log-lined sawdust paths. A few beds had shriveled tomato vines and dried beanstalks in them, some covered in seaweed for winter, most ragged with witchgrass. I scanned for the familiar curve of Mama's brown back bending over the earth in her bandanna-print halter top, braids hanging below the half-moon of her forehead. The soil was cool under my toes, making goose bumps scatter up my shins. I was a young animal not finding the shape of its mother in the wild.

The air filled with the shushing of feathers, a flock of geese heading south, wings beating the sky in the ancient pattern of migration. One bird had fallen off the end, having lost the draft, his wings pumping to catch up. Honk, honk, he called, wait, wait for me. I could feel his heart beating in my chest as my neck arched to watch the dangling V disappear over the broken edge of forest.

I SENSED MOVEMENT, heard muted voices, and my feet led me to a lower plot beyond the farm stand, where Pam and Paul were pulling squash from the vines to load in a wheelbarrow.

"Hello, Lissie," Pam called as I approached.

"Hello, Lissie," Paul echoed.

Pam held the fleshy shape of a butternut squash in her hands, baby Mariah in a sling on her back. The fall air filled the space between us as if we were swimming in the pond—warmish on top, cold underneath.

"Where's Mama?" I asked, arms crossed over my chest, bangs heavy on my forehead. Pam and Paul moved slowly toward me, as if trying to catch a goat. Paul rested his hands on both knees so his eyes were at my level, his face boy-cute beneath a dark bit of beard.

"Your mother has left on a trip with Shiva," he said. "She took Clara but couldn't bring you. I'm trying to get ahold of your father."

"I want to stay here," I said, bracing my feet. They were bare and brown below my knobby goat knees sticking out of my shorts. "Stubborn as a goat," Mama always said. "Stubborn as a goat with horns."

"Well, of course you do," Paul said.

He looked over my head at Pam. Rocked on his heels.

If I were to copy a quote for that moment into my journal, as Mama used to do, it would be this:

We live from minute to minute, hour to hour, day to day, and at each point we are a little different. If there is no change, this is the open door to death. Life is a progression. It is not a standing still. It is either a plus or a minus.

—SCOTT NEARING

TWO DAYS LATER, unable to locate Papa by phone, Paul drove me in his red pickup to school. Brooksville Elementary was a low, white, many-windowed building. I walked through the double doors, down the empty hall, to the classroom shared by the third and fourth grades. From the safe island of my desk, I practiced holding my breath—one, one thousand, two, one thousand, three, one thousand—in case I needed to swim a long distance underwater to safety.

"Attention, please," Mrs. Clifford said, and cleared her throat before taking attendance. When she called my name, I raised my hand and said, "Here." She looked at me over the moons of her glasses and made a note on her list. "Such a sad little girl," said the thought bubble over her head.

Once everyone was accounted for, we stood with right hands on our hearts and recited the Pledge of Allegiance in perfect Maineglish. "Ah pledge-a-lee-gence to the flag, of-the-Un-i-ted-States-of-A-mer-i-cer, and to the-re-pub-lick-far-which-it-stands, one nay-ton un-dah God, in-vis-i-ble, with lib-er-dy and jus-tice-fa-all."

My mind drifted and wandered, following the trail of the never-ending story Frank used to tell me the spring of Mama's first leaving.

"Why does the story have no end?" I asked Frank that summer.

"Because the universe is a big circle," he said, nonsensically, it seemed. "With a circle, you always come back to the beginning and start over."

He drew a circle in the air with his finger, starting at the tip of my nose and coming back around to the tip of my nose.

"See," he said as my eyes crossed on his finger.

Frank said everyone knew this was true. For example, he quoted the poet T. S. Eliot, who, he said, went to Milton Academy and Harvard like him: "And the end and the beginning were always there / Before the beginning and after the end." That didn't make much sense either, but made me think of how Papa said his classmates used to josh, "T. S., Eliot," meaning "Tough Shit, Eliot," when things weren't going his way.

I pictured Papa as he looked the last time I saw him, across the space under the ash tree by the woodshed, lifting firewood in his arms to bring into the house before saying good-bye. His breath came out in clouds in the early-morning air. My throat tightened, knowing he was going to leave. I wanted to run out to tell him how much I loved him and to hug him, but I didn't do any of those things because I was mad he was leaving. Now I wished I'd held on to Papa; his certainty was the one thing I could trust.

"Melissa."

Mrs. Clifford's voice came from far away.

"Melissa," she said again. "Your father is here."

I looked up, and the room narrowed into focus. Papa was standing outside the window of the classroom door, his silvering hair and blue eyes catching the light. The other kids were silent as I slid out of my desk and followed Mrs. Clifford through the door for good. In a few years, Papa would be granted custody of Clara and me, and he and Gerry would raise us, with our new little brother Ian, in Massachusetts. Our homes, from there to Texas, Vermont, and eventually back in Maine, would never be home like that little house in the woods, but they would always be safe.

Outside the door of the classroom, Papa opened his arms to pull me into a hug. I realized I'd been holding my breath. As it released, I began to cry.

Epilogue

THE LAST TIME I saw Helen, she read my hands, of course. Scott stopped eating nearly ten years earlier, taking his last breath eighteen days after his hundredth birthday, and in the coming fall, Helen would crash her car along the narrow roads of the cape and pass on to her next life, too. I'd returned to the farm for the summer of 1995, lost in the way of those living at home in their twenties, seeking something in the past that might mend me. Papa had returned five years earlier to find the orchard alive and the fertile earth from the 1970s waiting for him beneath tall grass, overgrown alders, and creeping rose-hip hedges. The ragged clearing was making way—with the help of my new stepmother, Barbara—for the greenhouses, gardens, and modern house of Four Season Farm, eventually featuring farm stand and apprentices anew.

It was the first time I'd lived on the cape since childhood and I was on a pilgrimage with my sister Clara—seven years younger, but an old soul—to see the woman who'd been a symbolic, if distant, grandmother to us.

By then, the Nearings' legacy had attained the aura of curious oddity, a throwback to the youthful rebellions of the 1960s and '70s, and as with most gurus, they'd revealed their fallibility like the rest of us. One of our neighbors liked to say that the Welcome sign at the Nearings' should instead read, "Scott's dead, Helen's in Florida. Get a life." But when Helen bemoaned her dwindling followers, Papa told her she simply needed to live a little longer, evidence pointing to the return to the land as a cyclical urge in history.

The small community the Nearings founded not only survived but was thriving anew, the land on either side of us peopled with former neighbors and apprentices, now with electricity, running water, phones, and Internet, though an outhouse or two for good measure. Every Wednesday, to this day, the neighbors come together amicably, and often quite raucously, for a sauna and potluck, hosted by each in turn. Other apprentices and visitors, too, are spread across the country, many with their own farms, carrying on the dream in their own manner.

Clara and I found Helen in the greenhouse, age ninety-one, active as ever, onion-skin hands still in constant motion, pruning and tying up tomato plants, continuing to work even as she took stock of us, these few remaining children from the past. As a way of greeting, Helen reached out and clasped my hand in a leathery grasp so similar to the one in her old kitchen twenty years earlier. There was still the dusky smell of books in her short granite hair, the puffiness under her eyes and chin as she looked down, the clucking of her tongue on the roof of her mouth.

"How old are you?" she asked, pressing the pad of my thumb.

"Twenty-six," I said, feeling quite ancient.

"Young," she said. "Young for your years. At that age I'd already met Scott-o, was already started on my life. What are you doing now?"

"Not sure," I confessed, lacking the skill to bullshit someone who would surely see right through it.

"Well, at least you're in possession of yourself." She nodded and gave me back my hand, again leaving the reading undone.

So she read Clara's instead, commenting, I think, that her career line was rather weak. Clara rolled her eyes, resigned to her current fate of joblessness. She would go on to have a family and successful organic farm of her own, but that was still years away.

Helen just clucked her tongue.

"Your life is only just begun," she said to Clara. "The lines of the hand can grow and change, you know."

I didn't fully understand what she meant then, but I do now.

The lines of our hands, and of our lives, are not predetermined and final, but can change as we do. We are, in fact, already creating what we will become.

NOW WHEN MY sister and I go to Cape Rosier to visit Papa—Gumpa to the grandkids—we might go with our husbands, Robbie and Eric. My young twin daughters, Heidi and Emily, and Clara's boys, Bode and Hayden, run out to the garden to find their grandfather with his shock of white hair and eyes still as bright blue as theirs. They pull candy carrots from the greenhouse to eat on the spot, and help him plant hopeful rows of seedlings in the dark soil, as the white-throat calls out spring's return.

"We were young and strong and we were running against the wind," Papa says of the homesteading years, now that much of the past has composted to foster the present. Over the years,

Papa's books on organic gardening and his enduring enthusiasm for healthy soil have inspired many people of all ages and backgrounds, no less his own family, to grow their own vegetables in ways that feed the soil, as well. Even Skates's conservative relatives are known to admit, "Eliot turned out all right."

Mama, too, has made her way to peace. Grana Sue, as the kids call her, is often found sewing squares of fabric into elaborate quilts, "in the Batcave," as my step-dad Tom refers to the studio in their comfortable home in Cambridge, Massachusetts. In the halo from the lamp, she reaches out with a sure hand, arranging the swatches in combinations that ease her soul, trying perhaps—like me—to unite the pieces of the past into a pattern that makes sense of things. Here, this print reminds her of a shirt she had then, with a blue fleur-de-lis pattern; this one of a dress she sewed for Heidi; here, the cloth she used for the chambray Russian peasant's shirts that Papa so loved. As the pieces come together, she thinks of her grandchildren accepting her so trustingly, and realizes that with the release of her secret guilt she can learn to love like them again, without fear of loss.

"Time present and time past," T. S. Eliot wrote, "are both perhaps present in time future." But in the end, all we really have is the present.

It was Pam who recently reminded me of the day before Heidi's passing, when Heidi and I had been playing and Heidi fell in the pond. Pam, who heard the crying, came and brought Heidi up to the house, but never said anything to Mama, not wanting to add to her worries, and so the incident was forgotten. I gasped at the recollection. Those two days had long ago blended in my mind, leaving me thinking I'd been there at the pond, that we'd fought and I'd splashed her and she died. That everything that happened was my fault. Now I, too, have been set free.

"This is the use of memory," Eliot also said. "For liberation—From the future as well as the past."

Someone once told me that as raindrops fall toward the surface of a pond, the water actually rises up to meet the drops—a magnetic attraction of sorts—welcoming the rain back into itself. When I think of my sister Heidi that day, reaching for her little boat, I can see the water rising up with joy to meet her, to take her back, and I no longer begrudge it. Joy is what remains.

Acknowledgments

This book is offered in gratitude to so many people. To my parents, Eliot and Sue, who chose to live as they did, and Helen and Scott Nearing, who inspired them. To my sisters Heidi and Clara; my stepmothers Gerry and Barbara; my stepfather Tom; my half brother Ian and my stepbrother Chris; my mothers-in-law Jean and Barb and my father-in-law Dotson; my siblings-in-law Robbie, Kelly, Kim, Michelle, and Rich; and my nephews Bode and Hayden. And to Prill and David, Skates and Skipper, Eunie, Nell, Lyn and Lucky, Martha, and John. It was my wonderful husband, Eric, who said this was the book I needed to write and gave me the support to do so, and our twin daughters, Heidi and Emily, whose birth pushed me to understand my own childhood in order to better celebrate theirs. They are lucky indeed to have five grandmas, three grandpas, and many aunts, uncles, and cousins.

Milton Academy and the University of Vermont did their best to civilize me and send me out into the world. Ian Baldwin, an old family friend, was an early voice of encouragement on this book, along with the teacher and editor Scott Sutherland, and the members of my Friday morning writers' group, Jen Hazard, Cathy Holley, Caroline Kurrus, Victoria Scanlan Stefanakos, and Lindsay Sterling, plus readers Catharine MacLaren and Audrey Wong and cheerleaders Basha Burwell and Peter Behrens. I could not have written this memoir without the memories of the many friends, apprentices, and Akiwabas my family has known over the years, in order of appearance: Mary, Susan and Carl, Susan and David, Keith and Jean, Chip, Brett, Kent, Michèle and Frank, Greg, Michael, Anner, Sandy and Larry, Pam and Paul, Rob, Peter and Jeannie, Mark and Mia, and the memory of Stan. Also Tony Stout and David Gumpert.

L.L.Bean provided gainful employment when I was writing this book. A lucky coincidence introduced me to the lovely editor and writer Bridie Clark, who referred me to Rob Weisbach, the dear wise agent who helped turn a draft into a publishable book and found it a great home with Jonathan Burnham at Harper-Collins. Everyone at Harper has been exceptional: my editor, Gail Winston, with her gentle and always insightful touch; Jason Sack with his eternal patience; designers Christine Van Bree, Archie Ferguson, and Eric Butler; and Beth Silfin in legal, Leah Wasielewski in marketing, and Katherine Beitner and Tina Andreadis in publicity.

Thank you all.

Illustrations

All photos are courtesy of the author unless otherwise noted.

About the Author

As a freelance writer, **Melissa Coleman** has covered health, gardening, food, art, and travel. She lives in Freeport, Maine, with her husband and twin daughters.